TENNIS IN NORTH CAROLINA

Printed in the USA

Published by

Heritage Histories
1289 Fordham Blvd., Suite 271
Chapel Hill, N.C. 27514

10 9 8 7 6 5 4 3 2 1

ISBN# 978-0-9851585-1-4

Noonan, Troupe
Tennis in North Carolina: Celebrating Our History

Book design by Josef Beery.

HERITAGE
HISTORIES

TENNIS IN NORTH CAROLINA

CELEBRATING OUR HISTORY

Troupe Noonan

The North Carolina
Tennis Foundation

To all the tennis players of North Carolina:
this book is dedicated to the tens of thousands of dedicated coaches,
teaching pros, NCTA staff, players and selfless volunteers who have
made North Carolina a tennis haven for over 125 years.

Acknowledgement

When my friend Cy King called me to inquire about my company, which publishes custom books, I thought the history of tennis in North Carolina was not a likely subject. I did not know the North Carolina Tennis Foundation or the North Carolina Tennis Association. Tennis was my first career, so I have a long history in the sport, but I have never run across a more dedicated, forward-thinking group of enthusiasts and volunteers. I learned there was quite a story, and they were committed to seeing it told.

The first acknowledgement goes to Carlyle Lewis, whose "green book" *History of North Carolina Tennis*, produced in the late 1970s, represents a nearly limitless compendium of results, information and anecdotes. Lewis's work lives in this one. Similarly, Grady Elmore, Mary Garber and the many other scribes who covered the sport over the last 50 years will hear echoes of their voices in these pages, as will the many people who gave of their time for interviews, or to provide memorabilia.

The primary committee of NCTA executive director Kelly Key Gaines, Cy King, Billy Trott, and Judy Utley worked tirelessly reading drafts, providing me information, and penning parts themselves. Thanks to all of them for their constant input. Indeed Billy and Judy are essentially co-authors of parts of this book, providing expertise and copy on play in the 1960s and league tennis, respectively. A special mention must be made of Catherine Reid, Billy's legal secretary, who ran down and typed up extraordinary amounts of information.

Others on the committee and off, like Andy Andrews, Herb Browne, Mark Dillon, Paula Hale, Gene Hamilton, John Peddycord, Bo Roddey, and Keith Stoneman, provided information, support, and friendship. Every person I interviewed was gracious, and I only regret I couldn't get to everyone who was willing to give of themselves for this project as generously as they give to the game.

At the NCTA Gwenda Priest, Mary Lloyd Barbera, Marianna Dunn Bryce, and Matt Gottfried all helped whenever I asked, and I asked often for names, information, phone numbers, research materials, office space, images, and a thousand other things. Never once was anyone too busy to help.

Josef Beery of Josef Beery Graphic Design Inc. conjured his usual wonderful design magic.

In our office, Tracey Lee Jones provided her usual excellent support in transcribing and proofreading, and Dave Weller, as always, was the consummate editor.

I hope the book is worthy of its subject, both the game and the people who play and support it in North Carolina. It has been a special gift to me to reconnect with a sport and people with whom I'd lost touch. I hope you, the readers, get as much enjoyment out of perusing this special story as I did compiling it.

Troupe Noonan
President & Publisher
Heritage Histories

Foreword

In the fall of 1976 the President of the North Carolina Tennis Foundation, Marshall Happer suggested to longtime volunteer Carlyle Lewis that he should put together a book about the history of tennis in North Carolina. Two years later *North Carolina Tennis History* was published through the volunteer efforts of many people who chronicled the players, the facilities, the events and the organizational efforts that made tennis in North Carolina thrive. The cost of the book was mostly paid for by Lewis and the proceeds from the sale of books were part of a very successful fundraising effort to build a North Carolina Tennis Hall of Fame addition at the J. Spencer Love Tennis Center in Greensboro. The new wing would also house the offices for the North Carolina Tennis Association.

The last page of the book included the following when it was published in 1978 :

> *The Need is Great*
> *North Carolina has an estimated half million people regularly playing tennis. The tennis program in our state, which includes over 75 sanctioned tournaments each year, a free film library, numerous publications, teacher's clinics for high school, college, and recreational coaches and annual rankings in all age categories, is conducted by volunteers through the North Carolina Tennis Foundation, a charitable corporation, and the North Carolina Tennis Association, a non-profit corporation. The North Carolina Tennis Hall of Fame was founded to honor North Carolina players and administrators who have achieved excellence and brought esteem to our state. At the present time the administration of these programs is being handled through temporary office quarters in Raleigh and at various volunteer's homes across North Carolina. Our Hall of Fame has no present home.*

A lot has changed since 1978. There are not many copies of that original green *North Carolina Tennis History* around today, and the old office space at Spencer Love has long been abandoned for the beautiful Harold T. and Mildred F. Southern Tennis Center Building which now houses the North Carolina Tennis Hall of Fame and the administrative offices of USTA North Carolina and the North Carolina Tennis Foundation. Tennis enthusiasts from across the state again showed their generosity in supporting the capital campaign to raise funds for the new building along with the establishment of the Emily Preyer Endowment which supports grants for junior scholarships as wells as grants for new programs, outreach and inclusion and adaptive programming.

Tennis has boomed in North Carolina. The number of people playing the game has skyrocketed. New clubs and public tennis centers have been built. New programs have been introduced and expanded as the game has been democratized through the use of the National Tennis Rating Program for league and tournament play. The new QuickStart format is taking hold as the way to introduce young children to the sport through Ten and Under Tennis. There are more and more opportunities to participate in tennis both as a player and as a volunteer. More North Carolina players are competing successfully nationally and internationally. The future is bright.

Three years ago the board of directors of the North Carolina Tennis Foundation decided to look into the possibility of publishing a new book professionally written that would update our 120 year history to the present day and to commemorate the 50th Anniversary of the founding of the North Carolina Tennis Foundation. We were most fortunate to connect with Tim Noonan with Heritage Histories. Tim is a longtime resident of Chapel Hill who started his career as a player on the men's professional tennis tour. He has subsequently become a very accomplished writer and the owner of a niche publishing company. Tim's longtime love of tennis and familiarity with tennis in our state was a natural fit. The deal was struck.

Our book project committee adopted the mission statement, "Promoting the Future by Preserving the Past." We feel that this has been accomplished through the exhaustive research efforts and creative writing skills of Tim Noonan and the committee members who assisted him, the many people who were interviewed and the generous support of those who contributed funds for the publication of the book. Tennis in North Carolina has a rich tradition and a storied history. Through the narrative, the sidebars, pictures and the extensive appendix we hope that we captured the vast accomplishments of so many who have contributed to our sport. The task has been challenging and we hope that we have kept any oversights to a minimum.

Please enjoy *North Carolina Tennis: Celebrating Our History*.

On behalf of the North Carolina Tennis Foundation Board,

Jeff Joyce
President 2008-10

Bonnie Vandegrift
President 2010-2012

Ted Reese
President 2012-2014

NORTH CAROLINA TENNIS FOUNDATION BOARD MEMBERS 2008-2012
Keith Richardson, Rocky Mount (now Rock Hill, SC); Vicki Everette, Winston-Salem;
Richard Holderness, Greensboro; Cy King, Raleigh; Susan Love, Charlotte;
Jeff Joyce, Asheville; Herb Bolick, High Point; Peggy Golden, Sanford;
Paula Hale, Greenville; Rich Preyer, Hillsborough; Mildred Southern, Winston-Salem;
Billy Trott, Raleigh; Andy Andrews, Raleigh; Herb Browne, Charlotte;
Henry Hostetler, Greenville; Bonnie Vandegrift, Asheville; John Peddycord, Winston-Salem;
Judy Utley, Greensboro; Keith Stoneman, Charlotte; Ted Reese, Holly Springs;
Pender Murphy, Charlotte; Alex Rucker, Winston-Salem

TABLE OF CONTENTS

**Chemistry Professor
Francis P. Venable**
Built his tennis court behind
University of North Carolina
President Kemp Plummer
Battle's house.

**Professor Venable's Tennis
Court in Chapel Hill c. 1884**
This sand court was the first tennis court
in North Carolina and is now the site of
Alderman Dormitory.

Tennis Comes to North Carolina

IN THE QUIET summer of 1884 in Chapel Hill, North Carolina, had you been strolling east down dusty, deeply rutted Franklin Street, perhaps after buying some jelly beans or marshmallows at kindly old Dr. A.A. Kluttz's store, you would have certainly enjoyed the shade from the leafy canopy stretched overhead from trees on both sides of the street. Taking care to avoid the horse droppings, you might have strolled on, reflecting on how good it was the university had opened again 12 years before, after closing during the Civil War, or pondering the presidential race that fall between Democrat Grover Cleveland and Republican James G. Blaine.

After passing the vine-covered Episcopal church, Chapel of the Cross, and reaching Raleigh Road, you might have turned right past the modest president's house, the second in the life of the university, set well back on the left and presently occupied by Dr. Kemp Plummer Battle. Further down Raleigh Road, well behind Battle's house and across from the boggy

pasture on your right,[1] you might have paused at the curious sight of 25-year-old chemistry professor Dr. Francis P. Venable, broad handlebar mustache dripping with sweat, grading a large plot of land and vigorously spreading sand about.

Venable, who in 16 years would become UNC's 11th president and move into Battle's house, was building what is now thought to have been the first tennis court in North Carolina. Venable had become enchanted with the game several years before while pursuing his doctorate at the University of Göttingen in Germany, and had become intent on bringing it back to America.

The game of tennis at that point involved the familiar rectangular court[2] and a set of rules that were very similar to the game we know today, but the net was badminton height, at five feet high on each side, and the service boxes still ran 26 feet deep from the net. It was only two years earlier, in 1882, that London's All England Club had adopted the dimensions by which we recognize courts today—nets three feet high in the center and service boxes running only halfway

A. A. KLUTTZ,
DEALER IN
STAPLE AND FANCY
GROCERIES,
FINE CONFECTIONERIES,
FRUITS, STATIONERY,
Cigars, Tobacco and Gent's
Furnishing Goods.
MINERAL AND SODA WATER
ON DRAUGHT.
CHAPELL HILL, N. C.

Franklin Street, 1890s
Except for the muddy road and lack of cars, strollers enjoyed a bucolic setting not very different from today's.

to the baseline. As Venable had left Europe in 1881, before the All England Club modernized the court, it is likely he first built his court with the old high nets and deep service boxes, but the first pictures from 1892 showed it with modern nets.

A LOVE GAME
In the 1890s, Chapel Hill's Sallie Anderson possessed a very popular private court, but the regular stream of players was said to be more directly attributable to Sallie's allegedly fascinating and flirtatious daughter, Mary, a reigning belle of the day, than to the unquestioned merits of the new game of tennis.

Venable's passion spread, and Venable and his friends founded the University Lawn Tennis Association. Over the next 15 years, as many as 15 courts were laid out on campus, most of them south of Gerrard Hall in the corner of today's quad. By 1899 students and faculty alike were energetically playing the new game.

Pinehurst and Western North Carolina

As courts were popping up in Chapel Hill, similar sand clay courts, both red and white, appeared at hotels in the resort communities of Pinehurst and Asheville. Pinehurst's first court seems to have been constructed on the property of the Holly Inn in 1895, with other courts following at the Carolina Inn, the Carolina Hotel, and the old Pine Grove Hotel. By the turn of the century, it was common to see women in long dresses and parasols and gentlemen in sport jackets wielding wooden racquets with unevenly shaped heads, enjoying genteel social tournaments in the mild winter climate of the Sandhills.

From Pinehurst, tennis spread throughout the area. A private court was built in Aberdeen on Page Hill, and another by J. Talbot Johnson at

An Early Game in Pinehurst
The Pinehurst area was one of the first regions of the state to which the game spread in the late 19th century.

Early Western North Carolina Players
The Sylva Collegiate Institute tennis club in Jackson County, N.C., c. 1921

Orleans Lawn Tennis Club brought the game to other venues as far away as Waynesville and even the Kenilworth Hotel in Sulphur Springs, just north of Mount Airy.

Asheville also continued to build. In addition to courts built in 1903 at the Mayview Manor Hotel and Cottages, in 1912 the new Asheville Country Club built three excellent sand clay courts, and in 1913 the Grove Park Inn offered two sand clay courts for their guests. In 1915 the new Asheville YMCA sported four sand clay courts, right in the downtown district. Local business people could play tennis after work, shower at the Y, and be home at a reasonable time for dinner.

his residence. The Highland Pines Inn in Southern Pines built a court and there were soon several school courts in town. [3]

On the other side of the state, in Asheville, Tench Coxe's Clondyke and Cornelius Vanderbilt's Biltmore estates each featured a court by 1898. In a departure from the norm when few courts were public, Asheville built three courts at Aston Park and two at Montford Park. No fee was required to play.

As it did in the Pinehurst area, activity quickly spread beyond Asheville to the rest of western North Carolina. Summering Charlestonians from South Carolina added courts to their estates in Flat Rock, near Hendersonville; four grass courts were installed both at the Eseeola Lodge in Linville and at the Highland Country Club, which were patronized by visitors from Atlanta, Nashville, Birmingham, and other southern cities seeking relief from the summer heat. Summer visitors from the New

WHOOPS!
In 1903, when Mr. William Raoul and his son Thom opened the Manor Hotel and Cottages on Charlotte Street in Asheville, they built one clay court, but, perhaps mistakenly, oriented it east and west. Not a problem...on cloudy days.

PLAYING ON A SAND COURT
The early courts, often referred to as "sand clay," didn't play like today's common green clay courts. If you played on Venable's court in 1884, you might find some surprising bounces if it hadn't been packed tightly or rolled recently.

Charlotte

Charlotte was late starting, but when it did, most tennis centered around clubs and private courts there as well. The hub of tennis in the 1930s was a privately owned club consisting of five courts

Grove Park Sand Courts
The Grove Park Inn built two sand courts in 1913.

on Baldwin Avenue that was run for many years by the Moseley family. The city's top tennis was played there until the pro, Corwin Gelwick, went to teach at the Myers Park Country Club. The Charlotte Country Club had pro Abe Barrett before World War II for a few years, and then Bill Lufler after the war. Lufler subsequently took successful college positions at Davidson, Presbyterian, and Miami of Florida, and ended up the pro at New York's famed West Side Tennis Club, home for decades of the U.S. Nationals.

Raleigh & East

Shortly after the turn of the century, tennis was initially played in Raleigh on private courts. The Drake family, Judge Winston, and the Brown Shepherds, all on Blount Street, had courts. Publicly, the YMCA, St. Mary's, and Peace Institute had courts. Around 1910 the Carolina Country Club on Glenwood Avenue put in two clay courts below the 18th green. In 1928 a group of enthusiasts led by Bob Winston built four courts and a clubhouse on Dover Road and christened them the Raleigh Tennis Club.

Early Piedmont Triad Courts

In the then small towns of the North Carolina Piedmont, courts were built by prominent families on private land. As pointed out by tennis enthusiast Gray Smith of Winston-Salem, "The first court in Winston was built in 1905 in the yard of [tobacco magnate] R.J. Reynolds. In the early 1920s, the Hanes family donated the land for Hanes Park, which was built next to Reynolds High School, and which has served as the home for numerous

tennis events, large and small, for many years."

In neighboring Greensboro, the first court is believed to have been built privately by textile magnate Caesar Cone on the family's land. The Cones and other prominent Greensboro families were to be major benefactors of tennis across the state for decades to come. The

Bo Roddey
The first North Carolinian to play on the U.S. Junior Davis Cup team where he paired up with Tony Trabert.

CHARLOTTE'S PLAYERS

The two best players to come out of the Queen City in the early part of the century were Bob Crosland, who played out of Myers Park, and Teddy Burwell, a member of Charlotte Country Club. Crosland won five Charlotte City Championships between 1926 and 1931, and was the first North Carolina men's singles champion in 1927.

Teddy Burwell was a bit younger than Crosland, winning the state high school singles and doubles titles in 1927 and 1928. He won the Old Dominion tournament in Richmond with Julian Robertson in 1929 before heading off to the University of the South, where he was a finalist in the NCAA's and then a Rhodes scholar. Burwell went on to win four state titles and five national titles overseas. He was ranked 17 in the nation in 1932, and was the first North Carolina player to go deep in a Grand Slam event,

Teddy Burwell

Bob Crosland

reaching the quarters at Wimbledon. Later he won senior titles on grass, clay, and hard courts.

Another top Charlottean, Bobby Spurrier, uncle of famed football coach Steve Spurrier, won the state high school singles and doubles for Charlotte Central between 1939 and 1941, and went on to play number two behind Vic Seixas at UNC.

"There just wasn't a lot of tournament play," said Bo Roddey, perhaps the top Charlotte player of the post-war generation, "except perhaps for the mid-Atlantic, which drew players from all over the east for about seven or eight years in the 1930s."

Roddey grew up with the four Keesler brothers, who had their own court, and Heath Alexander. "We tended to dominate the state juniors in the late '40s," said Roddey. "Three of us were usually in the semifinals of our age group up in Greensboro."

In 1948 Roddey became the first Tar Heel ever to play on the national Junior Davis Cup team, where he played doubles with Tony Trabert. At tournaments he suffered close losses to Pancho Gonzalez and Budge Patty. He would have a distinguished playing career before heading to medical school.

THE "MOST FAMOUS" PRIVATE COURT IN RALEIGH

Shortly after World War II, not more than a half dozen still-playable tennis courts remained open to the general public. To ameliorate this problem, George Geoghegan decided to refurbish the court behind his White Oak Road home.

The court had been built in the early 1920s by Dr. Hubert Royster when he developed the neighborhood. Completely surrounded by a forest of 100-year-old oak trees, the site was lovely and private. Geoghegan built a three-tiered wooden bench, which led to the facetious name "Royster Stadium."

Royster Stadium became a busy weekend venue for an entire community of memorable characters in the 1950s and 1960s such as Judge Frank Dupree, Joe Cheshire, James Dorsett, Dr. Sidney Martin, and George London, who played with unorthodox strokes, unconventional racquets, and much chatter.

Neighborhood Hot Spot
Dodge Geoghegan, George's son, rolling the court at "Royster Stadium" on White Oak Road in Raleigh.

city's central location, plus local enthusiasm for the sport, has contributed to its role today as the permanent home of the N.C. Tennis Association and the Hall of Fame of the N.C. Tennis Foundation.

Smaller Towns

Many towns in the more rural areas of the state were fortunate to have great tennis enthusiasts when the sport was in its infancy in the early 20th century. Typically, the first court in town was built by a family, rather than by the town or a local club, and often courts were built in the backyard out of local red clay with fences and nets made out of chicken wire and other agricultural supplies. Over time, a great deal of effort was required to maintain the courts, and most fell into disrepair as play gradually switched to clubs, colleges, and public facilities.

Some notable early courts were those of the Memory family in Columbus County, Prof. George Paschal in Wake Forest, the J.C. McNeill family in Scotland County, and the Winstead family in Roxboro.

In Wilmington, early courts were located at Robert Strange Park at the corner of 8th and Anne Streets. Charles Boney, who played on the state high school championship team in 1942, recalls that a German immigrant named Gerken faithfully rolled and limed the three red clay courts every day. In the late 1940s, impromptu teams from other towns in the eastern part of the state would play matches there. Across town, Dr. Hubert Eaton built and maintained a court and program that eventually assisted in

BEECHMAN ALFORD
Much of the tennis played in Raleigh for 40 years fell on the shoulders of Beechman Alford, an African-American who never played the game. Alford personally constructed and, for decades, maintained the tennis courts at NC State, the old Raleigh Tennis Club on Dover Road, and even Royster Stadium.

the development of great players such as Althea Gibson and Lenward Simpson.

The same story played out for decades all over North Carolina.

Early Competitions

About 25 years after Dr. Venable sank the first court into North

Hanes Park, Winston-Salem
Built in the 1920s, Hanes Park has been a mecca for every day play and major competitions ever since.

Early College Players
Senior class at the Women's College of the University of North Carolina, Greensboro, 1921.

Carolina's mucky red clay in Chapel Hill, formal competitions began to flourish around the state.

The very first organized tennis championship, the Midwinter Championship, was held in Pinehurst in the fall of 1911. "Pinehurst enters the field this year with [its first] annual Championship…which soon promises to occupy a place equal in importance with golf and trap shooting," noted the optimistic January 7, 1911 issue of *The Pinehurst Outlook.*

In the roaring 1920s, when Pinehurst was in its heyday for wealthy northern tourists, the tournament changed its name to the North and South Championships, moving the schedule to mid-April so as to attract big-name players. Indeed, players such as Bill Tilden, Vinnie Richards, John Van Ryn, Harold Throckmorton, U.S. Davis Cup captain Howard Voshell, and others played until the North and South

TILDEN'S FAVORITE COURT
The old Raleigh Tennis Club courts were acclaimed by Bill Tilden, who once played on them, as the best natural clay courts he had ever seen in the world.

was discontinued at the beginning of World War II.

Asheville jumped into the competition fray a year after Pinehurst, in 1912, shortly after Mr. and Mrs. Clarence Hobart began summering in the area. Hobart, runner-up for the U.S. men's singles in 1891, and men's and mixed (with Mrs. Hobart) national champion many times over, brought to town a great deal of knowledge about organizing tournaments. Together with Stanley Howland, Hobart established "The Annual Open Tennis Tournament for the Championship of the Carolinas" in 1912 at the Asheville Country Club, one of the first major United States Lawn Tennis Association-sanctioned events. In 1928 the event was moved to the Biltmore Forest Country Club, where it remained until being discontinued in 1969.

The great Bill Tilden was a frequent visitor to North Carolina tournaments.

Myers Park, Charlotte
A program from one of the many tournaments held over the years at Myers Park.

Biltmore Forest Country Club, 1922
Site of the Championship of the Carolinas from 1928 to 1969.

The Southerns and a USLTA Circuit Come to North Carolina

In July of 1919, North Carolina's growing tennis reputation was recognized when the Asheville Country Club was given the honor of hosting the prestigious Southern Tennis Championships, the top regional tournament in the South. The tournament was a success, and the new Biltmore Forest Country Club served as host from 1922 to 1925 when the Asheville School for Boys assumed the role of tournament host. This transition of such a prestigious southern tournament from one site in North Carolina to another could be considered the beginning of what was to become North Carolina's prominence and leadership on the broad southern stage.

In 1938, the Southern Championships returned to Biltmore Forest Country Club. Due to continuous rain, the matches were moved to a makeshift indoor court. All events were completed except the men's finals between Ernie Sutter of New Orleans and Charles Harris of West Palm Beach, Florida. In 1940 the Southern Men's Open was held at Myers Park Country Club and the Charlotte Country Club. UNC star Bitsy Grant defeated teammate Archibald Henderson in the finals.

Around the same time that the Southerns were first returning to North Carolina, in the mid-1920s, the USLTA established an amateur southern circuit, and looked to North Carolina to play a role. Beginning in the winter in Florida, sanctioned tournaments were scheduled each week, allowing nationally ranked players to work their way northward and arrive in time to play the Eastern circuit. The schedule included Palm Beach; Jacksonville; Augusta; Pinehurst; Asheville; Hot Springs, Virginia; and White Sulphur Springs, West Virginia.

The Asheville tournament, the Western North Carolina Open Championships, was first held in April of 1926 at the Asheville Country Club. Top national players such as Voshell, Tilden, and Japanese Davis Cup player Tacky Harada competed annually with top North Carolinians such as Reeves Rutledge, Tench C. Coxe, Jr., Bretney

Archibald Henderson Meets the Queen
North Carolina's Archibald Henderson met Queen Mary and Queen Elizabeth at Wimbledon in 1945 during an interservice match between the US and the British Empire.

THE WINSTEAD COURT

In the late 1930's Samuel and Kate Winstead commissioned a court to be built near downtown Roxboro. A local contractor, Mr. Frank Wilson, reportedly used mules to level the surface which he built using clay, sand, and dirt from his construction sites nearby. The fence was chicken-wire reinforced with wooden planks. According to Barden Winstead Jr., the Winstead's grandson, the court "became a unique 'gathering spot' for local friends and foes from many walks of life who met there to unwind, relax, tell stories, laugh, and occasionally see a tennis point worth watching."

Smith, F. C. Ivey, Dick Covington, Bob Crosland, and Caesar Cone. Mrs. Charlotte Chapin was among the competitors who played in the women's division. The public was invited to enjoy these outstanding matches

Caesar Cone
One of John Kenfield's early Greensboro players in the 1930s.

at no charge, and in the first year particularly enjoyed a thrilling semi-final encounter in which Tilden beat George O'Connell 15-13, 6-2 before going on to win the championship.

The State Closed Championships: A Greensboro Institution

If the locals wanted some respite from the top stars carpetbagging to win their tournaments, starting in 1925 they could compete in the North Carolina State Closed Championships, first held at the Raleigh Tennis Club on Dover Road. Charlotte produced the state's first singles champion that year when Bob Crosland topped the 24-man field by defeating Hugh Lefler of Raleigh in a three-hour marathon, 11-13, 6-4, 6-1, 3-6, 6-3. Mrs. G. Ward Finley of Chapel Hill won the women's singles, Lefler and Jasper Memory of Raleigh won the men's doubles, and Mrs. Finley and her husband won the mixed.

The state tournament eventually moved to Greensboro, beginning at the Sedgefield Country Club in 1935 and subsequently moving for a long run at the Greensboro Country Club. Much later, it moved to Greensboro's Latham Park, then the J. Spencer Love Tennis Center, and finally to other cities such as Raleigh and Chapel

Hill. Players from the 1940s and 1950s still associate the tournament with the Greensboro Country Club.

For years, Greensboro was blessed with prominent families who served as leading patrons of tennis not just in their city but also for the entire state, and their efforts led to Greensboro becoming the fulcrum of tennis in the state. Families such as the Preyers, the Holdernesses, the Cones, the Armfields, the Loves, the Kavanaughs, the Harrises, the Davenports, and others promoted the game both financially and otherwise. For instance, when the State Junior Closed was played there, many of these families graciously housed and fed junior players from across the state.

"The North Carolina State Closed in Greensboro was always over Labor Day weekend," said Jack Warmath, doubles champion many times over with numerous partners. "It was held in Greensboro because that was central and we had the best tennis situation. We had the best courts.

"The Greensboro Tennis Association ran the tournament with the help of the Recreation Department," Warmath continued. "We had good crowds. It was the tennis event of the state, held at Greensboro Country Club until the early '60s when it went to Latham Park."

"The State Closed was the tournament that players across the state trained for and most wanted to win," said Billy Trott, one of Raleigh's top players in the 1960s.

Other tournaments too numerous

JULIAN ROBERTSON PLAYS TILDEN
Salisbury's Julian Robertson, himself a good player, recalled a match he played against the world's best player, Big Bill Tilden, in Atlanta in 1925. "Early in the match, when not many spectators were present, Tilden hit easy balls to my forehand—the strongest part of my game—and I put them away...Suddenly I was leading 3 to 1 in the first set.

"When the word got around, in no time Tilden had the crowd standing around our court. Suddenly with a grin, he really applied the pressure on me with all his force and strategy, and before I knew it he had won the match 6-3, 6-1."

Julian Robertson

NC State Tennis Club, 1920
Tennis was organized as a varsity sport two years after this photograph of recreational players at the college.

to mention sprang up around the state, but no discourse would be complete without mentioning one of the longest-running tournaments in state history, the City of Asheville Tennis Championships, which began at the Asheville YMCA on Woodfin St. Park in 1928 and continues more than three-quarters of a century later. Legendary Dick Covington won the first six titles, and two of the next three. Eventually the tournament moved to Aston Park, where it is played today.

Tennis in Schools and Colleges

In 1912, University of North Carolina professor Dr. Louis Round Wilson got university president Dr. Francis

Greensboro's Jack Warmath
Warmath won the state doubles with numerous partners and was one of the first officers of the North Carolina Tennis Association.

P. Venable to allocate $600 for a university Extension Division, with one-third of that amount earmarked for the beginning of the North Carolina High School Athletic Association. State championships were held in football and track in 1913 and tennis soon followed with the first boys' championship in 1916. Women's high school tennis did not start crowning champions until 1970.[4]

College tennis was also getting its start in the early part of the century. In 1907, when Wake Forest College was located in the town of Wake Forest outside

Arriving from Atlanta, Bitsy Grant
Started a flood of top players arriving at UNC from outside the state.

of Raleigh, the tennis team used the lone court in town, located in Professor Paschal's yard. Despite this handicap, E.B. Earnshaw and H.M. Poteat led Wake to Southern Intercollegiate titles. Eleven years later, in the fall of 1918, when freshman Jasper Memory enrolled, there still was only one court in town, but

Courts at NC State, 1920s
A popular Raleigh venue before private tennis clubs. Zoology building is in the background.

as he recalled, "In February 1920 some of us organized a Tennis Club with 60 members, and I was made Manager, with broad powers. We pitched in $3.00 apiece, and with the $180.00 built in two months the four sand-clay courts in the field north of the library." By the late 1920s, Memory

was coaching successful Wake teams led by John Vernon of Burlington.

Although the University of North Carolina had a tennis association from almost the moment Venable strung his net, the sport did not attain varsity status until 1908. By 1925, it is said, there were as many as 40 to 50 sand courts on campus, although not all were maintained.

Carolina had some good teams in the early years of the century, but it didn't have a varsity coach until 1927 when candy magnate John Kenfield was hired from the Lake Shore Country Club in Chicago. "Like most incoming coaches, he didn't care too much for those who wouldn't be around much longer, so Coach Kenfield didn't spend much time with the seniors," remembered Greensboro's Caesar Cone, who played number 3 in 1928.

Under Kenfield's guidance the sport rose to great prominence at Carolina. His teams were unbeaten in nine out of 11 years between 1930 and 1941. It was not until 1940, however, that tennis was deemed a major sport at UNC, a recognition the team repaid a few years later by running a national record winning streak of 67 matches in a row, which stood until the late '40s.

Most of UNC's top collegiate

BABY RUTH
Coach Kenfield taught tennis in the Chicago area, while serving as vice president of the Curtiss Candy Company. While with Curtiss, he was responsible for naming the "Baby Ruth" candy bar.

The Legendary John Kenfield
UNC-Chapel Hill's first tennis coach, he coached his teams to 17 conference championships in 28 seasons. His teams won over ninety percent of their dual matches.

Homegrown Talent

The Davidson College team of 1947 represented the core group of North Carolinians that would soon rise to prominence: From left to right, front row: Lenoir Keesler; Teddy Keesler, Buck Archer, Captain; Jerry Robinson; Bo Roddey. Back row: Clyde Stroup, Manager; Glenn Turpin; Whit Cobb; Mike Williams; Don Hatch; Coach Bill Lufler.

Charlotte's Herb Browne

State champion and then active volunteer in North Carolina tennis for fifty years.

players were from out of state. Future Davis Cupper Bitsy Grant from Atlanta was the greatest star of the early Kenfield years, and he was followed by future Wimbledon champion Vic Seixas of Philadelphia in the late 1940s. In 1958, Don Skakle, one of Kenfield's former players, took over as coach and continued the winning tradition set by Kenfield. Kenfield's son, John, Jr., an excellent student of the game and a man of strong principles, began coaching at NC State in 1954 but refused to recruit high school prospects because he felt that recruiting was inconsistent with a university's academic mission. He left in 1966 to coach at Dartmouth.

In the 1946-1950 era, Davidson's tennis team came into prominence with a squad composed of mostly native North Carolina boys. In 1950 this group

won the Southern Conference Team Championship by defeating UNC 5 to 4. Charlotte star Bo Roddey, playing for Davidson, defeated UNC's Clark Taylor 6-4, 6-3, 6-2 for the singles title, and teamed with Durham's Whit Cobb in the doubles to beat Taylor and Charlie Rice 6-2, 5-7, 6-4, 6-3.

Many top college players were attracted to the game but did not fully blossom at tennis because they played multiple sports. For instance, Davidson's Cobb was a multisport athlete who was voted into the North Carolina Athletic Hall of Fame ahead of golfer Arnold Palmer. Semi Mintz played tennis and set NCAA basketball records at Davidson; Jim Donnan played tennis and was the quarterback on a bowl-champion football team at NC State; Charlie Shaffer played tennis and basketball at Carolina; and, later, John Lucas of Durham played tennis and basketball at Maryland and eventually played in the NBA.

Teaching Pros

Teaching pros were few and far between in the early decades of the 20th century. As a sport that was not year-round, tennis could scarcely support year-round teaching professionals. Outstanding players like Harris, Cobb, Roddey, Warmath, and Charlotte's Herb Browne were learning their games on their own or from personal mentors.

In the mid-1950s there were still only a handful of pros in the state, the most prominent being Harry Brown in Southern Pines, Dick McKee in Charlotte, Charles Rice at Biltmore, and Don Skakle, who held the position at Old Town

Top North Carolina Players, 1940s
Bo Roddey, Heath Alexander, Bob Spurrier, and Teddy Keesler at the Roanoke Exchange tournament in 1947.

Country Club in Winston-Salem and the Greensboro Country Club simultaneously. College players such as Browne, who taught at the Greensboro Country Club while he attended UNC and Harvard Law School, often taught in the summer.

Coming Together, 1946-1961

While tournaments abounded in the first half of the 20th century, they largely operated in a vacuum, on a purely local or regional basis, or occasionally as a part of a national enterprise, such as the USLTA Southern circuit. With the exception of the State Closed tournament in Greensboro, very little happened on a statewide basis.

"North Carolina is a very long state," said Billy Trott, a lawyer and longtime tennis volunteer. "From Wilmington to Asheville is a huge distance, and players just didn't communicate with each other. Players in Raleigh went to tournaments in Virginia and the Middle Atlantic

area; if you lived in Charlotte, you would go to tournaments in Atlanta or even Columbia."

As tournaments became more established in the 1930s through the 1950s, players improved, and interest in the game spread; however, like today, many people who didn't have the time or talent to compete against the top players still wanted to play. Regional competition between cities within regions—a precursor of today's league play—gradually developed.

"There were three regions in North Carolina—Eastern, Piedmont, and Western," said Winston-Salem player and volunteer Mildred Southern, who is as responsible as anyone for the growth of tennis in her city. Organized tennis in each of these regions developed as a result of tireless work by, in most cases, a couple of dedicated individuals, and with a lot of help from many other volunteers and supporters in the area.

"In all these regions there were

John Allen Farfour
Owner of Music and Sports store in Goldsboro, Farfour was the father of tennis in eastern North Carolina.

Next Pages →
1941 news photo of junior players at Charlotte Country Club.

Starting Young

AT CLUB—Above is Coach Bill Lufler's squad of junior tennis p
row, left to right, Mary Gibbon, Sally Labouisse, Evelyn Woods, Anne
Jean Roddey, Virginia Smith. Front row, Louis Rose, Channing B
Roddey, Dewey Keesler. Doll is at the national boys meet in Culver,
Hartsville in the Carolinas, Jean Roddey defending her title in the girls
Hartsville.

s at the Charlotte Country club—all 15 years of age or under. Back
erett, Jean Morehead, Jean Newcombe, Jean McVee, Carolyn Tillett,
, Bobby Doll, Heath Alexander, Lenoir Keesler, John Crosland, Olive
, this week. Jean Morehead, Jean Roddey and Virginia Smith are at
ision. Oliver Roddey, Lenoir Keesler and John Crosland are also at

1941

Dick Covington
Dick was a champion from Asheville and a major benefactor of tennis in the western part of the state.

top people in place," noted Vicki Everette. "There was Dick Covington in Asheville, Mildred Southern and John Peddycord in Winston-Salem, John Allen Farfour in the eastern part of the state, Buck Archer in Shelby, Marshall Happer in Raleigh. These were people who loved the game and did not mind helping out."

The Eastern Carolina Tennis Association

Prior to World War II many towns in eastern North Carolina had active programs and already sponsored some intercity play. In the fall of 1945, as the war was winding down, Lionel Weil, Jr., of Goldsboro, C.R. Council of Raleigh, and Billy Harrison of Rocky Mount met to discuss expanding the activities. Along with John Allen Farfour, owner of Music and Sports Sporting Goods in Goldsboro, a longtime local champion and tournament organizer, this group created in the spring of 1946 one of the first major regional associations, the Eastern Carolina Tennis Association, to promote tournaments and competition between interested communities. With the dearth of tournaments at the time, this regional league they created was critical in providing an opportunity for the best players in the eastern part of the state to compete against each other.

During the ECTA's first year, Beaufort-Morehead, Goldsboro, Kinston, Rocky Mount, and Wilson

Eliza Coxe
Perhaps North Caroliona's first great female player, Asheville's Eliza Coxe won the North Carolina state championships nine times and the Southerns seven times between 1927 and 1938. She also excelled in swimming, golf and polo.

participated in home-and-home matches. The Beaufort-Morehead City team augmented its team with some good players from nearby Camp Lejeune. Raleigh and Rocky Mount tied for first, and Raleigh won a playoff match held on the UNC varsity courts.

Raleigh then scheduled a follow-up match in Chapel Hill with a team from Charlotte to determine the state champion, and their luck ran out. Harvey Harris won the only match for Raleigh over Eddie DeGray, both former players at UNC. Bob Chapman, former number one player at Duke, played the number six position for an extremely powerful Charlotte team, which also included Bo Roddey, Bobby Spurrier, and Teddy and Dewey Keesler. From 1946-1978, the Raleigh team would gain the upper hand, dominating by winning the ECTA League competition 24 times.

Also in 1946, Goldsboro, Kinston,

Raleigh, Rocky Mount, and Wilson fielded teams in the ECTA women's league, using a format of four singles and two doubles. Wilmington eventually replaced Kinston in 1947 and, like Raleigh in the men's league, dominated the competition.

In addition to the adult ECTA leagues, a junior league program was also established. Lee Adams from Goldsboro was charged with forming this league in 1946, which in its initial season consisted of teams from Goldsboro, Rocky Mount, and Wilson. Teams from Wilmington, Raleigh, Kinston, and Chapel Hill were added over the next several years.

Early on, leagues provided an outlet for the best players to compete against each other on a team, with matches usually played at public courts throughout the region. The ECTA was "a pretty big deal," said Trott, who played on Raleigh's team as a junior in the 1960s. "During that era there were people who played at parks, clubs, or college courts, but they didn't play outside of that location unless they were asked to play in the ECTA, which was for the top players. So the ECTA ran the leagues for these top players. Typically you'd have about eight guys and you'd play just like a college match with six singles and three doubles."

"Both men and women competed in the early leagues…. There were many hotly contested team matches over the years," wrote C.R. Council of these early competitions in *North*

Carolina Tennis Today, "many matches going down to the night match before a winner was decided. Some teams even did a little pre-match scouting of upcoming opponents, as well as getting information on the lineups to be used." Certificates were awarded to each town listing the name of participants, with Raleigh listing 27 players. "The general approach," wrote Council, "except for maybe a few grudge matches, was to use as many different individuals as possible…and still win." Eventually A and B leagues were formed, and some of the larger towns had a team in each league.

C.R. Council
Tenacious player and one of ECTA's original officers.

The Western North Carolina Tennis League

Building on its early tennis history and subsequent activity, much of which was generated by Dick Covington, the Western North Carolina Tennis Association came into being about eight years after the ECTA. "A meeting was held in my home in the spring of 1954 to form a league," reported Newton's John Tate. "A full schedule was played that summer on a home-

Favorites Chalk Up Wins In Junior Tennis Tourney Here

One Seeded Player Falls In Opening Round Of Tourney

The favorites for the most part racked up victories as play got under way here yesterday on the Forest Hills courts in the Eastern Carolina Tennis Association Junior Championships.

All four seeded performers in the junior boys singles gained the quarterfinal round. The two seeded junior boys doubles team posted victories in opening-day play.

Top-seeded Ed Caviness of Goldsboro, second-seeded Richard Makepeace of Sanford, third-seeded Ken Tew of Southern Pines, and fourth-seeded Gordon Brown of Durham gained quarterfinal berths in the junior singles.

The lone upset of the day came in the boys singles when unseeded

East Carolina Tournament, 1955

Left to right: Joanna Holloway and Whit Cobb of Durham, Eion Felton and Marshall Happer of Kinston.

and-home basis," with teams from places like Shelby, Hickory, Newton, Morganton, Elkin, Statesville, and Gastonia. Asheville joined in 1955 and Charlotte in 1956.

Tate was the first president of the league, serving from 1954-1956. "We played every other Sunday and played each team twice," said

Shelby's Buck Archer, a top player and volunteer. "After the league was over the last year, we had a tournament on Saturday and Sunday, September 4 and 5 in Shelby, and played all matches to the semifinals. The semifinals were played in Morganton."

After a brief hiatus between 1957 and 1959, the league was reorganized with teams from Newton, Hickory, Morganton, Shelby, and Gastonia. In 1960 Gastonia dropped out, Asheville re-entered, and Statesville joined.

By 1962, with Johnny Huss serving as president, the field included teams from five areas: Newton, Statesville, Mooresville, Elkin, and Charlotte. "It took plenty of work to keep the league going, but Jay Shepherd, John Tate, and I were determined not to let the league die," stated Huss in *North Carolina Tennis History.* Such notable players

Regional Powerhouse

Shelby's tennis team from the late 1930s, left to right: Dick LeGrand, Tom Gold, J.L. Suttle; Buck Archer; Pig Hollard; and Russell Laughridge.

as Buck Archer, Norm Chambers, Frank Love, J.L. Suttle, Roscoe West, Bob Light, Norman Jarrad, and Dick Covington competed in the Western Carolina Tennis League.

Asheville participated as a league team in the WCTA, but curiously, given its long history of tennis activity, the Asheville Tennis Association was not officially organized until April of 1961. The purpose was to coordinate the Asheville City Recreation Department, YMCA, and other local organizations interested in promoting tennis.

The Roanoke Tennis League

On June 9, 1948, the Roanoke Tennis League was formed at Woodbourne Plantation near the small town of Roxobel in a section of the state referred to as the "Far East." The original teams, Rich Square, Aulander, Tarboro, and Enfield all played on dirt courts. In *North Carolina Tennis History,* Tom Norfleet reported that "teams were added in 1949 and 1950 to include Roanoke Rapids and Williamston, and for the first time matches were played on black asphalt. This type of surface quickly wore the covers from balls, causing them to float and sail in long three-set matches."

"The worst crisis of the Roanoke Tennis League came in 1951 when teams dropped out and many league tennis players switched to golf. An extensive search for new teams brought in Farmville and even included Franklin, Virginia, which played on composition courts, something new for league players. Robersonville joined the

league in 1952 and Williamston, Roanoke Rapids, and Enfield soon returned. Robersonville won five league titles between 1956 and 1963 with Maurice Everette leading the team.

While the North Carolina environment of seasonal play was not necessarily as conducive to producing players who aspired to the national level as, for instance, Florida or California, the tennis milieu throughout the state was warm, encouraging, and highly competitive for players in the midsized cities and small towns throughout the state. Decades before today's highly popular league tennis, successful and competitive leagues such as the ECTA and WCTA, or smaller groups like Roanoke, catered to the top players in their regions.

The North Carolina Tennis Association

In 1949, supporters of tennis statewide came together and formed the North Carolina Tennis Association (NCTA), the precursor of today's organization.

The NCTA, the first statewide tennis organization in North Carolina, was formed "in a meeting in Chapel Hill of tennis players and supporters from all over the state," noted William Blackburn in *North Carolina Tennis History*. "The Association's first

Buck Archer
Founder of Shelby Tennis Association and mentor to local players, including Tim Wilkison.

Whit Cobb
Cobb was a basketball and tennis player for Davidson and Southern Conference athlete of the year in 1950.

President was Hughes Davis of Greensboro. C.R. Council of Raleigh was named Vice President for the Eastern area. Other officers elected were Burt Arey of Greensboro, Vice President for the Piedmont area; Bo Roddey, Sr. of Charlotte, Vice President for the Southern area; and Roy Jones of Hendersonville, Vice President for the Western area. Whit Cobb was also a president in the early 1950s. "The Association soon became a member of the Southern Tennis Association," continued Blackburn, "and began to furnish leaders to that organization."[5] That tradition continues today.

Unfortunately, there is little information about the Association's activities in its first ten years. That information gap would diminish as time went on as a result of the efforts of one journalist, Grady Elmore, who began "writing up tennis happenings," as he put it, while he was a sportswriter at the *Smithfield Herald* between 1952 and 1954. "Then I started doing some tennis columns at the *Winston-Salem Journal* in 1954-56, and

Grady Elmore
One man publicity department for NCTA in the early years.

began a column on a weekly basis at the *Raleigh News and Observer* from 1957-69." As the game and the Association developed and grew through the middle part of the century, there would be no more earnest supporter or focused chronicler than Grady Elmore.[6]

Early African-American Tennis

It is an unfortunate legacy of our country that, more often than not, African-American players were not allowed to participate in USLTA-sanctioned tournaments. As a result, in 1916 a group of African-American businessmen, college professors, and physicians, along with representatives from more than a dozen African-American tennis clubs, met in Washington, D.C., to form the American Tennis Association (ATA). The first ATA National Championships, consisting of three events (men's and women's

AFRICAN-AMERICAN TENNIS CLUBS IN NORTH CAROLINA IN 1928

Cosmopolitan Club, Rocky Mount	Alpha Tennis Club, Raleigh
Smithfield Tennis Club	Algonquin Tennis Club, Durham
Wilmington Tennis Club	Wilson Tennis Club, Enfield
Kittrell Tennis Club, Kittrell College	Winston-Salem Tennis Club
New Bern Tennis Club	Capital Tennis Club
Central North Carolina Tennis Club, Laurinburg	

singles, and men's doubles), were held at Baltimore's Druid Hill Park in August of 1917.

In North Carolina, African-American tennis was vibrant, with a dozen neighborhood clubs—such as the Alpha and Capitol Clubs in Raleigh and the Algonquin Tennis Club in Durham—listed statewide in 1928.[7] The state also produced top African-American players like Nathaniel and Frank Jackson of Laurinburg, who won the ATA doubles championship in 1931.

A prominent North Carolina native, Dr. Hubert Eaton, would rise to become president of the ATA. Dr. Eaton, who was born in 1916 just four days after the ATA was founded, trained as an ob-gyn at the University of Michigan and became a force for integration in both the medical and tennis communities, but his most famous contribution to the game of tennis came on the court he built in his backyard at 1406 Orange Street in Wilmington.

Gibson and Eaton
Wilmington's Dr. Hubert Eaton, right, with the great Althea Gibson, whom he helped mentor during her high school years.

Irwin Holmes, Jr.
Irwin Holmes Jr., the number two ranked African-American player in the country, broke the color barrier at NC State on both the athletic field and in the classroom. He was most proud of the latter.

A junior, intercollegiate, and national ATA champion in the 1930s, Eaton not only played the game while practicing medicine but also mentored youngsters. On August 24, 1946, Eaton and his good friend Dr. Robert "Whirlwind" Johnson, who would later become famous mentoring Arthur Ashe in Lynchburg, Virginia, saw the young Althea Gibson play in New York City and hatched a plan not only to develop her as a champion, but to help break the game's color barrier. Althea would move to Wilmington to live with Dr. Eaton and attend Williston High School during the school year, and live and practice tennis under Dr. Johnson in Lynchburg during the summers.

"As an ob-gyn," said Dr. Eaton's son, Dr. Hubert Eaton, Jr., "he couldn't get away to travel with her like Dr. Johnson could, so he just worked with her here in Wilmington on the court out back."

Althea later declared, "I owe the doctors a great deal. If I ever amount to anything, it will be because of them." In 1950 Althea integrated the US Open, which was then played in Forest Hills, N.Y. Seven years later, she won it.

FIRST AFRICAN-AMERICAN AT NC STATE: CAPTAIN OF TENNIS

Irwin Holmes, who had been ranked as high as the number two African-American tennis player in the country in high school, but had to sue to enter NC State, became State's first African-American athlete in the 1955-57 school year, playing tennis and running track and becoming the tennis team's co-captain in his senior year.

Holmes expressed loneliness as the only African-American on campus. Once, on a drive back from a competition against North Carolina at Chapel Hill in which Holmes had been the only NC State player to win a match, the team was denied service unless Holmes ate outside. The team refused to eat there and left.

Dr. Eaton is in the North Carolina Tennis Hall of Fame alongside a neighbor, Lendward Simpson, who started playing on Dr. Eaton's court when he was just eight. Simpson, a protégé of Arthur Ashe's, became an ATA champion and the youngest man ever to play at the US Open in Forest Hills.

In addition to Wilmington, Durham was a focus of African-American tennis in the early years, with the Algonquin Club on Fayetteville Street hosting many junior tournaments. By the late 1950s, youngsters Bonnie Logan, who won the ATA Women's Championship from 1964 to 1970, and Sylvia Hooks, Logan's sometime doubles partner and a finalist to Logan at the ATA, were promising a

David Lash
Tennis and football coach Lash gave selflessly of his time and resources so kids in Winston-Salem could be introduced to tennis.

bright future for African-American players in the state.

No discussion of tennis in North Carolina would be complete without mention of David L. Lash, who coached tennis at Carver, Atkins, and East Forsyth High Schools in Winston-Salem, winning seven state championships and 14 western championships. He also coached the football team to two state championships and nine western championships and the basketball team to two state championships and six western championships.

It is arguable that tennis was his first love. As a tireless promoter of the sport, he was active well after his retirement teaching and promoting the game, and using it as a vehicle to enrich the lives of kids in Winston-Salem. "He would give kids rackets and bring them all to the courts to get them started," said his wife, Wilhelmina. "It's what he lived for."

It was the David Lashes, John Allen Farfours, Dick Covingtons, Buck Archers, and countless others who positioned North Carolina for its spectacular future in tennis in the second half of the 20th century. ❧

NCTA Adopts Revitalized Plan

Clark V
Head I
Campa

Piedmont Tennis Association Set; Lewis President —

Preliminary Plans Made To Open Action In May; Two Loops Formed

BY TOM NORTHINGTON
Staff Sports Writer

Tennis in the Piedmont area of N
ceived a badly needed sho

Net Notes

Feb. 21, 1960
N & O

State Asked to Hold '61 Southern Tourney

By GRADY ELMORE

e Southern Lawn Tennis
ciation has been quick to
nd to the new flow of
y in the North Carolina
s Association. A sugges-
has been mad that this
hold the Sout
next year.

rt S. Piatt
LTA secret
nry T. Cl
e new NCT

ur next
give th
ation, W
h to h
nships
at an
n has
ctio
ay
er
ery
hard work.

ments and subsequently better recon
players, young and old.
The Chapel H

seasons, with Shelby, Gastonia,
Hickory, Newton and Morganton fielding teams. In the East,
besides the bigger Eastern
Carolina Tennis Association, the
Roanoke Tennis League has
been functioning for more than
10 years. Roanoke members last
Washington, Tar-
McGuire has expressed great confidence in Stanley
many times. He'll give it a long thoughtful look before
he makes Ray the 'sixth' man. And if that does happen,
look for Ray Stanley to be the playingest sixth man
you ever saw.

Tennis Outlook Bright For N. C.

Members of the North Carolina Tennis Assn. who met
recently in Chapel Hill gave enthusiastic support to a
plan to bolster tennis in the state. If the response of
the 50 or so delegates in Chapel Hill is any indication
of the reception the plan will have throughout the state,
then N.C. tennis is on its way up.
The essence of the plan is to stimulate interest
throughout the state instead of just certain areas. Officials feel it can be done by extensive youth programs,
more publicity, formation of new leagues and just plain
hard work.
It calls for encouragement by means of

OFFICERS — Huddling
the North Carolina Tennis
are the new officers: (left
president; Burk In-

gram, Winston-Salem, secretary-treasurer;
Dr. William Powell, Asheville, Carlyle Le
Grady Elmore, Raleigh. An expanded p
was proposed. (Staff Photo by Bob Allen

1959 Annou

Growing the Game: 1961–1977

THE BUSINESS OF THE GAME

The North Carolina Tennis Association Reorganized

IN **1950**, Dr. Henry T. Clark, originally of Scotland Neck, North Carolina, was named the chief administrative officer of the newly formed Division of Health Affairs at the University of North Carolina.

Tennis is the best sport of all.
- DR. HENRY CLARK

In overseeing the expansion of the UNC Medical School and the North Carolina Hospital over the next 16 years, Dr. Clark became one of the chief architects of the North Carolina public health system, which came to be recognized as one of the finest in the country.

A 1937 graduate of UNC, Clark had been a member of the golf team while in school. As a freshman he distinguished himself by scoring an eagle in his first match, and once shot a 31 on the back nine at Hope Valley Country Club in Durham. When he returned to Chapel Hill in 1950, however, he found himself without the time to play golf, turned to tennis, and fell in love with the sport. "Tennis," he said later, "is the best sport of all."[8]

It was indeed fortunate, therefore, that Clark would bring both his love for tennis and his own considerable organizational abilities to the table to help transform the somewhat vestigial NCTA into a large and effective statewide organization. "He came into the statewide tennis scene," wrote North Carolina tennis scribe Grady Elmore, "very much like his first serve—a very crisp cannonball."

President of the Eastern Carolina Tennis Association in 1959, Clark identified an obvious need for a broader and more dynamic statewide organization, and invited over 50 tennis leaders from 20 communities from across the state to a meeting at the Carolina Inn in Chapel Hill in January of 1960. Citing the earlier efforts to organize a statewide organization in 1949, he said, "It was clear that if this attempt to create a viable NCTA was to be more successful than previous abortive attempts, some concrete program objectives had to be set and a few people found who had the organizational ability and drive to carry them out."

Chapel Hill's Dr. Henry Clark
Revitalized the moribund North Carolina Tennis Association in 1960 and then created the North Carolina Tennis Foundation the next year.

CLARK PRESIDENT

N. C. Group Plans To Pep Up Tennis

CHAPEL HILL—(Æ)—A plan to revitalize tennis in North Carolina was presented and enthusiastically accepted at a meeting of members of the North Carolina Tennis Association here Friday night.

Close to 50 representatives were on hand and pledged full support to the plan evolved by Dr. Henry T. Clark Jr. of Chapel Hill.

Clark, former president of the Eastern Tennis Association, was elected to succeed Francis J. Fitzjohn of Charlotte as NCTA president.

The plan called for an all-out effort to encourage more participation among the younger players, organization of a new league to be called the Piedmont League, increased publicity through the various communication media and a state association meeting at the time of the state closed tournament in Greensboro this August.

Other officers elected were Grady Elmore of Raleigh, vice

president; Lewis Carlyle of High Point, vice president; Dr. William Powell of Asheville, vice president; Berk Ingram of Winston-Salem, secretary - treasurer; Gil Stacy of Charlotte, district representative to the Southern Lawn Tennis Association.

1959 NC SINGLES RANKINGS
Men's: 1—Daniel; 2—Bob Green, Durham; 3—Ed Hudsins, Greensboro.

Women's: 1—Mrs. Raymond Jones, For Bragg; 2—Miss Joanne Cooper, Charlotte. 3—Mrs. Burke Davis, Greensboro.

Veterans': 1—Bill Carrigan, Greensboro; 2—Gil Stacy, Charlotte; 3—Henry Clark, Chapel Hill.

Junior Boys': 1—Charles Shaffer, Chapel Hill; 2—David Morgan, Asheville; 3—Stanley Cocke, Asheville.

Boys': 1—Jim Causey, Davidson; 2—Ken Oettinger, Chapel Hill; 3—Ray Stallings, Goldsboro.

Junior Girls': 1—Joanne Cooper, Charlotte; 2—Dasha Morgan, Asheville; 3 —Sally O'Rourke, Charlotte.

Girls': 1—Sally O'Rourke, Charlotte; 2—Gay Williams, Charlotte; 3—Jane Davenport, Greensboro.

It was of course obvious to everyone that Clark himself possessed the requisite organizational ability, as well as the energy and desire, and they elected him president. "He was," said then recently graduated UNC player Herb Browne, "an extraordinary leader."

After the meeting in Chapel Hill, Clark wrote the Southern Lawn Tennis Association's secretary, Bobby Piatt, about four objectives the reorganized North Carolina Tennis Association had set, and the individuals tasked with carrying them out.[9] First on Clark's list was public relations.

> "(1) Grady Elmore, a sports editor of the *Raleigh News and Observer* and one of the new Vice-Presidents, has responsibility for seeing that tennis is given full coverage in the North Carolina press during 1960. Grady has already demonstrated his ability and interest in this field with an excellent tennis column in his own newspaper during the past two years."

Of this objective, Clark wrote, "My own feeling is the single most important thing the NCTA can do this year to promote tennis in North Carolina is to develop a news service.... Some real drum-beating is in order and we are fortunate that we have a 'Pro' willing to work in this area." The pro, of course, was Elmore, who had founded the *North Carolina Tennis News* in 1959. Indeed, it was Elmore's mailing list that served as a principal tool of the early association.

"Elmore," continued Clark, "has done a wonderful job of assembling the tennis news from around the state and distributing it in weekly bulletin form for use in the Sunday newspapers and the state radio and television stations. In addition, his bulletin has been going to some 160 individual friends of tennis in these parts."

Elmore, who eventually became the dean of North Carolina tennis writers, recalled this beginning. "I became active in the ECTA, serving as president one year, and then Henry Clark talked me into turning my weekly column into a North Carolina Tennis Association newsletter when he took office and really got the state organization humming. That meant writing (cutting a stencil), reproducing, addressing and mailing responsibilities for the first few years. The N.C. Recreation Commission helped me one year with production and distribution, and NC State University let me use an addressograph another year in the Coliseum. Most of the time I was working at home, and spending my own meager funds when needed, until the Foundation took over and Henry got Phil Schinhan to handle the 'factory chores.'"

Indeed, Elmore, with his

newsletter and columns, provided the mortar for the bricks Clark and other volunteers were assembling into the North Carolina Tennis Association.

Continuing in his missive to the SLTA's Piatt, Clark noted:

"(2) Carlyle Lewis (Madison Throwing Co., Madison, N.C.) is another Vice President and he has responsibility for the organization of a Piedmont league."

To Clark's way of thinking, both the eastern and western regions were already reasonably well organized. The organizational gap lay in the middle, and so he looked to Lewis. In February of 1960, therefore, a month after the NCTA meeting in Chapel Hill, Lewis called a meeting at Greensboro's Mayfair Cafeteria and formed the Piedmont Tennis Association, becoming its first president. "A" and "B" Leagues were formed using the same six singles and three doubles format used by the ECTA and WCTA leagues. Competition between nine cities began in April. Charlotte won the "A" league that summer beating Winston-Salem and Greensboro; Burlington won the "B" league over Thomasville, Lexington, Asheboro, High Point, and Madison. The Piedmont Tennis League eventually fielded ten teams in the league competition.

North Carolina now was among the very few states with intercity league play from one border to the other, an especially impressive feat given the vast distance between North Carolina's westernmost counties and eastern beaches.

The third point Clark related to Piatt:

"(3) Dr. William Powell (412 Doctors Building, Asheville, N.C.) is a third Vice-President and he has responsibility for energizing the youth program in North Carolina."

In an effort to expand the horizons of North Carolina's junior players, Clark charged Powell with

Newsletter Number 1
The first communications from the new NCTA were informative but not slick.

NORTH CAROLINA TENNIS ASSOCIATION............Net Newsletter

FOR RELEASE Sunday a.m. newspapers   No. 1--Feb. 14, 1960

While restrictions are being placed on the "Big Game" in tennis on the national level, the newly re-activated North Carolina Tennis Association is making strides toward making the game bigger in this state.

A giant step in that direction will occur Wednesday.

The Piedmont Tennis Association and league will be organized at a meeting at 6 p.m. Wednesday, Feb. 17, at the Mayfair Cafeteria in Greensboro.

Carlyle Lewis of High Point, a NCTA vice-president who has promoted the project, said representatives from about 12 cities are expected to attend, including: Greensboro, Charlotte, Winston-Salem, Burlington, High Point, Thomasville, Lexington, Asheboro, Albemarle, Shelby, Madison and Salisbury.

A men's league is planned, and the league's championship team will meet the winner from the Eastern Carolina Tennis Association for state honors later in the summer.

"We might have two leagues," Lewis said, with the larger cities of Winston-Salem, Charlotte, Greensboro and Burlington perhaps comprising one circuit.

The Eastern Carolina Tennis Association, which has been in existence about 15 years, was made up of Chapel Hill, Raleigh, Rocky Mount, Goldsboro, Kinston and a combined Southern Pines-Sanford club last season. In past years such cities as Durham, Wilson and Wilmington belonged.

A president and secretary will be elected for the new Piedmont League at the meeting, Lewis said.

Formation of the new association and league or leagues means immediate fullfillment of one of the major aims of the

Chapel Hill Team
Chapel Hill fielded a team to compete against other cities in early league play. Left to right, front row: Jasper Memory, Walker Lockett, Mel Jordan, and Malcolm Clark. Back row, Marvin Silver, Charles Shaffer Jr., Henry T. Clark Jr., and H.S. McGinty.

heading up the selection of two juniors who would be offered $200 each toward expenses for participating in the National Boys' and Junior Tournament at Kalamazoo, Michigan in July. Selection was to be based on performances in the North Carolina High School Tournament, in May; the Winston-Salem Invitational and the Southern Boys' and Juniors' at Davidson in June; and the State Boys' and Juniors' in Greensboro in July. That summer Harry Felton of Rocky Mount and Jim Causey of Davidson captured the first two awards.

Clark's fourth point:

"(4) Berk Ingram (Massachusetts Mutual Life Insurance Co., Winston-Salem, N.C.) is Secretary-Treasurer, and it is our plan that the routine and basic functioning of the NCTA be carried out from his office. A part of this

functioning will concern the collection of membership dues and the supervision of the USLTA player registration program with approximately 100 adults and 50 juniors registered with the SLTA and USLTA as the tournament season begins."

"Berk's goal," continued Clark, "is 200 adults and 100 juniors before the summer is over. As there were already 100 adults and 50 juniors registered, this represented a doubling of the membership. In addition, partly through NCTA activity, the North Carolina summer tournament schedule for 1960 is the largest in history with 9 major tournaments sanctioned by the SLTA and five others not yet having formal sanctions."

Of the challenge before him, Ingram wrote to Clark on February 29. "Our efforts this year will have to be spent to a great extent in building an organization, increasing our membership, and in creating in the minds of our members an image of what the great possibilities are for our association over a period of years. In effect, we will have to prove to these members that they have an active working association that will be on call and available to follow through on the various ideas which the members develop."

In short, Clark, Ingram, and others were being strategic. They didn't just want memberships to get bigger; they realized that if membership fees and contributions grew, the statewide organization would be able to afford to promote the sport much more aggressively. Growth would beget growth.

Clark's vision for the NCTA was an ambitious four-point program

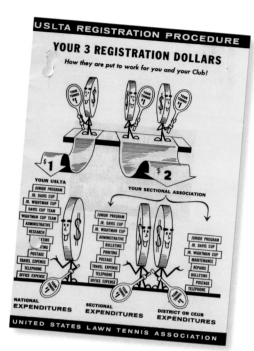

Clark immediately wrote Coach Don Skakle at UNC, "I think it would be a feather in your cap personally and a credit to UNC and to North Carolina tennis generally to hold the Southern Championships in Chapel Hill in June 1961. I can help in many ways but I think the initiative in the matter lies with you. Should we start off with a luncheon soon to include Chuck [Erickson] and Jake Wade and Billy Carmichael?"

Throughout this period of organization-building and beyond, Clark's letter-writing was indefatigable, not only in service to the NCTA and each and every objective, but even in terms of setting up team matches, writing on a junior's behalf, or any of a thousand other administrative matters with which he concerned himself. And Lewis, Warmath, Council, Ingram, Elmore, Farfour, Lewis, Covington, and

indeed, but Clark, who had spent the previous few years in a flurry of letter-writing and organizing, had built a foundation of volunteers and knew that they must be held accountable for following through. Upon the revitalization of the organization, he redoubled his efforts to make sure objectives were met, tournaments were held, members were registered, programs were started, and junior development would grow.

The Southern Lawn Tennis Association quickly took note of the new life in North Carolina. Piatt wrote Clark back on February 12, "At your next meeting I hope you will give this your earnest consideration. We would all like very much to have the Southern Championships held in North Carolina at an early date. Our association has a policy of rotating our sectional championships and to my knowledge it has been a very longtime since North Carolina has been host." This was a major offer by Southern that displayed confidence in Clark and the state.

CARLYLE LEWIS: PORTRAIT OF A VOLUNTEER EXTRAORDINAIRE

Carlyle Lewis was North Carolina's resident expert on getting a good tennis program going. He did more organizing in more places—and also become the number one player in more places—than anyone in the state's history. He organized tennis associations and programs in High Point, Burlington, Lexington, and Madison, helped get the Piedmont Tennis Association booming, and was a leader in the reorganization and revitalization of the North Carolina Tennis Association.

He served as president of associations in those four cities, the area, and the state, and also as secretary and treasurer of the N.C. Tennis Association for a decade and as Southern Tennis Association delegate for six years.

Carlyle Lewis
Lewis cut an impressive figure both as a player and as an administrator.

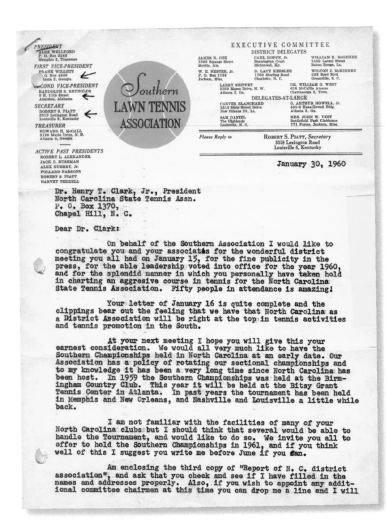

PRESIDENT
ALEX WELLFORD
P. O. Box 2245
Memphis 2, Tennessee

FIRST VICE-PRESIDENT
FRANK WILLETT
O. Box 4508
Atlanta 2, Georgia

SECOND VICE-PRESIDENT
RANDOLPH S. REYNOLDS
5 E. 11th Street
Anniston, Alabama

SECRETARY
ROBERT S. PIATT
3318 Lexington Road
Louisville 6, Kentucky

TREASURER
HOWARD H. McCALL
3120 Maple Drive,
Atlanta 5, Georgia

ACTIVE PAST PRESIDENTS
ROBERT L. ALEXANDER
JACK C. BURHMAN
ALEX GUERRY, Jr.
POLLARD PARSONS
ROBERT S. PIATT
HARVEY TERRELL

Southern
LAWN TENNIS
ASSOCIATION

EXECUTIVE COMMITTEE
DISTRICT DELEGATES

JAMES N. COX
1809 Bigazar Street
Mobile, Ala.

CARL HOPPE, Jr.
Bennington Court
Richmond, Ky.

WILLIAM R. McGEHEE
1602 Laurel Street
Baton Rouge, La.

W. R. HESTER, Jr.
P. O. Box 1185
Jackson, Miss.

D. LACY KESSLER
1709 Sterling Road
Charlotte, N. C.

WILTON F. McKINNEY
288 Byrd Blvd.
Greenville, S. C.

LARRY SHIPPEY
3100 Manoa Drive, N. W.
Atlanta 5, Ga.

DR. WILLIAM G. WEST
656 McCallie Avenue
Chattanooga 3, Tenn.

DELEGATES-AT-LARGE

CARVER BLANCHARD
1815 State Street Drive
New Orleans 25, La.

G. ARTHUR HOWELL, Jr.
461-6 Hass-Howell Bldg.
Atlanta 3, Ga.

SAM DANIEL
The Highlands
Louisville, N. C.

MRS. JOHN W. VEST
771 Porter, Jackson, Miss.

Please Reply to   ROBERT S. PIATT, Secretary
                                3318 Lexington Road
                                Louisville 6, Kentucky

January 30, 1960

Dr. Henry T. Clark, Jr., President
North Carolina State Tennis Assn.
P. O. Box 1370,
Chapel Hill, N. C.

Dear Dr. Clark:

 On behalf of the Southern Association I would like to congratulate you and your associates for the wonderful district meeting you all had on January 15, for the fine publicity in the press, for the able leadership voted into office for the year 1960, and for the splendid manner in which you personally have taken hold in charting an aggresive course in tennis for the North Carolina State Tennis Association. Fifty people in attendance is amazing!

 Your letter of January 16 is quite complete and the clippings bear out the feeling that we have that North Carolina as a District Association will be right at the top in tennis activities and tennis promotion in the South.

 At your next meeting I hope you will give this your earnest consideration. We would all very much like to have the Southern Championships held in North Carolina at an early date. Our Association has a policy of rotating our sectional championships and to my knowledge it has been a very long time since North Carolina has been host. In 1959 the Southern Championships was held at the Birmingham Country Club. This year it will be held at the Bitsy Grant Tennis Center in Atlanta. In past years the tournament has been held in Memphis and New Orleans, and Nashville and Louisville a little while back.

 I am not familiar with the facilities of many of your North Carolina clubs but I should think that several would be able to handle the Tournament, and would like to do so. We invite you all to offer to hold the Southern Championships in 1961, and if you think well of this I suggest you write me before June if you can.

 Am enclosing the third copy of "Report of N. C. district association", and ask that you check and see if I have filled in the names and addresses properly. Also, if you wish to appoint any additional committee chairmen at this time you can drop me a line and I will

The SLTA Takes Notice
Southern Tennis Association Secretary Bobby Piatt was an interested observer in the revival of the North Carolina Tennis Association.

New Net Officers
Carlyle Lewis, left, of High Point was elected president and Burk Ingram of Winston-Salem was re-elected secretary-treasurer of the North Carolina Tennis Association Friday night in a meeting at the Greensboro Country Club. Lewis succeeds Dr. Henry Clark of Chapel Hill as president.

a host of others were his willing correspondents and co-workers in service to growing tennis in North Carolina. The number of volumes these letters fill staggers the reader when he or she realizes that all these individuals had demanding, full-time, mostly executive positions in other fields. All were involved, but Clark was the hub of the wheel, the maestro of the entire tennis symphony in North Carolina in the crucial formative years of the late 1950s and early 1960s when success was not guaranteed.

Orderly Succession
In 1960 Carlyle Lewis of High Point became the second president of the new NCTA and Berk Ingram of Winston-Salem was elected secretary and treasurer.

"Henry Clark had to start from scratch in a situation where there was zero organization," noted Billy Trott. "North Carolina was later considered to have one of the best public health systems in the country and it probably goes back to him. I think he had that same vision for bringing tennis together across the state. Henry was the guy who united the state."

"Henry was accomplished in everything he ever did," said John Peddycord. "He was just amazing. But I think that was one of the reasons that North Carolina tennis has been so successful is because so many of our leaders were outstanding."

Underwriting the Growth: The North Carolina Tennis Foundation

Despite the hard work of volunteers, Clark realized early on that the NCTA could not meet its basic goals without at least some funding, and its more ambitious ones without a great deal of funding. The NCTA, however, was not even incorporated, and could not serve as the vehicle for receiving funds. In August of 1960, therefore, barely eight months after the newly reorganized NCTA took hold, Clark proposed a charitable organization parallel to the NCTA to finance, through tax-deductible donations, future statewide educational and other charitable activities, particularly helping local schools and parks departments promote tennis throughout the state. With tax-deductible donations, Clark noted at the annual NCTA meeting in Greensboro that "an active tennis program in every community in

North Carolina would be a wonderful objective for us."

The objectives were laid out as:

(1) The progressive expansion of tennis publicity in North Carolina via newspaper, radio, and TV;

(2) the development of little league tennis throughout the state;

(3) the sponsorship of tennis camps, workshops, and local clinics;

(4) the promotion of intercity team competition;

(5) the stimulation of more and better city and regional tournaments;

(6) the development of an advisory service to schools and communities launching or expanding their tennis programs;

(7) the development of a service to provide qualified tennis instructors to

Net Foundation Plans Talked At NCTA Meet

GREENSBORO (AP)—Plans for establishing a non-profit operating North Carolina Tennis foundation for the promotion of the sport in the Tarheel State were presented here Friday during a meeting of the North Carolina Tennis Assn.

And the incoming officers were given authority to go ahead with the idea of setting up such an organization as described by outgoing president Henry Clark of Chapel Hill. The latter was appointed chairman of a group to make it a reality.

Succeeding Clark as president of the NCTA was Carlyle Lewis of High Point. Berk Ingram of Win-

tennis for the past year: Clark Elmore and Susan Lewis of High Point being the recipients, the latter two for their publicity work

H. S. McGinty of Chapel Hill received a plaque as representative of his city winning the ECTA Class A team title. Whit Cobb of Charlotte carried off one for the Queen City which won the Piedmont a crown.

many communities during the summer months; and

(8) the provision of occasional prize trips to sectional and national tournaments for selected deserving youngsters.

A FAMILY AFFAIR

There were—and are — many unsung heroes among the tennis volunteers of North Carolina and that list includes many spouses and family members who pitched in to help.

Henry Clark's family was one example. As dedicated and indefatigable as Clark was in willing the NCTA into life, he would not have accomplished all he did without his equally tireless and dedicated wife, Blanche, and their children, Henry, Laura, and Anne.

Saddled with massive responsibilities in his day job, and without a personal secretary, Clark sought—and received—help from the troops at home. "It was a family affair," remembers son Henry III, a top player in his own right and now a professor of education

Henry Clark and Family

The Clark family in the early 1960s: (left to right) Laura, Henry III, Blanche, Dr. Henry Clark, Jr., and Anne.

at Virginia Commonwealth University. "There were many nights we sat around the dining room table, stuffing and sealing envelopes until all hours."

Blanche was of course the foreman of this work group. If there was a first lady of North Carolina tennis in the late 1950s and early 1960s, it

was Blanche Clark, but her efforts were mirrored by patient spouses all over the state who either pitched in to help, or waited at home while his or her significant other manned tournament tables, worked on ranking committees, or performed any of a thousand other services to the game.

Charter of the North Carolina Tennis Foundation

Underwrites the growth of the sport in perpetuity.

Clark's concept of a North Carolina Tennis Foundation was approved by some 80 people attending the August 1960 NCTA banquet, and a small action committee was appointed. Clark called upon Herb Browne, by then a young lawyer in Charlotte, to put together the framework for incorporating the NCTF as a nonprofit, tax-deductible organization for approval by the Internal Revenue Service. "I had gotten to know Henry when I was an undergraduate and the Chapel Hill league team he was on used the varsity courts," said Browne, who would go on to make many contributions to North Carolina tennis both on court and off, serving as an active NCTF board member through 2010. "I was probably the only attorney he knew who was also a dedicated tennis player."

The organization received its charter in December of 1961 "as a nonprofit educational and charitable organization. Its purpose is to encourage the development of amateur tennis in North Carolina as a healthful and wholesome recreational activity, a body and character builder for young and old alike." The first president of NCTF, elected in 1961, was J. Spencer Love of Greensboro, who had grown Burlington Industries into the largest textile manufacturer in the world. Most unfortunately, Love died of a heart attack while on court in Palm Beach in January of 1962, during his term of office. He was succeeded by Dave Morgan, Jr. of Asheville. Clark served as secretary and treasurer, a post he held through 1966, when he moved to Connecticut.

In November 1961, the key officers of the NCTA, the ECTA, the Piedmont Tennis Association, the WCTA, the Roanoke Tennis Association, and the NCTF met in Chapel Hill with representatives of the N.C. Recreational Commission and the N.C. High School Athletic

4C   High Point Enterprise, Sunday, July 3, 1960

SPENCER LOVE

'Never Too Old For Tennis, Says Piedmont Industrialist

By SUSAN LEWIS

GREENSBORO— You're never too old or too busy to play tennis, claims Burlington Industry's Spencer Love.

The 64-year-old head of the world's largest textile corporation says that playing tennis two or three times a week is one of the secrets for staying young.

According to Love, tennis can be more than a game — it can be a tranquilizer.

"Often when I'm tired or nervous from a hard day at the office, a good game of tennis sweeps out the cobwebs and relaxes me."

The textile magnate took up the game as a child, "knocking the ball around with the boys." He switched to golf in his twenties and thirties but returned to the court and racket in his forties for the sake of time.

"I found with tennis I could have more fun the quickest," he explains.

Nothing stops Love when he wants to play. He even recalls times when he's hacked in and shoveled snow off Greensboro courts to play.

His zeal for the sport in inclement weather once resulted in a wrenched back. He was playing on a hard court in Washington, D. C., when he slipped on a patch of ice the size of a pancake. The game was postponed.

Love never had any tennis instruction, "which accounts for my screwy game," he grins.

His unorthodox play has given him many occasions to smile. He was playing in Florida, when a spectator unknowingly remarked to Mrs. Love, "Who's that fellow over there? He's got the craziest game I ever saw!"

His partners and opponents say he's far better than he looks, however, and can outlast them all.

He has played with some of the best: former Davis Cup Pancho Segura and John Van Ryn; and Pauline Betz and Alice Marble, former national women's titlists.

He teamed with Australian Davis Cup player Rex Hartwig in '56 for a Pro-amateur round robin handicap in Palm Beach, place.

Love prefers doubles to singles. His favorite shot is a pass down the alley when his opponent is at the net. He says he has no special strategy and that his tactics depend on his opposition.

Long known as a patron of the court sport, Love has built been named honorary chairman of the North Carolina Tennis Association banquet to be held in August.

Love has no plans to quit.

"I'll keep playing as long as I can," he states.

At his present rate, it'll be some time before he retires to the sidelines.

SPENCER LOVE . . . Net Enthusiast

Mr. Tennis in the House!
Norm Chambers conducts one of his many clinics around the state as Mr. Tennis.

8—11   The News and Observer, Sunday, August 20, 1967

Net Notes

'Mr. Tennis' Program Produced Good Results
By Grady Elmore

Association, to map out even more aggressive objectives for 1962.

During the Foundation's first year, 126 people from across the state contributed over $1,400 for different programs. Weekly newsletters were sent to over 400 recipients, league play expanded to include some 35 cities, little league tennis was started in a few spots, and the summer tournament program in North Carolina was more active than any before it.

Takin' It to the Streets: Mr. Tennis

The unincorporated Association and the charitable Foundation both grew in the early years, meeting regularly in Greensboro as a middle point in the state. By 1967, Allen Morris, former Wimbledon quarterfinalist and many-time state champion, was president of the NCTA and began a new program which would have tremendous effect on tennis throughout the state. "One of the things a bunch of us did was create

"Mr. Tennis," said Morris. "[Mr. Tennis] was hired by the Association, and he used to go around and teach in small towns. We would pay for the expenses to do that."

Norman Chambers of Raleigh was the first Mr. Tennis in 1967, and he visited dozens of communities across the state, putting on clinics and training instructors who would carry on the programs after he left. Wingate College coach Ronnie Smarr, and Wake Forest stars Ken West and Mike Rubenstein later served as Mr. Tennis. "[They] would go to these little small towns who knew nothing about tennis or who wanted to have somebody come and teach the kids at the local park," said Morris.

This grassroots outreach, centered in public parks and recreation centers, would not have been possible without the organizing of the NCTA and the funding from the NCTF. Mr. Tennis reached numerous young players

and resulted in many additional sanctioned junior tournaments. Credited, at least in part, for the surge of tennis activity in the state during the 1960s, it gained national acclaim and international attention.

In addition to Mr. Tennis, over the years the Association and Foundation stimulated many additional tennis activities throughout the state, such as:

- Organizing and/or expanding regional and city tennis associations.

- Developing or expanding intercity tennis leagues.

- Activating and encouraging summer camps for youngsters in the state, including early camps at Atlantic Christian College and Pfeiffer College.

- Stimulating tennis activity in the public schools.

- Persuading many city and recreational departments to increase their emphasis on tennis.

- Offering expertise to local tennis development programs

- Assisting in staging tennis clinics in many communities throughout the state.

- Publishing the *North Carolina Tennis News.*

Marshall Happer: North Carolina's—and Later the Nation's—Tennis Czar

When Henry Clark left for Connecticut in 1966, another giant of North Carolina tennis appeared on the scene to take his place. Marshall Happer had learned to play tennis in his hometown of Kinston in the mid-1950s, was playing on ECTA league teams by the time he was 12, and was a state junior and high school champion. "I played tennis from the end of basketball season until Labor Day. Then you'd start basketball practice," he said. "That's about all the tennis you'd play. There were only a few junior tournaments in North Carolina. Mainly we were playing in-state and in the limited season."

After playing at UNC for Don Skakle from 1956 until 1960, Happer attended law school, then set up a private practice in Raleigh in 1964. A strong-willed administrator by nature, Happer soon began running junior tournaments in Raleigh in his spare time. "I can't believe I did it," he said much later with the hindsight of many years as a tennis administrator. "I had them on the six courts at NC State. I had boys and girls 12s to 18s, singles and doubles. It was unbelievable. We put them up in the dormitories at State. That was my first endeavor in running tennis tournaments." It was good practice, because later he would help run tennis on the world stage, serving in various capacities, including the unenviable job of hearing appeals by John McEnroe of disciplinary actions for bad court behavior.

After developing the Raleigh Racquet Club in 1967, Happer had a venue for putting on more tournaments. "In 1969 we had the Eastern Championships there, and again another year as well. In 1971 we had the state championships there. That was the year we opened the stadium court. We didn't have a clubhouse...just a funeral tent. But we had stadium court."

He got involved not only for the love of the game, like Clark,

but out of a sense of justice. "One of the reasons I got involved in the North Carolina Tennis Association is that I found out most of the adults were junior tennis parents." These parents, he pointed out, naturally filled a lot of committees...especially ranking committees. As a junior tournament director, Happer found this objectionable because, he said with disbelief, "These people were ranking their own kids!"

"Of course, if you get upset about something, somebody inevitably says, 'Okay, then, you fix it.' That's sort of how I got sucked into the North Carolina Tennis Association. We got a lot more people involved and we fixed it so nobody was ranking their own kids any more."

In 1974 Happer rose to president of the North Carolina Tennis Association, which he then incorporated. He also opened a dedicated NCTA office in the Raleigh Racquet Club, and hired Sally Wendt as the first state executive secretary. "Marshall was a great organizer and a real go-getter," said NCTA vice president Jack Warmath. "Very aggressive to get things done. He had a big impact on North Carolina tennis."

Honoring Our Own: The North Carolina Tennis Hall of Fame

By 1974, almost a decade and a half after the founding of the NCTA and the NCTF, North Carolina was honored by the Southern Lawn Tennis Association for having the most registered members in the south—1,511—the most member clubs in the USLTA—69—and the most sanctioned tournaments—67.

INDIVIDUAL CONTRIBUTIONS
Western Carolina's dean of tennis, Dick Covington, wanted somewhere to house his memorabilia. Consequently, he donated his entire estate to a foundation called the Irene and Dick Covington Foundation for the purpose of improving the Aston Park Tennis Center. With the money, Aston Park built a new clubhouse there, which displays some of Covington's memorabilia.

Upon Covington's death, Asheville applied to the Parks and Recreation Trust Fund, and along with a small grant from the USTA they built the clubhouse, display area, walking trail, and improvements, all thanks to Dick Covington's love of tennis.

That year represented another landmark when Mildred Southern was elected the first female president of the NCTA. Southern, in turn, hosted the first "Tennis Weekend" in Greensboro, where competitors, volunteers, organizers, teaching pros, and others attend. This showcase event is now held every January in Pinehurst, with hundreds of attendees coming together for hard work and good times.

Southern, yet another in what became a long line of extraordinary presidents, had started her career in tennis years earlier. "Somebody invited me to come to the North Carolina Tennis Association annual meeting early on, and I came," she remembered. "The whole meeting was about who gets what tournament. I thought it was a waste of time. I felt that we ought to be starting grassroots tennis, teaching juniors, and so many things that could be going on in all of the cities. So I was appointed chairman of junior tennis at that first meeting."

North Carolina was honored by the Southern Lawn Tennis Association for having the most registered members in the south.

By the time she was NCTA president she had developed numerous creative programs in Winston-Salem, and wanted to spread them to the other parts of the state. Thus, her annual NCTA meetings were different than that first one she had attended. "We wanted to have the meetings to get all of the cities to have representatives," she said. "We wanted someone that was interested in junior tennis to come, someone that was interested in adult tennis, someone who was interested in tournament tennis."

Southern, with support from Happer, John Peddycord, and many others, spearheaded the creation of the North Carolina Tennis Hall of Fame, to be housed at the then new J. Spencer Love Tennis Center in Greensboro. The Hall of Fame was created "to honor those persons who, by excellence of their activities in or connected with North Carolina Tennis, have brought substantial recognition and esteem to themselves and the State."

The first honorees in 1975 were North Carolina coach John Kenfield, Greensboro's Anne Martindale, Charlotte's outstanding player Bo Roddey, and native Chapel Hillian Archibald Henderson. Allen Morris, Dick Covington, and Carlyle Lewis were among the deserving recipients the next three years.

Greensboro's Anne Martindale
Named to the first class of the North Carolina Tennis Hall of Fame in 1975. She won numerous North Carolina state championships and later founded the Sugar Bowl junior tennis tourney in New Orleans, LA.

POCKETS OF THE GAME

Swing Through the Ball! North Carolina's Teaching Pros

Throughout the 1950s and 1960s, and into the early 1970s as the NCTA was gaining strength, North Carolina continued to suffer from a dearth of teaching professionals. The ones on hand, however, were outstanding. Among the most notable were Dick McKee in Charlotte; Jim Amaya in Shelby, a transplant from Colombia, South America; Robbie Smith at Sugar Mountain in Banner Elk; Maurice Everette of the Forsyth Country Club in Winston-Salem; Jim Winstead of the Greensboro Country Club; Jim Emmons of the Raleigh Racquet Club; Jim Haslam at the Chapel Hill Tennis Club; and Herb Bolick of Emerywood Country Club in High Point. Many of the college coaches, such as NC State's J.W. Isenhour, Appalachian State's Bob Light, and Wake Forest's Jim Leighton, also worked part time as teaching pros at local clubs in the summers.

In 1973 a core group formed the North Carolina Association of Tennis Professionals. The purpose of the NCATP, as stated in its revised constitution of March 12, 1978, "shall be to strive towards all objectives that are in the best interests of the members and the sport of tennis."

The NCATP committed itself to keeping high standards in the teaching profession, fostering "meetings, tournaments, idea exchanges, clinics, and technical publications for the welfare of the members," and on facilitating professional growth through job placement, standardization of contracts, and other such professional services. Emmons was elected the first president for 1973 and 1974, and was succeeded by Light for 1975, Isenhour for 1976, and Bolick for 1977 and 1978.

The NCATP also began to have tournaments of its own in 1975. Former UNC star Jim Corn of Shelby won the first year, followed by Dean Mathias in 1976 and 1977. Also in 1975, the United States Professional Tennis Association instituted for North Carolina the selection of "Tennis Professional of the Year." Winstead won the first year, followed by Smith of Asheville and Bolick of High Point.

The development of the NCATP was prescient because the number of professionals grew with the phenomenal growth of the game in the 1970s. By 1978 President Bolick estimated that there were nearly 80 full-time professionals in the state and some 20 others who devoted part of their time as a pro.

Jim Emmons
One of the NCATP's first presidents.

Mildred Southern
Founder of the Young Folks tennis program in Winston-Salem and as the first female president of the NCTA. Southern, an avid age group tournament player, holds numerous state age group titles.

ARTHUR ASHE VS. ALLEN MORRIS

Arthur Ashe, who was 21 in 1964 and ranked 6th in the world, up from 18 the year before, was in Greensboro with an ATA event, which was co-sponsored by N.C. A&T, according to Allen Morris. "They wanted to have an exhibition and called me." Morris was probably the only player in town who could play with Ashe, but he had to come out on his lunch hour from Burlington Industries for the match at the old Memorial Park. "There were a couple of hundred people there, including a lot of my buddies from work."

The buddies were rewarded: Morris won 7-5, 7-5. "Arthur was playing exhibition tennis," said the modest Morris. Despite the temper of the times, there was no racial backdrop to the match. "I knew Arthur," said Morris. "We'd been in tournaments together. He was a nice guy. And he always handled everything with such class. There were no racial overtones in the match. It was just tennis, and I think people enjoyed it."

African-American Tennis

African-American tennis was still beset by prejudice in the 1960s, with many players forced to play exclusively in ATA events and excluded from private clubs in North Carolina and elsewhere. Allen Morris and Arthur Ashe moved the needle in 1964 when they played an exhibition in Greensboro in what was thought to be one of the first times in Greensboro—which of course had been a flashpoint in the civil rights revolution—that white and black amateur athletes competed head-to-head.

In Wilmington, Dr. Eaton kept inviting youngsters over to his court, and Lenward Simpson led a group of young players in that city. Durham, however, became the real hotbed for African-American tennis in the 1960s and 1970s. The Algonquin Tennis Club on Fayetteville Street hosted many junior tournaments, with Mrs. Bess Whitted spearheading the organization. Dr. Cardozo McCollum, president of Durham's Blue

Allen Morris
Multiple state champion, Wimbeldon quarter-finalist, and coach at UNC-Chapel Hill.

Ribbon Tennis Club, "had a little juniors group going on with Coach Bear Easterling, who used to teach at Hillside," according to John McLean, an active Durham player and volunteer. Early on, this group "started off with paddle ball because they didn't have tennis rackets. Then Sam Moore made some racquets for the kids."

Durham Legend
Bonnie Logan, one of the most outstanding players in North Carolina history, won numerous ATA titles.

Like Dr. Johnson in Lynchburg, McCollum "would take his charges all over the country...to Baltimore, Atlanta, Detroit, New York," recounted McLean. Joe Williams, a good friend of Arthur Ashe's, got his start this way, and "he and Arthur would play each other on the North Carolina Central courts when Arthur was in town. Joe was a better player at one point, but Arthur had the better temperament," said McLean.

In the late 1960s, Williams made a name for himself in ATA circles, and a junior by the name of John Lucas, son of the principal at Hillside, began to emerge as a top junior player nationally. Among the girls, Sylvia Hooks and Bonnie Logan made splashes nationally. In 1972 Logan became the Althea Gibson of South Africa, breaking the color barrier in the South African Open Tennis Championships. Later that year she became the first African American on the Virginia Slims Tennis Tour, where she was followed by Hooks.

Tennis Gardens Bloom

The number of public courts, including a few destined to become among the most important centers for tennis in the state, exploded in North Carolina between 1961 and 1978. In 1975 Greensboro built the 13 clay courts of the J. Spencer Love Tennis Center. Keith Richardson, the Southern Conference Player of the Year representing Appalachian State, and John Lucas, the ACC Player of the Year representing the University of Maryland, opened the facility with an exhibition match. The J. Spencer Love Tennis Center, under the direction of Donna Sauls, went on to host such notable tournaments as the North Carolina State Adult Championships, USTA National Girls' 14 Clays, USTA National Boys' 12 Clays, and the Carolina Cup. The North Carolina Tennis Hall of Fame was housed there for a number of years.

In Raleigh, the 23 lighted hard courts of the Millbrook Exchange Tennis Center on Spring Forest Road came on line in 1978. The Joe White Tennis Center at Hanes Park was upgraded in 1973 and named for the former Parks and Recreation Director, who was also Mildred

Durham's John Lucas
John Lucas was an outstanding junior who went on to a stellar tennis career at the University of Maryland, and played on the pro tour before becoming a top player in the NBA.

Southern's brother-in-law.

Outstanding facilities often brought outstanding programming. The Joe White Tennis Center became a model of community grassroots programming, winning national recognition as Mildred Southern continued to be a driving force in the development of the many community programs held there under the umbrella of Winston-Salem Tennis, Inc. "I had gotten the Recreation Department's permission to use the Joe White courts on Saturday morning for clinics instead of just leaving it open to the public to use," said Southern. "We had a junior clinic, which we called 'Young Folks' tennis.

Joe White Tennis Center
Named for Winston-Salem's former Parks and Rec Director, the Joe White Tennis Center at Hanes Park became a center for both recreational and tournament competition.

HOW A COMMUNITY TENNIS PROGRAM STARTS

"In the summer of 1974, I went to be the pro at the North Hills Club," said former NC State player Cy King. "Marshall Happer and some other local community leaders had been lobbying the city to upgrade their tennis facilities and programs. In addition, people had been bugging the city about getting somebody to be full-time with tennis.

"I think the turning point was 1973 when the recreation superintendent and the assistant superintendent tried to run the city tennis tournament and it had not gone very well. They told me that they just got cussed out, and said, 'We're not doing this anymore. We're going to hire somebody.'

"So they called me." Fortunately for Raleigh and tennis in North Carolina, the position King thought was short-term and interim turned into a career.

We were trying to teach all of the juniors how to play, black or white, no matter." The Winston-Salem Parks and Recreation Department partnered with Winston-Salem Tennis, Inc. to run Young Folks tennis and numerous other state, regional, and national tournaments at the Hanes Park. In 1975, the same year she was president of the NCTA, Southern received special recognition from the USTA for developing the Young Folks program.

"Mildred felt that tennis was a sport for everybody, and that was all the work she did in Winston-Salem," said friend and fellow volunteer Vicki Everette. "That spilled over into the North Carolina Tennis Association. For her it was a matter of the game, not a matter of the country club."

With the building of public tennis centers came a new kind of tennis administrator: public tennis directors. While many club tennis pros were active in programming, their primary focus was on the court teaching lessons. Public tennis directors, on the other hand, were tasked with providing year-round tennis activities that reached all segments of the population. In most cases, these tennis directors spent the majority of their time not on the court, but in the office developing programs.

Cy King
Longtime City of Raleigh Parks and Recreation Tennis Director, Cy King was a leader in the CTA and league movements, and a behind-the-scenes force for the growth of the game in North Carolina.

Working with many of the local tennis leaders in their communities, these directors were instrumental in establishing and running many of the youth and adult instructional programs, leagues, and tournaments that are such a vital part of tennis in North Carolina. Their full-time status resulted in more off-season programming, with tournaments, winter workout excellence programs, and league play being scheduled in December, January, and February.

"Mildred [Southern] felt that tennis was a sport for everybody..."

In the 1970s John Morris at the Joe White Tennis Center, Donna Sauls at Latham Park and Spencer Love Tennis Center, Cy King at Millbrook Exchange Tennis Center, and Ed Ray at Oak Hollow in High Point were the first full-time tennis directors in their communities. In subsequent years, as new public centers were built in communities across the state, other notable directors such as John Walton at the Burlington Tennis Center, Henry Hostetler at Riverbirch Tennis Center in Greenville, and Parks Easter at the Bingham Tennis Center in Lexington joined the ranks.

Everybody Now! Community Tennis Programs on Public Courts

Community programs spread rapidly. "Winston-Salem started all of it, I think," said Southern of the trend toward active community programs. "That's when we tried to involve all of the other cities and bring them into it and get them started."

In Raleigh Cy King was hired as the first tennis director for the City parks system, and became one of the first to promote year-round tennis. He initiated winter workouts, "frostbite" tournaments in the cold months, and other innovative programs before indoor courts became common.

Laurinburg was another example of a top-quality public tennis center (four soft courts and eight hard courts) that provided a venue for player development. "They had some good players come out of Laurinburg," noted King. "Many of the great success stories have taken place in towns such as Lexington, Henderson, and Shelby, which produced players like Phil Head, Sally Schweppe, and Tim Wilkison. Many communities developed innovative programming before many of the national USTA programs even existed, so that's

another legacy in North Carolina tennis: we've had these pockets of small towns that produced some really good tennis players."

Private Clubs Join the Movement

Private clubs proliferated alongside public tennis centers in the 1960s and 1970s. Now one of the state's most prestigious clubs, the Olde Providence Racquet Club in Charlotte was founded in 1962 by Cliff Turner as a not-for-profit, member-owned club. Today it is located on a beautiful 55-acre campus and offers 27 outdoor clay (15 lighted), five outdoor hard, and five indoor hard tennis courts.

In the 1960s, "tennis was a secondary sport at traditional country clubs," said Marshall Happer. "The boards would say, 'If you make us angry, we're going to dig up the tennis courts and make them into a putting green.' So Olde Providence was the first tennis and swim club that wasn't a country club. That was the beginning of real tennis clubs in North Carolina."

Olde Providence gained its preeminent position in North Carolina not only for its outstanding facilities, but also for hosting prestigious events such as the Davis Cup, the NCNB Classic, U.S. Men's Clay Court Championships, World Team

Olde Providence
A lively scene at the Olde Providence Racquet Club.

Congratulations
Cliff Turner, founder of the Olde Providence Racquet Club, congratulates American Cliff Richey and Australian Bob Carmichael on an outstanding final at a pro tournament at Olde Providence.

in the state, the Chapel Hill Tennis Club, which was subsequently founded by Eastern Carolina Tennis Association players Bob Boyce, Mac McGinty, and Bill Blackburn. In 1967 six clay courts were built southwest of town. Eventually it grew to 18 outdoor clay courts, six hard courts, and four indoor courts. The Chapel Hill Tennis Club has also been home to numerous tournaments, such as the NC State Junior Closed and the Fall Adult Invitational.

Also in 1967, Happer made it three major new tennis-only clubs in North Carolina in three years. At the time, Happer was president of the Raleigh Tennis Club, an unincorporated association fielding a men's team in the Eastern Carolina Tennis Association. "We also staged tournaments periodically and paid to keep up the six clay North Carolina State varsity courts," he said. "They let us play our matches there."

By about 1965, the RTC needed to find a new venue. "NC State finally kicked us off. They said they could no longer let us use the varsity courts because they needed them for the students and the faculty."

Happer tried without success to get the city to build an enlarged and modern tennis center at Pullen Park. "We actually tried to play a year or two at the public parks in Raleigh and we tried to rent them, even tried to buy one, and we couldn't do that, so that led us to start the Raleigh Racquet Club."

"We incorporated with six courts in 1967," said Happer. A pool and swim house were put in by 1969, but with 200 families competing for

Tennis, and the Federation Cup. Olde Providence also catered to North Carolina only events, eventually serving as a regular host for the North Carolina State Closed Tournament for adults in certain age groups and the North Carolina Junior Clay Court State Open.

Though he left the state for another position in Connecticut in 1966, Henry Clark in Chapel Hill had put the wheels in motion to build the second tennis-only club space on six courts, more land was bought and more courts soon added.

Today, the Raleigh Racquet Club, situated on 36 wooded acres in North Raleigh, offers 17 outdoor clay courts, eight hard courts, a 10,000-square-foot clubhouse, and Raleigh's only indoor facility: eight clay courts. An anchor club in the North Carolina tennis scene, the club would host the Southerns and national tournaments, and its stadium court would feature exhibition matches by many of the world's leading players.

In 1973, five years after the Raleigh Racquet Club got its start, the Olde Forest Racquet Club was founded in Elon by a group of avid tennis players from Alamance County. Nestled in 15 wooded acres, it quickly became not only one of the most active, but also one of the most picturesque clubs in North Carolina.

In Asheville, a city out front in the early part of the century in terms of public tennis facilities with Aston Park, Buster Brown founded the Asheville Racquet Club in 1974. It was the first private club to be devoted primarily to tennis in western North Carolina. Brown, a Notre Dame tennis letterman, tour player, and national age-group champion as an adult, secured numerous important tournaments at the facility. The addition of a downtown center in 2010 eventually brought the number of indoor and outdoor courts to 40.

Chapel Hill Wins Cup

FT. EUSTIS — Chapel Hill defeated Fort Eustic, 6-3, Sunday and carried off the Sidney Banks Cup to North Carolina. The Tar Heels captured four singles matches and two in doubles to complete their conquest in the two-day tennis competition.

On Saturday Fort Eustis defeated the Cavalier of Virginia Beach and Chapel Hill defeated Byrd Park of Richmond.

In the consolation match Sunday Byrd Park edged the Cavalier, 5-4.

The contestants will move to the Cavalier courts this afternoon for a series of exhibition matches. The public is invited.

Chapel Hill 6, Fort Eustis 3
Singles—Malcolm Clark (CH) d. Richard Peters, 3-6, 6-3, 6-4; Charlie Shaffer (CH) d. Bill Shiver, 6-1, 0-6, 6-3; Jack Elliott (Ft. E) d. Marvin Silver 6-2, 4-1 default; Ronald Poindexter (Ft. E) d. Walter Lockett 6-2, 6-4; Mel Jordan (CH) d. Joseph Lerner 6-1, 6-0; Chick McClure (CH) d. Gerry Kreft 7-5, 6-3.

Doubles—Peter-Shiver (Ft. E.) d. M. Clark-Lockett, 6-3, default; Jordan-Shaffer (CH) d. Elliott-Francis Novitzky 6-3, 6-3; Jasper Memory-Silver (CH) d. George Jackson-Mai. Gen. N. H. Vissering, 6-1, 7-5.

Byrd Park 5, Cavalier 4
Singles—Phil Berry (C) d. Jerry Vankus, 6-2, 6-3; Gene Short (BP) d. Marshall Wheeler, 6-2, 6-3; Gene Gee (BP) d. Ed Kilgore, 6-3, 6-2; Garland Carlton (BP) d. Ralph Johnson, 6-3, 8-6; Mac Duke (BP) d. George Popper, 6-3, 6-2; Bill Bradt (C) d. Ernie Webb, 6-2, 7-5.

Doubles—Berry-Wheeler (C) d. Gee-Short, 6-2, 8-6; Frank Wells-Kilgore (C) d. Duke-Webb, 6-2, 6-0; Vankus-Carlton (BP) d. William Seidel-Lorenzo Sabin, 6-2, 6-2.

Milton Abbott, Cavalier tennis pro, presents Sidney Banks Cup to Captain H. S. McGinty of Chapel Hill team.

Tennis Coverage
Club competition received a lot of ink in the 1970s.

69TH ANNUAL SOUTHERN CHAMPIONSHIPS
JULY 8-14, 1974
RALEIGH RACQUET CLUB

Where It All Starts: Junior Tennis

One of Henry Clark's stated goals had been to promote little league tennis across the state. As Happer noted, junior tennis in the early 1960s was limited to a few tournaments and regional league play, but in 1963 NCTA State Chairman of Youth Tennis John Allen Farfour happily reported at the annual meeting that the number of teams across the state had increased from eight to 20.

This new opportunity to compete at the local level exposed more players to tennis. One of the first local junior league programs was developed in 1963 when the Raleigh Little League was organized with teams from Pullen Park, Jaycee Park, The North Hills Club, and the NC State Faculty Club. When the first Carolinas Juniors' and Boys' Team matches were held in Raleigh, local junior play saw an additional boost in Raleigh.

"There weren't that many tournaments then," remembered Tommy Dixon, former UNC star and longtime tennis director at Kildaire Farms Racquet Club in Cary. "There were maybe three or four that you could play, like the ECTA, the North Carolina Closed, the Sandhills tournament in Southern Pines, or the Greensboro Invitational."

Like many kids and adults throughout the state, Dixon and others in Raleigh were the beneficiaries of the efforts of a dedicated volunteer who sought no credit for his efforts. "During the summers when I was a kid my father would drop me off at the NC State courts at 8:00 in the morning and come back and pick me up at 6:00 at night," remembered Dixon. "There were about eight of us who would spend the whole day at the courts." Dr. Paul Bredenberg, an NC State philosophy professor, organized activities for kids at the courts. He taught free clinics every Saturday morning that were open to anyone who wanted to come. He set up a challenge ladder for us to play on and the top kids on the ladder formed a team to play matches in the ECTA junior league. We would play teams from Chapel Hill, Durham, Goldsboro, and Kinston. Dr Bredenberg would drive our team to matches in his old Volkswagen van. Nobody paid him. He just did it. It was a great experience."

There were numerous volunteers around the state like Bredenberg and

Raleigh Racquet Club
Raleigh Mayor Clarence Lightner, Dodge Geohegan and Charlie Morris at the groundbreaking for the new building. The club grew quickly to become one of the busiest clubs in North Carolina and hosted many important tournaments, such as the Southerns in 1974.

Tommy Dixon
One of UNC's top players in the 1970s and a teaching pro in Cary for many years.

Mildred Southern in Winston-Salem and John Allen Farfour in Goldsboro who fostered junior tennis one way or another.

In 1973, the Piedmont Tennis Association formed junior leagues with boys and girls competing across the region. Lexington, Burlington, Greensboro, Winston-Salem, Reidsville, and Salisbury all fielded

teams competing in the 18, 16, 14, and 12 and under age divisions.

In 1975 the Raleigh Parks system added a novice league to the already-existing Little League program. The league was for beginners and operated out of 14 park sites. Opportunities to compete were expanding and league play was not just for the better players anymore.

Junior summer camps added to the opportunities. Ed Cloyd held one of the first in the 1960s at Atlantic Christian College and there was another at Pfeiffer College. Starting in the 1970s, renowned Puerto Rican teaching pro Welby van Horn started tennis camps at Pinehurst; Mary Lou Jones, longtime coach at St. Mary's, had a long-running camp there, and Robbie Smith and Woody Blocher had thriving concerns in Asheville. At the same time, more and more junior

Paul Bredenberg
Bredenberg was one of tennis's unsung heroes, spending hours teaching kids to play on weekends and carrying them to competitions in his car.

Tennis Clinics
The North Carolina Tennis Foundation underwrote junior clinics throughout the state. Here youngsters learn the basics in Winston-Salem.

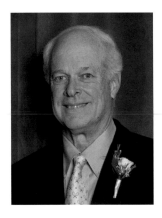

Keith Stoneman
Former UNC standout Keith Stoneman won the state title in 1971.

tournaments came on line. By 1975 junior tennis in North Carolina was increasing exponentially in all areas.

COMPETITIVE TENNIS

Ready... Play! Major Tournaments — Senior and Junior

The North Carolina Tennis Association's first major coup after reorganizing in 1961 came when Winston-Salem hosted the Southerns, the showcase tournament for the USLTA's nine-state Southern section.

The next year the North Carolina Open Tennis Championship became the North Carolina Invitational Tennis Championships. In 1967, 297 players competed in the State Junior Closed in Winston-Salem.

To create more out-of-state opportunities for juniors, the North Carolina Tennis Foundation first sent two, then four players each year to the Nationals in Kalamazoo, and Dr. McCollum and Dr. Eaton arranged for the African-American players to compete in ATA tournaments throughout the East. Other than these token efforts, however, relatively few players left the state to compete. In addition to lack of money, "we had no indoor courts," said Billy Trott. "Thus, while kids in other parts of the country played year-round, tennis was a half-year sport for many of our top athletes."

"Jim Corn, Tommy Dixon, and Lucas were some of the top players who did travel out of state to play tournaments," noted top junior Bobby Koury of his colleagues from the late 1960s. As early as 1963, Koury and his brother Chip played in the Sugar Bowl Championships between Christmas and New Year's in New Orleans. "But the majority of players," he said, "mostly played tournaments in North Carolina."

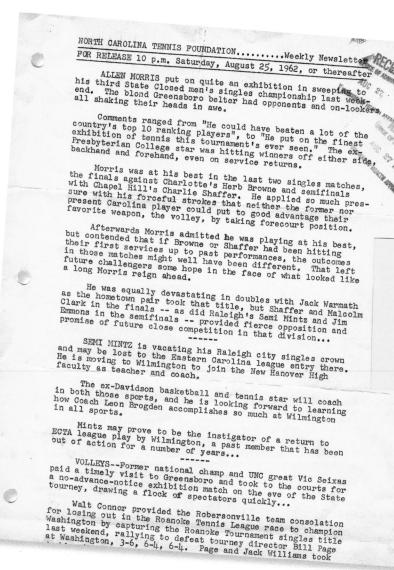

An Early Newlsetter
Early newsletters, produced by Grady Elmore, were long on information and short on graphics.

On the rare occasions when North Carolina's best juniors did go out of state, Trott notes that they faced obstacles because of the style of play they had learned. "Most top-level competitive play in the state was on clay courts. Most junior and adult tournaments in the state were on Har-Tru clay courts in Greensboro, Winston-Salem, Raleigh, Charlotte, and Asheville, and on red clay in Southern Pines. Top college matches in the state were primarily played on classic clay courts such as those by the old cemetery in Chapel Hill and below the steep bank at NC State. That's what people played on, so most North Carolina players developed baseline games suitable for slow courts."

The National Juniors at Kalamazoo was on hard courts, however, and many of the other major "national" tournaments were played in the northeast on grass, which rewarded offensive net play. When North Carolina juniors traveled to these tournaments, therefore, they played on fast surfaces, which did not suit their baseline games, and against players from the East, California, and the Midwest who had learned the game on fast concrete and asphalt courts that rewarded serve and volley play. "It was not a recipe for success," said Trott.

There was the occasional turnabout, he noted. "Sometimes 'name' juniors from California, Florida, or overseas would come to tournaments on slow North Carolina clay, and end up getting thrashed by a top North Carolina player like Gene Hamilton of Asheville, who

they may have never heard of."

Mildred Southern, again a pioneer, helped juice the pipeline for juniors to travel in the very early

> ### "Most top-level competitive play in the state was on clay courts."

1970s. "We got two buses and got all of the juniors that wanted to go to the Southern Tournament in Atlanta. They had a great time. All of the states were supposed to send people to play in those tournaments. Sometimes the juniors didn't get there unless someone was helping them. We just felt like in North Carolina that we ought to try to get our juniors down there."

Youth Versus Age

In the period from the late 1940s to the early 1970s, when winning the "State Closed" was the paramount goal for the state's adult players, Greensboro's powerful Allen Morris reigned for almost a decade as king of tennis in the state. Winning seven state championships, Morris employed powerful ground strokes to fend off challenges from contemporaries such as serve-and-volley player Herb Browne.

The "youth versus age" theme was then, as now, a hot topic in tennis. Inevitably Morris aged and was dethroned by youthful Gene Hamilton, who won four times. Hamilton was dethroned a few years later by a series of younger players: Bob Koury, Jim Amaya, and Tim Wilkison. Not lost in this youthful revolution, however, was the comeback by Keith Stoneman, who at the "ancient" age of 30, won in 1971.

Julia Anne Holt
Greensboro's Julia Anne Holt, who started playing in the juniors, won numerous state championships in the 1950s and 1960s, continued to pick up age division titles into the 21st century.

Top Junior and UNC Star
Raleigh's Billy Trott served North Carolina tennis as a dedicated volunteer for decades.

On the women's side, Anne Martindale, Audrey Brown, and Sarah Walters dominated over many years, each winning four state championships. Later, Joanne Cooper, Alicia Smythe, Julia Anne Holt, and Bonnie Logan each won two times.

As the number of players was beginning to increase rapidly and the post-war baby boomer generation was advancing, some significant changes were instituted to meet the growing demand for adult tournament tennis. Administrators recognized the difficulty faced by adults, with demanding jobs and families, in playing against younger players, particularly in the grueling North Carolina summertime heat and humidity.

For many years the major age differentiation for "senior" adult tournaments had been age 45, but in 1973 state championships began to be played in the 35s. Newer divisions became popular, and by 1979 state championships began to be played in multiple five-year age brackets over 35.

These new age brackets helped bring about an era in which the adult tournament tennis format blossomed all across the state, proving that competitive tennis can last a lifetime. Many new tournaments sprung up, and decades later there are over 100 adult tournaments played in North Carolina each year. The more recent advent of player ratings and the popularity of the league tennis format today afford an even greater range of opportunities for players of similar abilities to compete against each other.

The Game Flourishes Nationally—to North Carolina's Benefit

As the North Carolina Tennis Association was attempting to stimulate the game in North Carolina in the 1960s and 1970s, tennis around the country started to blossom, boosted to some extent by open tennis in 1968. The very next year Rod Laver won the Grand Slam, and stars such as Billie Jean King, Jimmy Connors, Ilie Nastase,

Gene Hamilton
Four-time state champion Gene Hamilton of Asheville confounded visiting out-of-state hard court players with a tricky clay court game.

and Chrissie Evert captured the public's imagination through expanded television coverage. In 1973 Bobby Riggs and Billie Jean King brought the sport into the mainstream with their widely publicized, globally viewed match at the Houston Astrodome. Public television showed night tennis across the country.

North Carolina rode the wave as more and more junior tournaments came on line in major cities. Beginning in 1972 with the Tar Heel Qualifier, which qualified top players for major tournaments at the next level, Winston-Salem again took a leadership role in developing tournaments, just as it had in developing junior programs. "We were doing the junior tennis and we were having tournaments," said Southern. "We even had family tournaments, father/son, mother/daughter. We had the open championship for the women's champion and the men's champion. We wanted to get everyone possible involved in tennis."

"We got our first national tournament in about 1975," said Winston-Salem volunteer and longtime NCTA executive John Peddycord. In 1976 the city hosted a "tennithon," with juniors playing from all over the state and raised $6,500 for junior development.

"Winston-Salem Tennis, Inc. had their own funding," said current NCTA executive director Kelly Gaines. "They ran tournaments with their money, and had fundraising. Neill McGeachy ran the Edgar B. out at Tanglewood and proceeds for that went to Winston-Salem Tennis, Inc., which provided all the volunteers."

In Raleigh in 1972, Happer brought the Southern

Championships to the Raleigh Racquet Club for the first year of a five-year run. "We paid $5,000 in player expense money. I gave everybody $40. I had a 256 draw in men's singles. We had women's singles and we had men's 50s singles and doubles and mixed. It was a big tournament."

Second, just as with the blossoming of public facilities and tournaments in larger cities, small pockets of players and tournaments soon began to proliferate in smaller towns throughout North Carolina. "Kinston was known for its big junior tournament," said longtime Greenville city tennis director and club owner Henry Hostetler. "Goldsboro had the Eastern Carolina Tennis Association Tournament. Elizabeth City had a great tournament as well."

Third, as the game continued to grow, some of the private clubs—notably the Asheville Racquet Club, the Chapel Hill Tennis Club, and the Raleigh Racquet Club—finally started to build indoor facilities. First they tended to be bubbles over one or two courts, then permanent buildings. And many of these were faster hard courts. This was a major development with lasting implications, because

Neill McGeachy
An early promoter of professional tennis in North Carolina.

Tennis Man
This unique trophy developed by the Raleigh Racquet Club for the Southern Championships was a popular and iconic symbol of North Carolina tennis.

49

with indoor tennis, tournaments could be held year-round, teaching pros could enjoy year-round employment, and juniors, with more teaching pros and year-round instruction, could have the same opportunities to develop as players in Florida, California, Texas, and similarly temperate regions, and on the same type of fast, hard courts on which more and more national tournaments were played. Players from the state began to learn fast court strategies.

The next generation of players—those in the 1970s—could all trace their rise to the availability of winter tennis.

The next generation of players—those in the 1970s—could all trace their rise to the availability of winter tennis. With year-round practice and tournaments, top juniors such as John

Sadri in Charlotte, Andy Andrews in Raleigh, Jane Preyer from Greensboro, and Camey Timberlake of Lexington finally began to enjoy opportunities to travel out of state and compete more effectively on a national basis. Even with the indoor courts, however, they likely could not have done it without the backing from the ever-stronger NCTA, NCTF, and an increasing cadre of excellent teaching pros.

When the USLTA—which dropped the "L" after 1975 to become the USTA—began to sponsor more and more age-group events, the NCTA, with its active tournament calendar, also added more and more sanctioned senior

Venue for the Stars
The Julian J. Clark Stadium at Olde Providence Racquet Club in Charlotte hosted the Davis Cup and many major events.

tournaments with age divisions five years apart.

The state tournament continued to be a hotly contested event, with the open division often won by top college-age players. Multiple winners included Andy Avram, Stephen Enochs, Stephanie Rauch, and most notably Wayne Hearn and Susan McDanald.

Special events grew as well. The Davis Cup was played for the first time in North Carolina in 1968 when the American Zone Finals were held on the Julian J. Clark Stadium in Charlotte's then new Olde Providence Racquet Club. The USA defeated Ecuador 5-0.

Three years later the Davis Cup Challenge Round started badly at Olde Providence when the wrong national anthem was played for the Romanian team. Then it rained incessantly, turning the club's clay courts into a swamp. When the music stopped and the skies cleared, the USA defeated Romania 3-2 on the strength of a stellar, come-from-behind performance by Frank Froehling.

In 1973, on the same court, Chrissie Evert, to that point merely a junior phenom, burst onto the international tennis scene by besting Françoise Durr of France and then world champion Margaret Court in an eight-woman invitational. Two years later, Arthur Ashe again visited North Carolina to play

an exhibition with Stan Smith in front of over 12,000 people in the Greensboro Coliseum. It was the largest crowd to ever see a match in the area.

In 1978 American Express put up $17,000 to sponsor ten satellite tournaments around the country. The tournaments themselves had to contribute $8,000 to meet a $25,000 tournament prize requirement. Happer, still running the Southerns at the Raleigh Racquet Club, found the $8,000 and changed the Southerns to one of the American Express Tournaments.

Happer was subsequently instrumental in turning the entire southern circuit into one of the early USTA satellite circuits, placing it on the calendar between the

Camey Timberlake
Awarded the first ever women's athletic scholarship at UNC. In the summer of 1973, Timberlake won five North Carolina titles in the span of a few weeks: the 18-under state singles title, the 18-under doubles title, the women's open, the women's open doubles and the mixed open doubles titles.

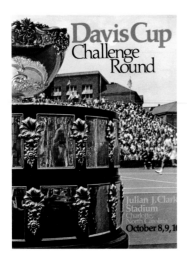

more established WATCH (World Association of Tennis Champions) circuit in Florida and the Missouri Valley Circuit. North Carolina was finally emerging from its isolation and becoming a part of the national tennis scene.

College Tennis

UNC, Davidson, and Wake had been the early tennis powers in North Carolina, with UNC perhaps occupying a spot first among equals in the very early years. For over eight decades following the first tennis ball being hit in Chapel Hill in 1884, much of the best

tennis in the state was played there. In an era before scholarships, top North Carolinians like Pinehurst's Bo Roddey often headed to Davidson and Wake, while UNC attracted top players from across the East Coast, such as Vic Seixas of Philadelphia

The advent of tennis scholarships in the mid- to late 1960s and early 1970s, together with the rapid transition from clay courts to hard, changed the face of college tennis in the state.

and Bitsy Grant of Atlanta, who sought the opportunity to play against one another in Chapel Hill. In 1967 UNC's Gene Hamilton was the first North Carolina native to win the ACC Singles championship. Among Coach Don Skakle's top players in the late 1960s and throughout the 1970s were O. H. Parrish, Jimmy Corn, and All-Americans George Sokol, Fred McNair, Rich McKee, and Billy Brock.

The advent of tennis scholarships in the mid- to late 1960s and early 1970s, together with the rapid transition from clay courts to hard, changed the face of college tennis in the state and brought greater competition and parity to the ACC.

By the early 1970s, Duke also had some good teams, most notably recruiting top national junior Mark Meyers of Louisiana, who won the ACC Singles championship in the early 1970s. During the same period, Wake Forest built some excellent records by attracting foreign stars such as Jim Haslam and Gary Cooper from Australia, Peter Pospisil from Canada, Eddie Prybl from Czechoslovakia, and Audley Bell from Jamaica. Several of

Present Ballboy, Future All-American
Stan Smith spearheaded the United States Davis Cup victory against Romania in Charlotte in 1971, but America's real secret weapon was 10-year-old ballboy and future NC State All-American Mark Dillon, just behind Smith.

these players had originally been recruited to Wingate by Ronnie Smarr. They teamed with North Carolinians such as Burlington's Bob and Chip Koury, Winston-Salem's Andy Avram, and Raleigh's Sammy Martin and Ed Parker, who was Wake's first scholarship recipient. At Davidson, the legendary Harry Fogleman continued Davidson's winning ways, begun in the 1950s with 183 wins against only 73 defeats in 11 seasons from 1961 to 1972. Under Fogleman, Davidson won every Southern Conference Championship but one between 1965 and 1971.

In 1968 NC State had hired former Appalachian player J.W. Isenhour, and he would bring the Wolfpack onto the national stage with players like Mark Dillon, Scott Dillon, and Matt McDonald from Charlotte, Bill Csipkay from New Jersey, John Joyce of Australia, Andy Andrews of Raleigh, and the best of them all, John Sadri of Charlotte, who would garner 86 NCAA singles victories in his career, lose a classic NCAA

singles final to John McEnroe in a legendary match, and eventually rise to number 14 in the world and the finals of the 1979 Australian Open.

"They had a good team the year before I came," said Andrews of the Sadri-anchored 1977 squad, which had registered a 17-3 record. "They

SADRI-MCENROE FINAL

The final of the 1978 NCAA between NC State's John Sadri and Stanford's legend-to-be John McEnroe remains perhaps the most famous NCAA match ever played.

McEnroe was an already well-known and brash Stanford freshman ranked number 15 in the world thanks to his reaching the Wimbledon semifinals following high school graduation; Sadri, a senior All-American from Charlotte representing the little-known tennis program at NC State, had gained some measure of fame by wearing his red NC State blazer and a black cowboy hat during the championships. "As his coach I agreed to it because of what he had meant to our program through his career," said NC State's coach, J.W. Isenhour.

Sadri had a wild card into the main draw of the US Open hanging in the balance plus the almost sure prospect of large monetary endorsements should he conquer the world's 15th ranked player on the way to the NCAA singles title. "In addition," said Isenhour, "there was the underlying fact that both these young men were great competitors and very volatile on the court.

"The level of play remained high for the entire match, with

the only service break of the day occurring in the third set, and the other three sets being decided by the 9th point of the 9-point tiebreak being used for NCAA play at that time."

Despite Sadri's 24 aces, McEnroe ultimately prevailed 7—6, 7—6, 5—7, 7—6 after 4¼ hours of play. Inside the match score, only one point (144-143) and one game (26-25) separated the two.

Eighteen months later Sadri reached the final of the Australian Open, on his way to a world number 14 ranking.

"It is still the best tennis match I have ever seen," said Isenhour. "I felt privileged to be personally involved."

John Sadri
NC State star particpated in perhaps the most famous NCAA singles final of all time.

UNC Team...

Before his untimely death, UNC Coach Don Skakle's teams won or tied for 18 ACC championships in 22 years, and major matches attracted huge crowds of spectators on the old clay courts on campus. Shown with his 1971 team, Forrest Simmons; Joe Garcia; Richard Hardaway; Freddie McNair; Bill Mears; Jim Corn; Terry Dukes; Richard McKee; and Mike Kernodle. In 1973 the team of McNair and McKee reached the NCAA doubles finals.

felt like that with one more good player they could win the ACC. So I committed to State." Coach Isenhour was right: with Sadri and Andrews leading the way, State broke Carolina's stranglehold on the ACC and won the ACC title in 1978 and 1979.

The rivalry was good for the game. "Don Skakle at UNC and Coach Leighton at Wake were the two guys who had the best reputations around here, and they always treated me nicely but they were always beating us," said Isenhour. "I didn't care how long it took, but I wanted to be able to walk up to those guys and shake their hands after we beat them." Of course, in his coaching and subsequent teaching around Raleigh, Isenhour's players brought him the ACC title and went on to succeed on the professional tour. A largely self-taught player who played at Appalachian State, he became a top teaching pro in Raleigh, and joined Skakle and Leighton as icons among North Carolina coaches.

Even with the rise of the other schools, by 1978 it was still Coach Skakle who owned the best won-

lost percentage record of any active collegiate coach in the whole country, 355-35 over 19 years; he was fourth in the total number of wins of any active coach. His teams had won or tied for 18 out of 20 Atlantic Coast Conference championships, compiling a 123-4 ACC record, and placed high nationally—the highest being 5th in 1972 and 7th in 1974.

Unfortunately, society was slow to place emphasis on women's sports programs prior to Title IX, the government regulation in 1972 that guaranteed equal opportunities for women in all educational programs, and that would give a large boost to women's athletics in general, and tennis in particular, all over the country. Women's tennis at the University of North Carolina had begun in the 1930s, for instance, but only as an intramural club for female undergraduates. Somewhat later, the club began to host informal extramural matches. Many of the larger universities did not even accept females for the first two years of college.

After Title IX, scholarships brought women to the major universities. UNC began a true women's intercollegiate tennis program in 1970-1971, when the university became a charter member of the Association for Intercollegiate Athletics for Women, with tennis designated one of six varsity teams for women.[10] Outstanding players included Laura DuPont, who was Mid-Atlantic Singles Collegiate Champion in 1968, 1970, and 1971, and Jane Preyer '72, who embarked after graduation on a successful professional career, including a win over Evonne Goolagong. Preyer later turned to coaching and won the ACC coach of the year title four times at Duke. In 1974 Lexington's Camey Timberlake received the first female athletic scholarship offered by UNC-CH. Future coaching legend Kitty Harrison took over the Lady Tar Heels squad in 1976, the beginning of a 22-year tenure.

Smaller colleges, like Wingate under Ron Smarr, which won two national championships in 1970 and 1971, kept pace with the powerhouses. And despite this dearth of major college women's programs, there were still a number of highly successful programs and players at smaller all-girls' schools. Peace College in Raleigh had a succession of outstanding teams and produced many successful players. Longtime Peace College president Dr. S. David Frazier saw that the

Title IX would give a large boost to women's athletics in general, and tennis in particular, all over the country.

co-educational schools at the time were slow to offer women scholarships in tennis and other sports. Just a year after Camey Timberlake was offered a scholarship to play tennis at UNC-CH, Frazier offered the first grant-in-aid to Ginger Lancaster Shields of New Bern. Many others followed, such as Mary Lloyd Hodges Barbera of Henderson, Leslie Lewis of Fayetteville, Bonnie Johnson of Cary, Susan Stanley and Diane Penesebene of Charlotte, and Nicole Nissley of Brevard. These women and others brought topnotch All-American honors to Peace College. The tradition continued into the 1990s with Peace College seeking the best women from the state of North Carolina. Not to be left out, Mary Lou Jones took St. Mary's to a prominent position among high school and

Kitty Harrison
Coach of the North Carolina Tar Heels from 1976 to 1998, she led the Heels to four conference championships.

NC State's 1979 ACC Championship Team
Bottom row, left to right: Andy Andrews; Carl Bumgardner; Scott Dillon; Matt McDonald. Top Row: Mark Greene; Allen Spizzo; John Joyce; Mark Dillon; Greg Hennemuth; Coach J.W. Isenhour.

college teams. The success of Mary Lou Jones's St. Mary's Tennis Camps each summer offered young women a chance to learn and then later compete on even footing.

LEAGUES

"Hey, North Carolina Seems to Have a Good Idea!"

By the mid-1970s, the popularity of tennis at the grassroots level forced the hand of the USTA, which tried to get out in front of the parade by helping to foster not just tournaments and junior development aimed at elite players, but broad participation in the game by recreational players who were not necessarily bound for the higher competitive ranks. In 1977, therefore, the USTA commissioned an independent marketing firm to explore new ways to stimulate the game among the general populace.

North Carolina had already provided the USTA its answer with its wildly popular intercity leagues across the state. At the time the number of towns entering men's teams in ECTA league play, for instance, had increased to 23 teams. Women from 15 towns in the ECTA region scheduled summer and intercity matches, and then drew up another schedule for fall with all but two of the same teams competing, plus six additional teams. Similar numbers appeared around the state.

In addition to the well-established WCTA, ECTA, and Piedmont Leagues, leagues like the Roanoke Tennis League grew and changed. "Tom Sayetta kind of led it in the '70s," said longtime Greenville

city tennis director and tennis club owner Henry Hostetler. "The Roanoke League was just a summer season thing for smaller crossroads towns such as Rich Square, Roxobel, Tarboro, Scotland Neck, and Enfield. It eventually gave way in the 1980s to the Downeast League."

By 1977 the Roanoke Tennis League counted ten teams, including towns such as Ayden, Jackson, Littleton, Greenville, Washington, Edenton, Elizabeth City, Plymouth, and Suffolk, Virginia. The league was always known for the high quality of play and for the emphasis on sportsmanship, underscored by a sportsmanship award given to a player selected by his teammates and competitors.

Finally, a plethora of smaller, more local leagues developed in the early and mid-'70s in imitation of the larger regional models. In Charlotte, the Queen City Tennis League was an organized women's league for clubs and other organizations. In Greensboro, the Gate City Tennis League, founded by Donna Rock and Linda Collins, eventually grew to four divisions based on skill levels, added additional clubs, and included park courts. Administration was assumed by commissioners that rotated between the clubs each year. Queen City and Gate City leagues still serve the communities today. Greenville and Elizabeth City had women's leagues and added mixed doubles in 1974 and 1976.

In the Triangle, two morning women's leagues dominated the action. The Capital Area Women's League included teams from Raleigh and Cary, with leadership rotating from club to club. The Triangle

League, administrated primarily by Faye Thomas and Liz Wagner of Durham, served a larger geographic area, including club and city teams from Raleigh, Cary, Durham, and Chapel Hill. Teams from Sanford entered as travel teams.

In 1975 Raleigh City Tennis Director Cy King started yet another morning women's league that included both club teams and park teams. "This league was popular, and eventually this was the league that was converted into the USTA League in the early 1980s," said King. "We added other leagues along the way with spring weekday evening men's and women's leagues, fall mixed doubles leagues and summer World Team Tennis (WTT) leagues."

These Raleigh leagues all eventually fell under the umbrella of the Raleigh Area Tennis League (RATL), the all-encompassing name for the league program that the Raleigh Parks System ran at both parks and clubs throughout Wake County. The Capital, Triangle, and RATL are all still in existence.

North Carolina's was among the most active state organizations in the country, leading most states in tournaments, clubs, local leagues, and USTA memberships. In 1977 the USTA commissioned an independent marketing firm to study future avenues for tennis, including league play. When the firm handed in its report, it urged immediate adoption of a national USTA League program.

The USTA Center for Education and Recreational Tennis conducted a national survey in 1978 and the findings projected that there were approximately 500,000 current league participants across the country, a figure that further emphasized the incipient popularity of the league format.

Recognizing the Southern and Mid-Atlantic Sections as the biggest hotbeds of league activity, the USTA planned pilot projects in those regions in which teams competed within specified ability levels locally, and winners advanced to a playoff between the two sections.

For North Carolina, which enjoyed more league activity than almost any other state, the compliment was obvious, but it was a mixed blessing. For areas with little or no activity the idea was a godsend, but North Carolina already possessed mature local league play, and hence the execution was more problematic. "Dickie Tyler from Charlotte and I attended the very first USTA League meeting in Atlanta back in the late '70s, and the leaders were saying that league tennis was going to be the greatest thing ever," said Cy King. "But we had lots of leagues in place already before USTA Leagues were designed or thought of. We had long thought of it as a bottom-up phenomenon...a great idea in Winston-Salem, in Raleigh, in Greensboro, and it would filter up. Then the USTA came in."

King nevertheless went back to Raleigh, advertised yet another new league for the city—a USTA League—and duly registered potential players for the USTA League.

League Tennis Takes Off in North Carolina
Initial USTA League play draws a Greensboro area team.

North Carolina Tennis Giants
Left to right, Dick Covington, Whit Cobb, C.R .Council, Mildred Southern, John Allen Farfour, Dr. Henry Clark.

"Then I got a call from the editorial writer at the *Raleigh Times* who was going to write an editorial questioning why membership in a national organization was required to play in a public parks league."

The fact was that the USTA wouldn't simply adopt North Carolina's existing leagues. To participate in USTA Leagues, the players had to be USTA members. Moreover, the local leagues had to overhaul their tried-and-true formats to adopt those required by the USTA.

"I called Marshall Happer to get his advice on what to do," continued King. "He said that I had a bigger problem than I knew. The league, which was supposed to have been approved at the USTA's national meeting that month, had in fact not been approved, so I had to give everybody who had signed up their money back. I guess they got the cart before the horse." As for the existing local leagues, most league directors and players simply refused to convert, and ignored the USTA. The Triangle League, Queen City, and Gate City, and many others continued on independent of official oversight, operating outside of USTA, STA (Southern Tennis Association), or NCTA jurisdiction. It was an approach borne perhaps of one of sports' most fundamental strategies: never change a winning game! Despite these rocky beginnings in 1978, USTA League play would grow and dramatically change the face of local and statewide competition.

Promise Delivered

Like the start of USTA League play in the mid-1970s, the rise of the modern NCTA between 1960, when it was reorganized, and 1978 had certainly not been without hiccups. But due in no small part to Henry Clark's leadership, Marshall Happer's efforts in competitive tennis, Mildred Southern's pioneering work in junior development, and the work of a terrific number of volunteers such as the original vice presidents and a small army of others like Whit Cobb in Durham, Sam Daniel in Eden, C.R. Council in Raleigh, John Peddycord in Winston-Salem, Cliff Turner in Charlotte, and many more, the Association and Foundation delivered almost completely on their original goals.

"You had people in place," said Vicki Everette. "You had Dick Covington in Asheville, you had Mildred and John in Winston, you had John Allen Farfour in the eastern part of the state, you had Buck Archer in Shelby that played tennis. These were people who loved the game and did not mind helping out. Once they got all of those people together, then things took off."

The programs to send juniors to national tournaments jumpstarted a lot of young careers and led others out of state. By 1974 Grady Elmore's newsletter had expanded to a circulation of 3,600, restricted solely to contributors to the NCTF. Sanctioned tournaments grew from nine in 1961 to 75 in 1978, with a concomitant rise in players ranked in the Southern section and nationally. In 1974, shortly after Title IX was pushed through in the NCAA, Bev Culbertson headed up the NCTA's statewide committee for women's tennis. Membership in USTA was up to 2,900, but the total number of tennis players in the state by the late 1970s exceeded half a million, up dramatically from 20 years before.

As the 1980s loomed, the biggest initiative on the NCTA's plate involved a plan to raise funds to move the NCTA, along with the Hall of Fame, to the J. Spencer Love Tennis Center in Greensboro. More money than anyone could have imagined in 1961 would start to flow into North Carolina from the USTA's increased revenues from US Open television rights and the National Tennis Center. North Carolina players and tournaments would continue to play an ever larger role on the national scene, and leagues for players at all levels would begin to blossom as verdantly as tournaments for the top players had over the past couple of decades.

Had anyone had a crystal ball, they could have been amazed at what the next 20 years would hold.

Democratization of the Game: 1977–1995

THE STATE OF THE GAME

IN THE LATE 1970s, tennis was in its heyday. The open game had matured after a decade, and the public enjoyed unprecedented television coverage of colorful characters like Connors, McEnroe, Borg, Nastase, Evert, Navratilova, and Goolagong, whose popularity boosted the game on all levels. If open tennis and television dramatically changed the game in the 1970s, then money—and lots of it—and computers were the catalysts to growth in the 1980s and 1990s on both the national level and in North Carolina.

The money, of course, would not have happened without open tennis and television, but all these forces together had triggered so much growth that the game had outgrown its infrastructure in some key places, most notably the charming but antiquated old Forest Hills Tennis Club in Queens, site of the US Open. When a few aficionados took the subway out from the city to watch a relatively small group of amateurs compete in the U.S. Nationals before 1968, Forest Hills' homey atmosphere was wonderfully quaint, ideal for a fringe sport. When, however, the US Open began to attract tens of thousands of fans to see the stars who had transcended their once semi-obscure sport and become celebrities in the larger culture, the narrow pathways of the Club or the 100 parking spaces Forest Hills afforded the USTA for spectator parking became woefully inadequate. It was as if the Super Bowl were being held at the local high school stadium.

In early 1977, soon-to-be-president of the USTA Slew Hester was flying into LaGuardia Airport when he looked down on Louis Armstrong Stadium on the grounds of the old 1964 World's Fair, and had an inspiration. Negotiations with New York City and New York City officials followed, and the U.S. National Tennis Center, affectionately known as "Slew's House" opened in time for the tournament in 1978. The US Open had a new home.

The House That Slew Built
USTA chief Slew Hester, who rose up through the Southern Tennis Association, was the mastermind behind the new National Tennis Center in Flushing, which became the new site of the US Open, replacing the much smaller West Side Tennis Club in Forest Hills.

The Epicenter of U.S. Tennis
The new National Tennis Center brought in the dollars to the US Open that flooded down to the grass roots level in American tennis.

Headquarters
The J. Spencer Love Tennis Center, built in 1975, was not only the site of many tournaments, but the first headquarters of the Hall of Fame. Photo courtesy of Mark Falcon.

What seemed at the time like a phenomenon at the very pinnacle of the game in fact within a few years would dramatically alter the landscape of the game at its very roots…in places like North Carolina…because a virtual torrent of television money began—though not immediately—to flow from the US Open to the USTA to the sections. From sections, like Southern, the money would fall to more regional bodies, like the North Carolina Tennis Association, which in turn distributed funds to programs, associations, and organizations throughout the state in its mission to grow the game.

"The USTA I think for awhile reinvested its money back into the US Open," said current NCTA executive director Kelly Gaines. "It was a little bit of a delayed reaction, but after moving to Flushing Meadows from Forest Hills, TV money went crazy. But the revenues for the US Open, which in recent years have grown to the hundreds of millions, were not immediately available."

With so many more players playing in the past decade, a more equitable and democratic method of gauging skill level was required, and a more automated system of managing the increasing numbers of players and events was needed. The National Tennis Rating Program (NTRP), and the subsequent application of computers to everything from tournament entries to rankings therefore became the second and third hallmarks of the late-20th-century game, with an impact almost as significant as the new money.

THE BUSINESS OF THE GAME

The North Carolina Tennis Hall of Fame Opens at J. Spencer Love Tennis Center

In the late 1970s, the North Carolina Tennis Association was operating out of Marshall Happer's Raleigh law office, and the Hall of Fame had no physical home whatsoever. Happer and Mildred Southern therefore led a broad fundraising effort to construct a building that would house both the Association staff and the North Carolina Tennis Foundation at the J. Spencer Love Tennis Center in Greensboro.

Although the NCTF Board of Directors voted to delay opening the campaign until May, 1981, "The facility was completed in 1979 at a cost of about $80,000," said John Peddycord, a Wachovia executive and longtime volunteer. "We filled that new building with our Hall of Fame memorabilia from the previous inductees as soon as it was dedicated."

Southern, as president of the Foundation; Peddycord, who was president of the Association; former Association president Marshall Happer; and Jim Melvin, the mayor of Greensboro, were all on hand to make the dedication. North Carolina thus became the only state in the country to have a building for its state Tennis Hall of Fame.

With a formal office and the money already increasing from the USTA and from more members, the NCTA could finally, in 1979, hire its first staff member, Dru Michaels, who came on board as the part-time executive secretary when the office moved to Greensboro. In addition to managing membership, tournaments, rankings, and early leagues, Michaels served as the editor of the *North Carolina*

Mary Milam
The NCTA's executive director started managing rankings by hand and eventually oversaw the computerization of the office.

Tennis News. By 1982, Michaels's third year, the Foundation had been financing and publishing the *North Carolina Tennis News* for 23 years, and its Board wanted a broader communication to inform more people of the various tennis activities across the state. With mailing lists from the Association, therefore, the newsletter was sent for the first time to all 5,000 USTA members residing in North Carolina.

Mary Milam Arrives

Michaels left in 1982, and was replaced by Mary Milam. "It was mostly just a clerical job," Milam remembered. "The USTA had some programs. They weren't putting enough money behind them. Mostly everything was still about the US Open, and their staff was really still geared toward the US Open at that point."

"It was a tremendous amount of work for her," said volunteer Vicki Everette, "because we were trying to do the rankings and seedings and get the tournaments going. Mary did all of the paperwork for everything."

"I was working hard to rank players," said Milam, whose job basically centered around tournaments. In fact, in 1984 she volunteered to rank the 14-and-under age group. "I felt I needed to learn how to do the rankings," she said, "so I would fully understand the process when people called in with ranking questions."

Milam pointed out that the volunteers were critical. "I was the

NORTH CAROLINIAN MARSHALL HAPPER RISES TO THE TOP OF THE TENNIS PYRAMID

In 1981 Marshall Happer of Raleigh was named administrator of the Men's International Professional Tennis Council, the international governing body of men's professional tennis. He served in this capacity as essentially the commissioner of the men's pro tour until the establishment of the Association of Tennis Professionals in 1989, which resulted in the dissolution of the MIPTC. From 1990 to 1995 Marshall served as the executive director of the United States Tennis Association, the governing body of tennis in the U.S. After 1995 Happer continued to represent the USTA as an outside counsel negotiating television and sponsorship contracts for the US Open until his retirement in 2009.

only paid employee at the time, and everyone who ran our programs and did our rankings were volunteers," she said. "It was a nice little job. The work came into the office and went out to the volunteers."

NTRP Rating System for Leagues and Computer Rankings for Tournament Players

The explosion of players nationwide in the 1970s increased the demand for some sort of national rating system so that players could be grouped in tournaments and the newly developing leagues with others of like ability, and so teaching professionals could recommend appropriate games to visitors from other parts of the country. The earliest NTRP rating system was developed by the USTA in 1978 to supplant the traditional methods of classification—A, B, C, beginner, intermediate, advanced, etc.—and to unify dozens of additional different rating systems that were in use at the time. The USTA enlisted the help of the United States Professional Tennis Association (USPTA) and the International Health, Racquet & Sportsclub Association (IHRSA) and finally determined that the seven-level system, with descriptions of each level, was the best for achieving "better competition, on-court compatibility, personal challenge, and

"I'm ranked what?!!??"
A ranking sheet from an NCTA yearbook. Rankings compiled by hand took volunteers hundreds of hours.

19. LAURA WAGNER	DURHAM	22. CATHERINE LAND	GREENVILLE	STEPHANIE HARPER	WINSTON-SALEM
20. ROBIN BULLARD	LAURINBURG	23. SUSAN NEWBERRY	NEW BERN	JENNY MOUNTJOY	WINSTON-SALEM
21. HOLBROOK NEWMAN	WINSTON-SALEM	24. CLAUDIA CAMPBELL	FAYETTEVILLE		
22. CHANDY CHALLA	WINSTON-SALEM	25. STEPHANIE DONAHUE	WILMINGTON	MARY JAC KIZER	FAYETTEVILLE
23. ANH TA	HICKORY	26. CHRISTINE NASHICK	NEW BERN	WENDY SIMPSON	RAEFORD
24. BETSY BURCHFIELD	CONCORD	27. KIRSTIN OSBORNE	CHAPEL HILL		
25 BRETT MURPHY	WINSTON-SALEM	28. KIM BAYLISS-CAMBELL	NEW BERN	**GIRLS' 18 SINGLES**	
26. ELIZABETH GOLD	WEAVERVILLE	29. WENDY SIMPSON	RAEFORD		
27. HEIDI SMITH	BREVARD	30. CAROLINE INMAN	CHARLOTTE	*1. KIM KESSARIS	HENDERSONVILLE
		31. MILLIE MAXWELL	GOLDSBORO	*2. PAIGE FISHER	BATTLEBORO
28-34 ALPHABETICAL		32. MARY LAMURAGLIA	HIGH POINT	3. ANNA COLEMAN	LEXINGTON
		33. JULIE LERNER	CHARLOTTE	4. ANGELA CARROWAY	MORGANTON
ALLISON COLE	CARY	34. MARY JAC KIZER	FAYETTEVILLE	5. JILL POWELL	SHELBY
ABBEY LYERLY	HICKORY	35. ROBIN SZALANSKI	HICKORY	6. LAURA ROSS	CONCORD
LISA MANNING	WASHINGTON	36. PAM DAVIS	NEWTON	7. KANDI O'CONNOR	THOMASVILLE
CINDY MATTHEWS	EDEN	37. CARIE PETERSON	GREENSBORO	8. KIM VAUGHN	GREENSBORO
HELEN CHRISTY SANDERS MT. AIRY		38. JENNIFER EVANS	CHARLOTTE	9. HANI SIE	CHARLOTTE
KIM THOMPSON	CHARLOTTE	39. JANE FRYE	VASS	10. JOANNE BLACK	DURHAM
CAROLINE VINSON	GOLDSBORO	40. STEPHANIE HARPER	WINSTON-SALEM	11. THERESA SHEA	RALEIGH
		41. KATIE CARPENTER	WEST END	12. KAREN ROTHSCHILD	RALEIGH
35-41 ALPHABETICAL				13. KIMBERLY O'CONNOR	CHAPEL HILL
		42-46 ALPHABETICAL		14. LISA ORRINGER	CHAPEL HILL
SHELLEY BURGIN	NEWTON			15. MISSY FULMER	WASHINGTON
KIM COUCH	CHARLOTTE	ALLISON COLLINS	STONEVILLE	16. MARIA SWAIM	KERNERSVILLE
STEPHANIE LONG	CONCORD	JULIE DENISON	ARDEN	17. MIKKI VAUGHN	ARDEN
EMILY RASCOE	WINSTON-SALEM	BRIDGET McNEIL	ASHEVILLE	18. BECKY BRYSON	SHELBY
SHARON NASTASHA ROSS GREENSBORO		PEGGY MCNEIL	ASHEVILLE	19. DORIS WANGERIN	CARY
MICHELLE WATKINS	DURHAM	JILL WALKER	NEW BERN	20. DAWN KEYS	BOONVILLE
JENNIFER WEBB	CHAPEL HILL			21. JAMIE SHIPE	ASHEVILLE
		47-50 ALPHABETICAL		22. BETSY BYRON	GREENSBORO
INSUFFICIENT DATA				23. EMMY HULL	WILMINGTON
		LAURA EVANS	ST. PAULS	24. KRIS DONAHUE	DURHAM
RENIKA SHAW	GREENSBORO	JENNIFER GRIFFIN	GOLDSBORO	25. KATHLEEN MYERS	RALEIGH
		JOANN PAUTZ	MOREHEAD CITY	26. ASHELY HAMILTON	MINT HILL
GIRLS' 14 DOUBLES		SUSAN PROCTOR	ROCKY MOUNT	27. KELLY BAILEY	WEST END
				28. LAURA DAVENPORT	FAYETTEVILLE
1. MARGARET BRIDGER	WINSTON-SALEM	**51-60 ALPHABETICAL**		29. MARIA SHACKELFORD	BURLINGTON
ASHLEY McGEACHY	WINSTON-SALEM			30. CAROLINE MATTHEWS	CANTON
		MELINDA ALLISON	ASHEVILLE	31. KAREN ADAMS	CHARLOTTE
2. SUSANNAH COBB	CHAPEL HILL	PAM BEDFORD	KENLEY	32. CAROL KARP	
JENNIFER THOMAS	CHAPEL HILL	KRISTIN BOLCH	NEWTON		
		ANGELA CLONTZ	TRYON	**INSUFFICIENT DATA**	
3. HELEN SPENCER	BURLINGTON	TUCKER HARRELL	HOPE MILLS		
SCOTTI THOMAS	DURHAM	KAMI HOSTETLER	MT. HOLLY	STACEY SCHEFFLIN	MATTHEWS
		ELIZABETH JACKSON	FREMONT		
4. CINDY MATTHEWS	EDEN	SUSAN McNEILL	LENOIR	**GIRLS' 18 DOUBLES**	
CHRISTIE SANDERS	MT. AIRY	SENA PARRISH	RALEIGH		
		ANGELA PAYNE	MARS HILL	*1. DIANE PENSABENE	CHARLOTTE
INSUFFICIENT DATA				HANI SIE	CHARLOTTE
		INSUFFICIENT DATA			
* JENNY BOONE	RALEIGH			2. PEGGY McNEIL	ASHEVILLE
CHRISTY HEDGPETH	THOMASVILLE	LISA ADELMAN	GREENSBORO	BETSY BYRON	ASHEVILLE
		GWINN CARTER	SALISBURY		
		RACHEL JONES	ROCKY MOUNT	**BOYS' 10 SINGLES**	
GIRLS' 16 SINGLES		ALICA MARTIN	GREENSBORO		
				1. DREW MANER	WADESBORO
*1. JENEE CROSS	WINSTON-SALEM	**GIRLS' 16 DOUBLES**		2. QUENTIN HUFF	WINSTON-SALEM
2. SUSAN STANLEY	CHARLOTTE			*3. JIMMY JACKSON	CHAPEL HILL
3. SUSAN SAUNDERS	SALISBURY	1. MAREL SHAFFER	DURHAM	4. MARK FIELDING	WILSON
4. KAREN JOHN	HIGH POINT	SUSAN STANLEY	CHARLOTTE	5. CHRIS MENOCAL	WILMINGTON
5. MAREL SHAFFER	DURHAM			6. SCOTT TEUBNER	HICKORY
6. BETH CHOATE	MORGANTON	CO-2. KAREN JOHN	HIGH POINT	7. DAN PARHAM	ELON COLLEGE
7. TIFFANY HARDING	PROVIDENCE	BECKY KOPACK	HIGH POINT	8. JAY BRADLEY	WILSON
8. BECKY KOPACK	HIGH POINT			9. KEITH KESSARIS	HENDERSONVILLE
9. DIANE PENSABENE	CHARLOTTE	* CACY KINNEY	HIGH POINT	10. JOHN LAMPLEY	BREVARD
10. RENIKA SHAW	GREENSBORO	SUSAN SAUNDERS	SALISBURY	11. RASHAD SIMPSOM	GREENSBORO
11. NORI SIE	CHARLOTTE			12. ERIC SAUNDERS	SALISBURY
12. NICOLE NISSLEY	BREVARD	4. NICOLE NISSLEY	BREVARD	13. JAY GRIFFIN	LENOIR
	CARY	NORI SIE	CHARLOTTE		DURHAM

more enjoyment of the sport."

Many of the newly developing USTA Leagues the USTA and the NCTA were beginning to sponsor would benefit from the NTRP because league play is dependent on accurately gauging a player's skill level. As it turned out, the NTRP would indeed serve as the foundation for the growth of the leagues.

The computer was the other engine for growth in tournaments and rankings. Touring pros had been ranked by computer since the early 1970s, but in North Carolina, as in every other state, the process was undertaken, as Milam said, by volunteer committees, who sometimes took as many as 60 hours to produce rankings by hand for junior and adult tournament players. As ranking software developed in the early 1980s, however, the work gradually shifted from the individual and the committee back into the NCTA office. In 1988 the transformation was complete, and the NCTA announced that the rankings chairmen "have been replaced by a computer. It will be

our collective jobs to 'manage' and 'understand' this computer and its computer system, not to be managed by it."

COMPUTER-GENERATED RANKINGS

"It was scary at first," said Milam. "I was scared that I would 'break the computer.' You were afraid you would lose all the data you had just entered. And sometimes you did!"

"It was scary at first," said Milam. "I was scared that I would 'break the computer.' You were afraid you would lose all the data you had just entered. And sometimes you did!"

Milam simply had to grow with the job. "It became my responsibility to set up the programs," she said, "and over the years we updated our computers and printers about five times. The computer was a lifesaver," she admitted, because it offered more capabilities, which naturally created more programmatic opportunities.

As the money from the USTA increased, the work of longtime NCTA volunteer Treasurer, Tom

Deliberations
Jim Haslam, Mary Milam and Toni Adams compiling rankings by hand.

Peatross, became increasingly important. As the number of players grew, the programs proliferated, and the computers whirred, the NCTA found itself with responsibilities far beyond what could be handled by volunteers. "All of a sudden in the late 1980s a lot of people were going to work and had less time for volunteer activity," said Milam. "I think it would [have been] impossible to get volunteers to spend 60 hours on rankings as they once did."

Publications

Publications were another example of programs changed by the impact that the computer had on Milam's and others' responsibilities. "We didn't have a state yearbook when I took the job," said Milam. "When Southern stopped including districts in their yearbook, it fell to me to put out one for North Carolina." That first yearbook effort was in 1985, and it was a black and white, cut-and-paste publication, with no photographs and most of the type set on a typewriter. "I lined the columns up with a T-square and the printer reduced the copy to fit the page." Word processing and computerized publishing not only made the job easier but professionalized what had been a somewhat amateurish publication.

Editorial advances continued. Six years later, in 1988, the Foundation established the "Grady Elmore" Award, named for the Raleigh sportswriter who breathed life into the *North Carolina Tennis News* in 1960 at the

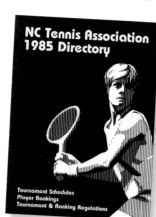

NC Tennis Association 1985 Directory

Tournament Schedules
Player Rankings
Tournament & Ranking Regulations

Mary Garber
One of the top sports journalists in North Carolina. The Grady Elmore Award, for which she was the first recipient, was one of over 40 writing awards she received in a seven-decade career, most of which she spent at the *Winston-Salem Journal.*

request of Henry Clark, and given for outstanding media coverage of tennis. The first recipient was Mary Garber of the *Winston-Salem Journal* in 1988, followed by A.J. Carr of the *Raleigh News & Observer.* In 1992 *North Carolina Tennis News* was subcontracted out to Ray Alley, who brought more modern design and changed the newsletter's name to *North Carolina Tennis Today.* Alley's publication brought news from the Association as well as tennis interest stories from across the state and region, including coverage of college and high school teams.

By the mid-1990s everything looked different, because tournament entries, rankings, publications... everything was computerized. "I feel very good that I was responsible for taking us into the computer age," admitted Milam.

POCKETS OF THE GAME

Juniors

The juniors continued to be a focus of both the USTA and the NCTA. In 1980 leagues were starting to appear when the NCTA Junior Tennis Council announced a Junior Team Tennis League program, but tournaments remained central for juniors. That same year, the Junior Tennis Council tried to standardize junior tournaments by forming a tournament aid committee made up of individuals who had extensive exposure to running tournaments, so that assistance could be provided to any tournament director or official across the state at any time.

Junior tournament play opportunities had grown exponentially in the last decade, and having a state ranking became a goal for most junior players. Junior league play provided many local players with an opportunity to get their first competitive experience or to supplement their tournament schedule, but their growth was made increasingly difficult by the emphasis that many players and parents put on tournament play. Nevertheless, new, mostly local or regional leagues were forming. In 1983 Greenville Tennis Director Henry Hostetler started the Down East Junior League with teams participating from Greenville, Williamston, Snow Hill, Washington, Rocky Mount, Kinston, Goldsboro, Wilson, and New Bern. Leagues in Raleigh and the Piedmont League continued to make strides.

The National Junior Tennis League, started by Arthur Ashe and Charlie Pasarell in 1968, was a precursor to junior leagues. The goal of the was to expose as many kids to tennis as possible, with a special emphasis on reaching kids who might not get a chance to be exposed to the game. Two of the first NJTL chapters in North Carolina were in Chapel Hill and Raleigh, which affiliated with the NJTL in 1980. Other cities followed suit, with leagues forming in Rocky Mount, Asheville, Greenville, and Durham.

In addition to local play there were also Regional Rallies with teams from North Carolina competing with teams from cities in South Carolina and Georgia. The NJTL program continues to this day with the goal of carrying on the legacy of Arthur Ashe, with an emphasis on introducing kids to tennis and, more importantly, stressing the value of education.

As with adult leagues, when USTA Junior Team Tennis came on the scene in the mid-1980s, there were local leagues already in place that were not affiliated with the USTA. As the NCTA began to promote the league on a statewide basis, the initial format was informal. Local leagues could affiliate with JTT, but USTA membership was not required, and there was no advancement for local league

THE VALUE OF A TEAM EXPERIENCE

Henriette Williams, from Raleigh, started participating in junior leagues at a young age. "My first team experience with tennis was with NJTL when I was about **Henriette Williams** ten years old, when my mom signed up my three siblings and me. I remember loving that I could finally play tennis, an individual sport, but have others competing along with me for a common goal. I believe it was this initial team experience that led me to love both high school and collegiate tennis."

Henriette became a top-ranked junior player, won the NCHSAA Singles Championship while on the Broughton High School team, and played number one singles for the University of Virginia.

Stephen Enochs
Winner of numerous national junior titles, Stephen Enochs was the best player ever to emerge from Greensboro until John Isner came along.

winners. Many local leagues joined and the concept began to take hold.

By 1995 there were 11 local leagues participating in Junior Team Tennis around the state. That was also the first year that a statewide jamboree was held with teams participating from across the state.

League play had a positive impact on many juniors who later became top-ranked players, and by the 1980s the top North Carolina juniors had aspirations beyond the state level. With good coaching, good facilities, and good support from the NCTA, North Carolina became known for producing top juniors at the national level. An impressive number of players won various USTA national singles or doubles championships in the 16s or 18s: Louise Allen, Chris Kennedy, Lawson Duncan, Stephen Enochs, Ashley Rhoney, John Yancey, Jim Rogerson, Woody Webb, J.J. Jackson, Peter Ayers, Ally Baker, Jonathan Stokke, Andy Orban, and John Isner.

Academies and Training Centers

The ruling public bodies found they had a great deal of help from the private sector in promoting junior tennis. There were a few famous tennis academies or schools around the country in the 1970s, the most famous being Nick Bolletierri's in Bradenton, Florida, but in the 1980s, outstanding but less expensive alternatives proliferated in North Carolina. J.W. Isenhour, retired from his job coaching at NC State, ran a top program at the Raleigh Racquet Club, and

J.J. Jackson
The Chapel Hillian became one of the top juniors in the country.

Woody Blocher in Asheville and Gary Johnson in Hendersonville continued to run two of the first and better-known junior academies in the state.

In support of these private camps, and with some of the earliest new moneys from the expanded US Open, the USTA started a summer tennis camp scholarship program, splitting the costs with the private individual camps that served as sites. In 1982, 22 tennis camps participated across the U.S., and North Carolina was home, disproportionately, to three of them: 4-Star Tennis Academies at Duke University, Davidson College Wildcat Camp, and the Smoky Mountain Tennis Camp at Cullowhee, N.C. Ten years later, in 1992, *North Carolina Tennis Today* was advertising many more camps throughout the state—not all of them scholarship camps, of course—but if a young person wanted a summer tennis camp experience, there was no better place to get it than North Carolina.

Despite all the support for junior tennis, by 1987 the *USTA* had become concerned that the United States no longer had the top tennis players in the world. A committee set up to address the issue suggested that national training programs be set up and supported by a national coaching system and scouting network. The committee proposed a national training camp, four to six regional, or area training centers (ATCs), and 100 local programs strategically located so that they would serve the entire United States. In addition, the USTA encouraged local excellence programs to be set up in every town and city in the country in order to develop participants for the ATCs.

Two years later, the USTA had developed the first of the ATCs in which local pros supported and trained by the USTA would select and train top juniors, and even arrange competitions with other ATCs. The Triad Training Center in Burlington was the first such USTA-sponsored ATC in North Carolina. Players were to be selected from 18 counties: Ashe, Watauga, Alleghany, Wilkes, Surry, Yadkin, Stokes, Forsyth, Davie, Rowan, Davidson, Rockingham, Guilford, Randolph, Montgomery, Caswell, Alamance, and Moore. Participants paid $150 for the 50-hour program. The curriculum,

Isenhour's lessons last lifetime

J.W. Isenhour
John Isenhour was both a top college coach and a top teaching pro.

TENNIS CAMPS ADVERTISED IN NORTH CAROLINA IN 1992

BLUE STAR CAMPS (J)
Hendersonville, N.C.
Coed (9-17). 7 courts.
4:1 ratio.

ALL-STAR TENNIS CAMP (J)
Guilford College,
Greensboro, N.C.
Coed.

DAVIDSON COLLEGE (A,J)
Davidson, N.C.
17 courts. 4:1 ratio.
Weekly sessions.
Juniors (9-17).

FOUR STAR TENNIS ACADEMY (J)
Duke University,
Durham, N.C.
Coed (9-18).
24 courts (2 indoor).
4:1 ratio. 1, 2, 4.

GATOR TENNIS CAMP (A)
Brevard College,
Brevard, N.C.
Coed (9-17). 6 courts.
5:1 ratio

JOHN NEWCOMBE TENNIS CENTER (A)
Fairfield
Sapphire Valley
Sapphire, N.C.
10 courts. 4:1 ratio.

MARY LOU JONES TENNIS CAMP (A,J)
St. Mary's College
Raleigh, N.C.
12 courts. Girls (6-18).

SMOKY MOUNTAIN TENNIS CAMP (J)
Western Carolina
University
Cullowhee, N.C.
Coed (9-18).
6 courts. 5:1 ratio.
June-August.

TAR HEEL TENNIS CAMP (J)
University of N.C.
Chapel Hill, N.C.
Coed (10-17).

WELBY VAN HORN TENNIS AT PINEHURST (A,J)
Pinehurst Hotel and Country Club
Pinehurst, N.C.
36 courts (4 indoor).
3-4:1 ratio.
Juniors (8-17).

WESTERN CAROLINA RACQUET CLUB (A,J)
Black Mountain, N.C.
4 courts. 3:1 ratio.

(A=ADULT, J=JUNIOR)

THE TRIAD AREA TRAINING CENTER

Herb Bolick

The Triad Area Training Center utilized the courts at Elon College, Olde Forest Racquet Club, and the City of Greensboro Parks and Recreation Department.

Donna Sauls, tennis director for the City of Greensboro and a member of the NCTA Board of Directors, was director. Richard Holderness, also on the NCTA Board, was chairman of the Triad area organizing committee, which included Sauls, Herb Bolick of Olde Forest Racquet Club, and Tom Parham of Elon College, who was responsible for making the successful application to USTA. Bolick, who attended a national seminar for coaches in Indianapolis, Dean Mathias of Greensboro, and Adam Brock of High Point, were coaches. John Eatman, former college coach at UNC-Charlotte and a leading N.C. senior player, was the head scout charged with selecting the 20 participants, and he was assisted by Parham and Jane Preyer, Duke women's tennis coach and a former top 100 player on the women's pro tour.

balls, T-shirts, USTA banner, and scouts' expenses were paid by USTA.

By 1993, North Carolina added two additional ATCs in Raleigh and Charlotte.

Schools

The NCTA realized that supporting junior tournaments was only half the battle, and that encouraging the game in schools was critical, so in 1989, the NCTA Board of Directors approved a program—*Adopt a School*—designed to provide every North Carolina high school and middle (or junior high) school a USTA membership. Generous NCTA members were encouraged in the newsletter to select a school, complete a form, and donate $25.00 of the school's membership. The school would then receive a letter from NCTA announcing the membership and

the name of the patron providing it. The program was very successful.

College Tennis

The democratization of the game reached lower into the college ranks. No longer were the major Division I schools in North Carolina—UNC, Davidson, Wake, Duke, NC State, etc.—the only story, or even the lead story. NAIA schools, led by coaches like Tom Parham at Atlantic Christian (now Barton) and Gayle Currie at Guilford, followed Wingate's example in the 1960s and started enjoying unprecedented success on a national level, beginning with Atlantic Christian's NAIA national championship in 1979. Two years later, in 1981, Currie and Guilford repeated the feat, sharing the title with the team from Grand Canyon.

In 1982 Guilford's Tarjo Koho, a freshman from Finland, compiled

1981 NAIA Champs!
Guilford women's 1981 NAIA championship team from 1981, left to right, head coach Gayle Currie; Stacy Cook; Kerry Kennedy; Lili Carpenter; Tammy Strickland; Kris Lajeskie; Sue Ireton; Shirley Dunn.

Two time Champ
Tom Parham won national titles at both Atlantic Christian and Elon.

a 31-0 record and won the NAIA singles title, as the team finished second. Atlantic Christian won again in 1984, sharing the title with Southwestern Missouri State. It was the 13th time that Atlantic Christian had won the District 26 title and qualified to go to the Nationals.

That same year, two products of the North Carolina junior tennis, Lawson Duncan and Louise Allen, playing for Clemson and Trinity of Texas respectively, won the Marriott National Collegiate Tennis Classic held in California in January. Also that year, Gayle Currie was named Carolina's Conference Coach of the Year, the NAIA District 26 Coach of the Year, and the NAIA National Coach of the Year by the Intercollegiate Tennis Coaches Association, a recognition of the fact that for the previous five years her teams had placed in the top five at the NAIA National Tournament.

Parham moved to Elon in 1985, and in 1988 one of his players, Duane Johnson, a senior from nearby Graham, was named to the NAIA Scholar Athlete team for the second time in his career. Over the next six years, Andreas Faehlmann and Peter Linstrom would repeat this feat. In 1990, Parham repeated his earlier success when Elon won the NAIA national championship.

Coach Bill Madrey, having coached outstanding teams for years at both St. Augustine's in Raleigh and Johnson C. Smith in Charlotte, again worked his magic in 1993 at Barber-Scotia College. The Sabers, a program only two years old, posted a 19-1 mark, losing

Texas Bound
North Carolinian Louise Allen became a champion for Trinity University in Texas.

LOUISE ALLEN & LAWSON DUNCAN

Trinity's Louise Allen (from Winston-Salem), recognized as the best woman college player at the time, proved it by winning the singles and, with Trinity number two Gretchen Rush, the women's doubles title at Marriott's National Collegiate Classic in California in 1982. The pair went on to win the NCAAs.

Clemson's Lawson Duncan won the men's singles, and later was runner-up in the NCAAs to Mikael Pernfors in 1982.

Tennis writer Richard Evans made a visit and wrote that he was impressed with the on-court behavior of the college players he saw.

BEST BALL MACHINE IN THE WORLD MADE IN NORTH CAROLINA

In 1973 NC State engineering student Alfred Yarur designed an improved tennis ball machine that enabled players to practice as if they were playing against a live opponent. The prototype was tested at the Raleigh Racquet Club with the help of head pro Jim Emmons. The machine was called the Playmate. Yarur's concept has been greatly enhanced with computer technology and robotics to make his Morrisville-based company, Metaltek, the world leader in designing and building tennis ball machines. Since its inception the company has sold over 25,000 machines worldwide.

Flying Eagles

The North Carolina Central tennis team won the Central Intercollegiate Athletic Association title ten times between 1949 and 1988. From 1949 to 1975 the Eagles won five CIAA championships, four MEAC championships, two NAIA District 26 championships, and one NCAA Eastern Regional championship.

only their last regular season match to NCAA Division II power Hampton Institute. "That was a disappointing season-ender," said Madrey of the Hampton loss, "but all in all I'm very, very satisfied with the performance." The Sabers won their NAIA district championship and advanced to the NAIA championships in Kansas City.

"I think of that period of time—the 1980s—as the golden age of the NAIA," said Parham. That golden age ended, in Parham's opinion, for two reasons. First, there was an influx of foreign players at U.S. colleges and universities. "If you didn't have the internationals," he said, "you didn't win. When you went to Kansas City, there were 256 players and 32 seeds, and 30 of the seeds were suddenly international." Parham himself found Swede Roland Thornqvist, who led the Elon team to the national title and went on to have a stellar career when he transferred to UNC. A two-time All-American, Thornqvist was also the first player to win college's Rafael Osuna Award for sportsmanship twice.

Second, as smaller teams got better and better, they looked to move up in the competitive ranks. "About 1992 or 1993," said Parham, "the NAIA teams started defecting for the NCAA Division II—all the Elons and High Points and Guilfords, all those guys. They became Division II schools. Some of them still are. Elon is Division I. Atlantic Christian, now Barton, is still Division II."

Beginning in the late 1980s

The democratization of the game reached lower into the college ranks. No longer were the major Division I schools in North Carolina—UNC, Davidson, Wake, Duke, NC State, etc.— the only story, or even the lead story.

Duke's men's and women's teams began to dominate the ACC. Several North Carolina players, such as Charlotte's Peter Ayers, who is now a teaching pro in Charlotte, contributed prominently to their success. In 1999 Duke's women's team won the NCAA championship. Fayetteville's Reka Zsilinszka, playing number three singles and doubles, was selected the tournament's Most Valuable Player.

Elon Tennis Center

The colorful Jimmy Powell Tennis Center at Elon, home of the Phoenix tennis teams.

College Tennis Facilities

While the major North Carolina colleges didn't haul in the national championships like their smaller counterparts, they started on a building spree. In 1985, UNC opened a new 16-court facility off Country Club Road near campus, the first of two they would open in a short time.

In 1987 Elon built a beautiful 12-court championship tennis center on the 150-acre campus, paid for by special funds and participants of the Tom Sawyer-Huck Finn Tennis Classic, an annual summer tournament held in Alamance County. Coach Tom Parham called it one of the finest among all NAIA colleges and universities in the nation. Elon now had more tennis courts in one complex than any small college in North Carolina. It was the Elon

Cone-Kenfield Tennis Center

The Cone-Kenfield Tennis Center at UNC boasts lush landscaping and a 6 court indoor facility.

tennis center that helped attract the USTA's eye for the first Area Training Center.

In 1989 Wake Forest opened the James P. Leighton Tennis Stadium, named for former coach and Intercollegiate Tennis Coaches' Hall of Fame member Jim Leighton, who led the Deacons to a record of 267-169-2 from 1962 to 1984. The facility, which included 1,200 permanent seats, 140 box seats, and five lighted outdoor courts, would serve as host to both Wake Forest home matches and numerous top-flight regional events, the first being the 1989 Flow Motors Invitational.

In 1992 UNC built the second facility, the Cone-Kenfield Tennis Center, off Skakle Drive in Chapel Hill. Boasting 12 outdoor courts and six indoors, the facility was named for benefactor Caesar Cone II, a 1928 alumnus who played tennis at Carolina, and John Kenfield, the legendary Tar Heel tennis coach who compiled a record of 434-30-2 in dual-match play from 1928-55, 15 Southern Conference championships, and two Atlantic Coast Conference team championships during his tenure.

Duke's attractive Sheffield Indoor Center was opened in 1990, followed by the renovation and renaming of the outdoor tennis complex the Ambler Center.

African-American Tennis

In the late 1970s and early 1980s, African-Americans were participating fully in the tennis boom, and, thankfully, without the discrimination at the tournament level that had forced many earlier generations of players, such as Hubert Eaton and

Namesake
In 1989 Wake Forest named the James P. Leighton Tennis Stadium for legendary former coach and Intercollegiate Tennis Coaches' Hall of Fame member Jim Leighton.

Lenward Simpson, out of USTA tournaments and into ATA events.

On a social and grassroots level, however, African-American tennis retained its cohesiveness in many areas. "In 1977, '78, '79, you couldn't get on the courts," said Anna Mercer McLean. "Cardozo McCollum and Sam Moore and Joe Williams started the Southeastern American Tennis Association tournaments about that time. These tournaments had adult, college leagues, and the juniors, and they were sanctioned through the N.C. Tennis Association. All the ACC colleges used to play."

In 1983 Durham's James Gaddy wanted somebody to play tennis with on a regular basis and organized the Rum Tennis Club with Charles Daniels, Larry Daniels, and Anthony Evans. There were no club dues and the original goal was to recruit two new members each year. A tournament was held the next year, and Gaddy won. In 1986, the name of the Rum Tennis Club was changed to the Magic Express Tennis Club, which became one of the largest African-American tennis organizations in the state. "The public parks had a lot of the folks that weren't in private clubs," said John McLean, Anna's husband, "so they became members of the Magic Express."

In 1985, two years after Gaddy started the Rum, a group of tennis players from eastern North Carolina—Rodney Bailey of Goldsboro, and Bobby Short and Marvin Hardy of Greenville—started a tournament, the Mahogany Tennis Classic, which was to be a rotating team tennis tournament with individual awards as well. Age brackets were not used because in the challenge matches everyone played each other, regardless of age.

The first Classic was held in Goldsboro in 1986 on July 4th weekend. Later, it was changed to Memorial Day weekend. In 1987 Mahogany rotated to Greenville and included an annual family cookout. In 1988 it went to Raleigh; in 1989 to Rocky Mount.

"The tournament moves around from each of the different locations," said John McLean. "It will go down the line to all of the different clubs and then it comes back to the original club that started it and then keeps going. It starts in Goldsboro and goes around until it makes it around."

The Magic Express kept pace, hosting its first benefit tournament in conjunction with WFXC-FM

Spreading the Game
One of the many junior clinics that funds from the USTA helped spawn.

Foxy 107/Operation Breakthrough for the Homeless in 1990. The METC continues each year to give proceeds to organizations such as the South Durham Youth Athletic League and the Coalition for Battered Women.

In Greensboro noted civil rights leader Dr. George C. Simkins supported the game he loved to the extent that the indoor tennis facility at Barber Park was eventually named the Dr. George C. Simkins, Jr., Tennis Pavilion.

Communities

Tennis started in the late 19th century in North Carolina in communities like Chapel Hill, Pinehurst, and Asheville, and blossomed in the early part of the 20th century in others like Greenville and Charlotte. As it boomed in the 1970s and 1980s, it continued to flower in individual communities, and usually, as had been the pattern since the start, as a result of individual missionaries dedicated to growing the game in their areas.

As an example, Henry Hostetler, tennis director for the Greenville Recreation Department, realized

Henry Hostetler
Henry Hostetler, former Greeneville City Parks and Rec Tennis Director, has been one of the NCTA's most valuable administrators and volunteeers.

the local junior high did not offer a team, so he sponsored one through the department. Competing against other junior high teams from Kinston, Wilson, Goldsboro, Murfreesboro, and Chapel Hill between 1980 and 1985, the girls' team did not lose a match for five years. Hostetler worked hard to encourage other towns that had no junior high teams to sponsor a team through their recreation department. "No other city had had a tennis director east of Raleigh until they opened up a position around 1981," said Hostetler, "and I was fortunate enough to get the position."

Also in eastern North Carolina, Bobby Taylor and Donald Clark from Snow Hill founded the North Carolina Recreational Tennis Players' Association, with low entry fees for tournaments to encourage participation. By 1993 the Association was offering over 40 tournaments per year for thousands of players.

Raleigh and Winston-Salem continued to sponsor a plethora of junior and adult programs out of the parks and recreation offices. In Raleigh, city tennis director Cy King even acted as something of a traffic cop. "If a new pro moved into town I would try to help them anyway I could. I would send kids to other pros to be in their programs. My job was to get programs going, get people interested in tennis, and then if they got interested, they could join a club."

In the west, in Hendersonville, Ralph Wingerter began giving tennis lessons to children at a local park in 1989, then expanded into Henderson County and the Henderson County YMCA. He also started a competitive eight-

A large group of stalwart senior players emerged....These players loved the thrill of competition and devoted long hours playing their beloved game.

team Junior Team Tennis League for youngsters aged 8-18 living in Henderson County.

In short, the early "angels" of the game—Dick Covington in the west, Henry Clark in the Piedmont, John Allen Farfour in the east, and others like Carlyle Lewis and Whit Cobb—had by the 1990s spawned disciples who were scattered all across the state, starting clinics, leagues, tournaments, and teams, sometimes with money coming down from the NCTA, and often with funds from their own pockets.

COMPETITIVE TENNIS

Tournaments

While the local and state tournaments continued and grew, professional tournaments also proliferated in North Carolina in the 1980s and 1990s. Before the computers took over, however, managing the scheduling and sanctioning of tournaments across the state was a chore.

Paula Hale was one of the Mary Milam's most critical volunteers in this area. "I'm not sure how I initially got involved," said Hale. "Mary or somebody on her staff asked me to help with the sanction and scheduling the tournaments in North Carolina back in the 1980s. Basically it was

THE HANES PARK BRIDGE: A BRIDGE TO THE FUTURE

In Winston-Salem's Hanes Park a beautiful stone bridge arches just slightly over the lazy water of Peters Creek. Every June for over 40 years, every North Carolina junior who has aspired to play at the next level has crossed it to the 14 clay courts at the Joe White Tennis Center on the other side.

For decades prior to the early 1970s, the bridge was not central to North Carolina tennis. To that point, every North Carolina junior who wanted to play in the national championships had to enter the Southern Closed Championships to qualify. In the early 1970s, though, the Southern Tennis Association began limiting players who wanted to play in the Southern Closed Championships to a quota based on the percentage of Southern junior memberships held by each state.

Each state had to desig-nate a person or a committee to select players. In North Carolina, Mont Graham would pick a quota of eight players. With the explosion of players, however, North Carolina started the Tar Heel Qualifier in Hanes Park, and players now compete not for Graham's selection but a spot on a post-tournament endorsement list published by a committee of selectors.

For 40 years, then, ambi-tious juniors have left cars parked across the street at the Central Y or on West End Boulevard, gathered their rackets, wristbands, and water jug, passed six hard courts, and crossed the bridge, hopefully on the way to the Southerns and then the national championships.

Once over the bridge, play-ers check in at a courtside tent, manned for years by Dottie Peddycord and Sue Peatross. Longtime tourna-ment committee members Alex Rucker, Tom Peatross, John Peddycord, and Glenn Moore have made sure play-ers had t-shirts, court times, and plenty of bananas. And for over 25 years, Mildred Southern kept a close eye on all as the tournament's referee.

Entire families spent years attending the Qualifier as each of their children aged through the process. Will Fanjoy of Statesville brought daughters Laura and Meg and son Thomas year after year. He boasted that he had spent every first weekend in June in Winston-Salem for almost 15 years. Blount and Dargan Williams could say the same thing. Raleigh's Williams fam-ily had four children, Judson, Henriette, Hampton, and Rankin, all exceptional players going deep in the draws year after year.

Future national champi-ons—Greensboro's John Isner won the Tar Heel Qualifier

Kim Kessaris

five times—and national con-tenders also hit the first ball toward that quest across the bridge—Tommy Paul, Patrick Kypson, Kaitlin McCarthy, Ally Baker, Adu Kodali, Ryan Noble, Sarah Taylor, Stephen Enochs, Louise Allen, J.J. Jack-son, Kim Kessaris, Thad Lang-ford, Susan Saunders, Michael

Thad Langford

Leonard, Cory Ann Avants, Mary Lloyd Hodges, Helen Graham, Scotti Thomas, Helen Spencer, Quentin Huff, Nori Sie, Jim Latham, Jay Pul-liam, Michael Pittard—the list goes on and on.

For every North Carolina junior player, the trail to a potential national champion-ship began each year as that player crossed the bridge to the Joe White Tennis Center at Hanes Park. It is a place to see friendly faces from tournament volunteers to life-long tennis friends. It all waits, across the bridge.

Connection to the Future

At some point every junior tennis player in North Carolina likely crosses the Hanes Park Bridge on the way to the Joe White courts in Winston-Salem.

Maurice Everette

Bev Earle

big, long, handwritten sheet of paper. Tournaments would submit an application and we'd schedule it. You did it by hand. This was way before Internet and computers."

Continuing the rapid expansion of tournament opportunities begun in the 1970s, a state championship was awarded in the men's 80s, and a mother/daughter championship was awarded in 1985. As age brackets were expanded, championships began to be held in multiple cities and at different times.

The computer eventually livened things up, freeing Hale and Milam from their long handwritten sheets, and by 1990 there were seven NTRP Tournaments — meaning they were for players with an NTRP rating — in places as small as Boiling Springs and as large as Charlotte, and with names like the Piedmont Indoor and the North Carolina Tennis Festival.

A large group of stalwart senior players emerged, including Maurice and Vicki Everette, Bobby Heald, Mary Lou Jones, Buck Archer, Liz Wagner, J.W. Quick, Bev Cansler Earle, Norman Chambers, Al Griffin, Mildred Southern, Peggy Golden, and many others. These players loved the thrill of competition and devoted long hours playing their beloved game. More and more adults from North Carolina also played in tournaments out of state, some winning

Out in the Sun
Reidsville's Mont Graham was one of the many volunteers who ran tournaments, served as lines people, and generally did whatever was needed to keep tournaments running.

"gold balls" at the national level.

One of the NCTA's biggest tasks involved not only upgrading the quality of tournaments, tournament directors, and officials, but also preventing multiple tournaments from being held at the same time in the same area. The NCTA's Ellen Lyon, and later Jane Scott, took over the chore, and were ably assisted by active volunteers Mont Graham, Barbara Melvin, Paula Hale, Emily Styers, and Joan Cox in these important but often difficult tasks.

As the 90s progressed, some of North Carolina's top players were able to test their mettle against younger pros in small professional tournaments in places like Elkin and Rocky Mount, and in the Flow Motors Championships in Winston-Salem.

In terms of international events, in 1991 Charlotte's Olde Providence Racquet Club hosted the U.S. Men's

Multi-tasker
Mary Lou Jones made her presence felt with her playing, coaching and directing her junior camp at St. Mary's, one of the first in the state.

Clay Courts, one of the first national championships to be held in the state. The club followed up in 1993 by hosting the U.S. Davis Cup zonal qualifying match against the Bahamas, the first time it had held a Davis Cup event since 1971, when the U.S. successfully won the championship final against Romania. Andre Agassi had been one year old at that time, but he was now scheduled to lead a four-player U.S. contingent, including Malivai Washington, Patrick McEnroe, and Richey Reneberg, onto the same Julian J. Clark Stadium Court. The only difference was that for the Bahamas tie, a hard court was put down in place of the normal clay because the faster surface would favor the Americans. Choice of surface is always a prerogative of the home team. Agassi won his first match, and when the U.S. clinched it in the doubles, he flew out before the final rubbers, angering some of the local fans. The rest of the team pulled out a 5-0 victory anyway.

Special events were also plentiful in the 1980s and 1990s. In 1980, for instance, North Carolina players edged Virginia players 5-4 for the 15th annual Otis Jones Cup tennis competition between North Carolina and Virginia. In 1987 the North Carolina women's team brought home the silver by winning the first Southern Senior Team Cup Matches held at Hilton Head, S.C., in early April. The men's team came in second, close behind Louisiana.

Beginning in 1990, the Legends came to Raleigh, Pinehurst and Landfall, with players like Ken Rosewall, Roy Emerson, and Cliff

Drysdale. The national senior 75s and 85s, played in Pinehurst, brought back long flannels and proof that "The competitive spirit beats strong well into the senior years of tennis," according to the *North Carolina Tennis News.*

In junior competitions, the North Carolina Junior Davis Cup squad won one national competition in the mid-1980s, and, in contrast to the 1960s, North Carolina's best juniors competed widely throughout the country.

Team Tennis

Billie Jean King's creation, World Team Tennis, made several appearances in North Carolina, starting

Tom Wilkison, aka "Dr. Dirt."

Longtime Pro
ACC champion and longtime pro at MacGregor Downs in Cary, Bobby Heald became a leader among North Carolina's teaching pros.

in 1987 with the Charlotte Heat based at Olde Providence and playing in what was then the one-year-old Domino's Pizza Team Tennis League. Coached by Karl Coombes, team members included John Sadri, Mike DePalmer, and locally-based alternate Tim Wilkison. In its first two years, the Heat won consecutive World Championships. Unfortunately, victories did not prove financially rewarding, and in 1992 the Heat folded, despite moving to the Charlotte Coliseum in 1990.

The Heat was not the only North Carolina team in the league, as the Raleigh Edge was formed in 1989. Owner Duane Long asked Wilkison to coach but "I couldn't be the coach," said Wilkison, by then one of the best players North Carolina had ever produced, "because it was going to take time away from my regular job, so I turned it down."

The Edge put a lot back into the game with tutoring programs for inner-city youths and other community programs. Wilkison eventually took an ownership position, but unfortunately, after the 1993 season, despite the presence of Hall of Famer Tracey Austin and a balance sheet in the black, the team was shut down.

In 1994, Charlotte re-entered the fray with the Express, announcing seven home matches to be played at Julian Clark Tennis Stadium at Olde Providence. Coombes was again the coach, and Charlotte fans enjoyed visits by players such as Björn Borg, Martina Navratilova, and Jimmy Connors, before it too finally stopped play in 1996. "We had some good fans," said the team's principal owner, G.A. Sywassink, "but we didn't have enough of them."

World Team Tennis also sponsored local and regional competitions, and North Carolina, always a strong league and team state, participated with recreational teams across the state.

Teaching Pros

By 1993 the North Carolina chapter of the USPTA had grown to over 200 professionals, and was forming a new state chapter with Steve MacDermut as president. This was basically a reorganization under the national organization to ensure that pros could provide certification and other services to their colleagues more efficiently across the state.

LEAGUES

Despite all this junior development, tournament activity, and local programs, the advent and growth of USTA League play represented the biggest story of the 1980s and 1990s. USTA League play expanded to such an extent that it competed with tournaments and local leagues for courts and participants, and has dramatically changed the nature of competition and increased the opportunities for play in North

Carolina and the rest of the country.

The USTA unanimously adopted a national league program—after a false start or two—at its annual meeting in 1980 on the strength of successful pilots in the Southern and Mid-Atlantic sections in 1978.

The official program initially consisted of league play for 5.5, 4.5, and 3.5 levels with a two singles and three doubles format. Michelob Light was the title sponsor and Wilson was the official ball. There were 13,000 participants and the first national championship was held in Chicago.

The existing local leagues proved to be an initial obstacle for the new USTA Leagues, and in the first year that North Carolina participated in USTA League play, only two programs took hold in North Carolina, one in Hendersonville and one in Winston-Salem.

In May of 1981, in the first-ever state championships for league play,

women and men competed at two different locations. The women's team from Hendersonville defeated the Winston-Salem team 3-2 at the Wake Forest Indoor Courts in Winston-Salem. The men's team from Hendersonville won in Hickory, defeating the team from Winston-Salem. Both teams entered the sectional playoffs in Atlanta.

The USTA Leagues would prove to be something of an overwhelming force, over time, and North Carolina's traditional league system ultimately paved the way. "There was a history in North Carolina that enabled the leagues to succeed here

...the advent and growth of USTA League play represented the biggest story of the 1980s and 1990s.

A SUCCESSFUL LEAGUE

"When I came in 1981 to the city director's job," said Henry Hostetler of his time in Greenville, "Danny Phillips and I talked about getting the Eastern Carolina Tennis Association going again. We thought we needed to change the whole name of it.

"We started a new thing and called it the Downeast Tennis League in about 1982, starting with six women's teams in the eastern Carolina area: Greenville, Washington, Rocky Mount, Wilson, Tarboro, and Kinston.

"When Dru Michaels

came calling, we jumped on the USTA bandwagon. I was sold on leagues at that point and we had a 5.5 team fly to Kentucky to play one match, lose and go home! That was my first bad taste of league tennis but it convinced me to get involved and try to make a difference. I saw what a great thing it was," says Hostetler.

"I convinced Gay Pratt, then state league coordinator, to let Greenville host the State League Championships. Again, it was not a round robin. Seven hundred players

came to Greenville that weekend. Matches started on Saturday at 8:00 a.m. and ended on Sunday at 8:00 p.m. No rain! Greenville became excited and league play in the Downeast was on the rise!

"In 1988 the USTA Downeast League consisted of 24 teams from Wilson, Greenville, Tarboro, New Bern, Rocky Mount, Jacksonville, Kinston, and Washington playing 2.5 to 5.0 levels. We grew from those six teams to over 1,500 players," said Hostetler.

Stalwart Volunteers

Dru Michaels, the NCTA's first paid executive secretary, Barbara Melvin, an NCTA sanctions and schedule chairman, and Donna Sauls, tennis director for Greensboro Parks and Rec, have been among scores of individuals who have dedicated hundreds of hours to North Carolina tennis.

the way they did," noted Cy King, former director of tennis for the Raleigh Parks system. "The early local leagues existed along with age group tournaments but USTA Leagues opened the door to a competitive team format based on specific skill levels while adding the element of advancement."

After the initial resistance, the local league players eventually joined the USTA Leagues. "Those local leagues players would have been there whether the USTA came along or not, but the USTA took a lot of players from around the state, and kind of unified all of them."

In the 1980s, the state league coordinator and the local league coordinators were all volunteers. Dru Michaels, executive secretary for NCTA, actually organized the first USTA League program in North Carolina and acted as the first state league coordinator. She appointed Gay Pratt of Laurinburg in 1985. Dale Dickerson followed Pratt, and in 1988 Judy Utley accepted an invitation from NCTA executive Secretary Mary Milam to serve as the state league coordinator. "That was my first experience with all of the leaders and USTA Leagues at the time," said Utley, who had managed the Gate City League in Greensboro and captained a USTA League team. "I was hooked. I loved it.... I thought it was so much fun. I liked everything about it. There wasn't anything I didn't like."

The leagues in North Carolina, of course, grew against the backdrop provided by the USTA, which not only grew but expanded its offerings. By 1983 USTA Leagues, even before North Carolinians had fully embraced the program, boasted 50,000 participants nationally from all 17 sections. In 1984 Volvo North America replaced Michelob Light and new levels were added over the next several years. Penn Racquet Sports began its continuing association with league tennis as the official ball of the league program.

By the end of the decade, participation nationwide had grown to almost 125,000 players in 12 divisions and was still growing.[11] Combo doubles, allowing players of different levels, and senior leagues for players over 50 became the newest divisions.

As a result of the growing complexity of the job, Utley was the last of the totally volunteer state league coordinators. By the end of 1980, participation in the USTA League program in North Carolina had grown to the point that the role of state league coordinator exceeded volunteer expectations and a part-time staff person was hired to work in the NCTA offices as state administrator for the national program.

Busy Day at the Courts
Watching league play from the porch of the Olde Providence Racquet Club in Charlotte.

Vicky Bethel filled that position until Nell Barksdale took over as a full-time staff person in 1993. Barksdale commented, "I loved my job, I liked everything about it except having to tell a 2.5 player at championships that they had been disqualified. They were thrilled to be told they were too good but felt they let their team down.

"I was so thrilled when the 3.5 Senior Men's team from Little Washington won the sectional championships. They were such a nice bunch of guys and, lo and behold, they won the national championships that year." Getting people into the right league, according to their level, was a challenge when so many levels began to be offered. In the 1980s verification of one's self-rating was a requirement to enter the program until many pros across the state stepped up to the plate to hold verification clinics in local communities prior to the beginning of the league season. The chief verifier of the

state organized and staffed these clinics to make sure players had the opportunity to attend a clinic. Don Woodfield, Steve MacDermut, and Kin Roseborough each served as chief verifier, traveling all over the state and spending countless hours helping organize local clinics with a minimum of three verifiers at each clinic. Gene Blackwelder and Lindsay Pratt were also part of that early team who contributed by giving their time to provide clinics across the state.

Local league coordinators have served as the league's driving forces, and North Carolina has a rich history of local league coordinators who served their communities for many years. Some of those legendary coordinators included Lynn Goldberg—Raleigh; Henry Hostetler—Downeast; Anna Martin—Wilmington; Ruth Bondurant—Pinehurst/Sandhills area; Sol Flynt—Charlotte; Iris Ham—Lake Norman; Donna Barger—Foothills area; Suellen

BROWNIES
Mark Lindsey, a pro who served as an NTRP verifier, recalled, "The system was great at putting players in general playing levels where they could compete with others of similar ability, but it was not without its challenges. Players did not always agree with the assigned rating and would get upset with the pros if they didn't get the rating they wanted, often offering brownies for bribes, while claiming 'you just ruined my life' if the bribe didn't work!"

83

Volunteer to Leader
Asheville's Bonnie Vandergrift would rise from enthusiastic league player to volunteer to NCTA and NCTF president.

McCrary—Piedmont area; Bonnie Vandergrift and Pam Hymer—Mountain area; and Tammy Brown—Durham. Without their passion and dedication, the league program would not have had the consistency and continuity needed to be successful in those early days of development and later years of change.

By the end of the decade, technology allowed the verification process to be replaced with computer-generated ratings based on a system originally called Compurank, a USTA computer-based mathematical system which assigned ratings based on direct and indirect comparison of match results in the local league and at championship level. That addition in 1989 was just the beginning of applying technology to enhance the fun, fairness and competitive play for leagues.

By about 1990, the *North Carolina Tennis News* reported 15 USTA/Volvo Leagues statewide, 372 teams, and 4,056 players. That didn't count all the independent leagues. The state championships held in Charlotte that year required the use of six sites to accommodate all the action: Renaissance Park, UNC-Charlotte, Park Road, Freedom Park, Olde Providence Racquet Club, and Sugar Creek. Leagues had been around for ten years, tournaments almost 100 years, but no tournament had ever reached such a monumental size.

League Coordinators
Nell Barksdale, center, North Carolina's first full-time league coordinator, flanked by Elaine Hamilton, left former state league coordinator for Georgia and current executive director, and Ellen Lyon, longtime NCTA staffer.

The NCTA made a significant change when it moved the 1991 USTA League State Championships from Charlotte to Pinehurst, where the Carolina Inn, Sandhills Community College, and the Southern Pines Recreation Department all opened their courts. Long known as the "golf capital of the world," Pinehurst learned about USTA League tennis when over 500 players from all over the state descended on the resort for the event. In addition to staff from NCTA and local league coordinators working as site directors, local volunteers in Pinehurst, such as Bud and Margie Ruddle, worked tirelessly to make the players feel welcome and help tournament staff ensure that the championship was a first class event. Many players were thrilled to stay in the beautiful historic Carolina Inn and enjoy the July 4th weekend competing for a chance to advance to the sectional championships.

As a result of its success, Pinehurst became the home of the adult division championship for several years, creating a powerful incentive for many teams in local leagues across the state to practice hard and win locally just to get to go to Pinehurst.

By 1994, participation in the USTA League program at the national level reached almost 160,000 in the Adult and Senior divisions. Forty-eight percent of USTA adult members played league tennis.

By the mid-1990s USTA Leagues were beginning to fill up courts all over the state. "Lots of people were playing," said Jack Blankenhorn, longtime Raleigh tennis pro. "Not so much the upper-end players but more the 3.0, 3.5 players. Then they started doing mixed doubles in the summer and then combo doubles in the fall. So what you've got is continuous league play basically starting at the end of February through the end of November, and they almost overlap.

"If you're a pro at a club and your members played leagues, but you have people who wanted to have a tournament, well, you had to have courts available for league play. The courts weren't open weekends anymore."

Anna Mercer-McLean noticed the same thing happening on public courts in Durham. "Because we weren't members of clubs, we saw so much tournament play or so much play in general on public courts, that the courts were always full. Then you had this lull where there weren't as many people playing. Then all of a sudden more people were playing because of leagues and again the courts were full. People were playing on two leagues, or three leagues, or playing in other cities. The courts were just overwhelmed with league play."

By 1995, Milam's last year as executive director, the USTA League program had grown from about 700-800 participants in North Carolina in 1982 to over 6,000. "It is the biggest program the USTA has," she said at the time.

"The tennis that we grew up with had changed," said Blankenhorn. ❧

League Tennis Explodes
One of Charlotte's many enthusiastic senior teams.

Tennis Everywhere: 1995–2012

THE STATE OF THE GAME

IN THE EARLY 1990S, the USTA would make a decision to expand the USTA National Tennis Center (later named the USTA Billie Jean King National Tennis Center), which would have every bit the impact on tennis across the country and in North Carolina as the original decision to build the Center in the late 1970s.

Construction began in March of 1995 on the cavernous new Arthur Ashe Stadium, designed to hold more than 22,000 spectators, while the original Louis Armstrong Stadium was downsized to hold 10,000 people. Other courts were rebuilt with better access and more seating available for spectators, and the number of restrooms and food concessions, including a large food court, were also expanded. A year later, additional construction began on a new 245,000-square-foot, state-of-the-art multipurpose tennis pavilion near the east gate. The latest edition is Court 17, another small showcase stadium court with seating of about 3,000 enhancing the Open experience for all attendees.

Leagues!
Good times rule in league play.

The Arthur Ashe Stadium was completed in August 1997 with a grand opening for Arthur Ashe Kids' Day prior to the Open. The entire project was completed two years later, in 1999, allowing more than 33,000 people to visit the US Open daily. The USTA spent $285 million of its own money on the project, and in 2011 pays $1.5 million per year to rent and operate the more than 30 outdoor and 12 indoor courts. In addition to the US Open, the NTC annually hosts the Eastern Wheelchair Tennis Championships and the Mayor's Cup high school tennis championships, and conducts community tennis programs, summer tennis camps, group and private lessons, and USTA programs.

It is a center for tennis, yes, but also a portal through which more money than ever would flow into the USTA and trickle down to sectional, state, and local organizations. Those funds, combined with the demands brought about by the astounding growth of leagues, would trigger an ascending cycle in which the NCTA would grow

Bigger Still
Arthur Ashe Tennis Stadium was a new addition to the National Tennis Center in 1997, and brought even more money into tennis programs across the USA.

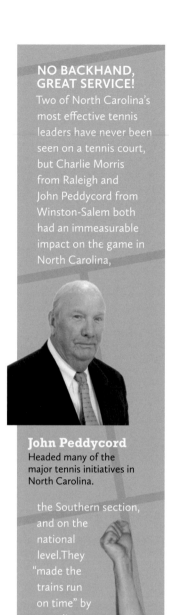

John Peddycord
Headed many of the major tennis initiatives in North Carolina.

to meet the needs of the game statewide, then sponsor even more programs and events, which would lead to even more growth.

THE BUSINESS OF THE GAME

In 1996, as the Arthur Ashe Stadium was under construction, Mary Milam retired after 13 years from what she called "a nice little job," although she agreed to continue managing some projects, such as the STAR ranking program, from her home.

That same year, longtime volunteer Vicki Everette was slated to be president of the Association, but was beset by anxieties. "I didn't want Mary to leave. I was used to her being there and I was new. I felt I hadn't had enough experience to work without an experienced executive director."

She was more than happy when Burlington native and NC State women's tennis coach Kelly Key came on as Milam's replacement. Even though Key's most recent team had been ranked in the top 40 in the country, "I felt like I was burned out," said Key, who relished the opportunity to unleash her

From Peace to State to NCTA
Kelly Key, later Kelly Gaines, brought extraordinary enthusiasm and competence to the NCTA executive director position.

considerable energy in a different tennis arena.

Because the NCTA staff had grown from one to four and the number of exhibits in the Hall of Fame (one for each inductee) had grown from 13 to 46, the Association quickly determined it was running out of office space in its three-room building at the J. Spencer Love Tennis Center in Greensboro. Initial plans for adding on to the building were put on hold, however, and the Hall of Fame Room was rearranged to provide space for Amy Franklin, the NCTA's new Program Director.

A program director was necessary because more and more players had become involved with USTA programs that required membership. In 1997 total USTA

Charlie Morris
Charlie Morris, who was also Marshall Happer's law partner, was widely recognized as one of North Carolina's most effective volunteer leaders. In 1995 The Southern Section of the USTA established the Charles B. Morris Jr award that recognizes volunteers who exhibit exemplary volunteer spirit at the local, state, sectional and national levels.

membership in North Carolina had reached 15,114 (11,361 adults and 3,753 juniors); adult-age group-sanctioned tournaments had declined, but the number of NTRP tournaments and junior tournaments had increased significantly. More importantly, leagues were still on a dramatic upswing, and hence so was overall participation.

Changing Communications

Despite the fact that computerization was by this time central to NCTA office operations, neither staff nor volunteers were totally aware of what the computer, combined with the Internet, could do. "I remember asking, 'Are we going to get email?'" said Key, now Gaines. "The answer came back, 'Who in the world would you email?'"

The advent of the Internet would bring a change to communications in the North Carolina tennis community, just as it would to everyone else. In 1996, the NCTA launched nctennis.com, and reported that people quickly started depending on it, logging 25,000 visitors in January of that year and 150,000 by June.

By 2002, Ray Alley's *North Carolina Tennis Today,* a privately owned publication partially supported by the NCTA, was feeling the pinch of this digital

December Issue, 1999

NORTH CAROLINA Tennis Today

VOL. 8, NO. 9 — *North Carolina's Tennis Magazine* — PRICE: $2.00

On The Inside

P2 *Tennis Isn't Dead, It's Actually Growing In Number Of Players In USTA!*

P4 *North Carolina High School Athletic Association Dual Team Champions*

P5 *Tim Wilkison Interviews John McEnroe At Nuveen Tour Event*

P5 *Video Tape Can Be*

North Carolina Tennis Today

Until it was supplanted by the internet, Ray Alley's *North Carolina Tennis Today* was the primary source for tennis news in North Carolina.

Madam President.
As president of the NCTF in 2004-2005, Paula Hale would oversee the plans to buy a new building and Hall of Fame.

competition, and would cut back to six issues a year. By 2003 the NCTA decided to stop the funding that had allowed *North Carolina Tennis Today* to be free. "As a means for communicating our North Carolina tennis news," said Kelly Gaines, "the Internet had become a more immediate and effective means of communication."

A New Home Realized; An Endowment Begun

In 1998 the NCTA could no longer make do at Spencer Love and moved its administrative offices out of the Hall of Fame building to a 1,900-square-foot office where it had secured a two-year lease.

Five years later, in January of 2004, Paula Hale, the outgoing president of the NCTA and the incoming president of the NCTF, was increasingly concerned about the inadequacies of the space the NCTA was renting in West Greensboro. "We were in rented space and bursting at the seams," she said. "We had been working with some potential partnerships to be able to partner with a facility to house our association offices in conjunction with something else." Prior to the January 2004 Tennis Weekend and Foundation Board meeting, Hale told John Peddycord and Judy Utley, "It's time for us to revisit this whole idea of a building."

"Vicki Everette had had plans drawn up years before," she explained later, "in anticipation of trying to build something." In 2004 Hale felt it was time to dust them off; the next day at the Foundation Board meeting, her proposal to get moving on the NCTF and Hall of Fame building project was met with enthusiasm. Judy Utley agreed to chair a building committee.

Unfortunately, the Foundation only had about $70,000 in the coffers at the time, and had only raised about $12,000 to $20,000 per year through an annual letter. This money was given out in community grants and to a few high schools. "We didn't do a lot because we didn't have a lot of money," said Hale. A fundraising committee therefore decided that a campaign was in order. Former North Carolina State All-American Andy Andrews, by then a commercial real estate developer in Raleigh and soon to be an active NCTF volunteer, agreed to serve as chair.

Over a glass of wine at the Carolina Hotel in Pinehurst in January of 2004, Utley, Peddycord, and Hale were discussing the need for a building when developer Ted

Andy Andrews.
NC State All-American and top touring pro Andy Andrews led the fundraising effort for the North Carolina Tennis Foundation. He now serves on the Board of the USTA.

Reese joined the discussion, only to walk away charged with finding creative financing that would work for both the Association and Foundation. The Foundation Board was enthusiastic about the

"We were out to raise money for the building, to recreate the North Carolina Tennis Hall of Fame, and to establish a tennis endowment fund."

building idea because it was perfect to house the Association offices, provide meeting and training space, and provide a home for the Hall of Fame and showcase for its inductees.

The fundraising committee divided the state into seven regions, each with a leader, and several theme committees. Hale chaired the community donor group and developed a plan for selling bricks for the front walk that could be personalized in honor of anyone the donor chose, so that everybody could be involved in some way.

Within a few months the building committee found an attractively

Harold and Mildred Southern.
Harold T. and Mildred F. Southern have made tremendous contributions to tennis at the local, state, section and national levels. Their unwavering support in both time and resources has benefitted all who play tennis in North Carolina.

priced vacant building in a string of commercial and medical buildings on Henry Street north of downtown, and closed on it in July of 2004. The idea was that the Hall of Fame would be part of the new building, but would be added at a later date. Eventually the decision was made to add to the campaign by including in the goal an endowment for tennis-related charitable purposes as a way to grow the game in communities throughout North Carolina.

"It would be a trifecta," said Andrews. "We were out to raise money for the building, to recreate the North Carolina Tennis Hall of Fame, and to establish a tennis endowment fund."

With the help of fundraising consultant John Bennett of Capital Development, the campaign was announced in January of 2005 with a goal of $1.5 million. Raising money took time. Hale noted, "the campaign planning committee was a year or so into planning in coordination with Capital Development before we ever received the first check." The real momentum was secured when the lead gift by Harold T. and Mildred F. Southern was given verbally on the eve of Tennis Weekend in January 2005. In October of 2005, eight months after the public launch, Hale announced that $1.35 million was in hand. Four months later, at Tennis Weekend in Pinehurst in January, the campaign was closed with $1.77 million, almost 20 percent over the goal.

Jeff Joyce
Longtime Parks and Rec official in Asheville, has been a stalwart volunteer for many years.

"What I really admire about North Carolina tennis is that this state is very well organized," said Andrews. "There was a core group that wanted to see this work."

Jeff Joyce, who worked on the campaign in western North Carolina, spoke directly to that organization. "They did a good job by having leadership teams in every area of the state," he said. "I served with Bonnie Vandergrift and Buster Brown. We had social functions to invite people to give money. It was just a wonderfully run campaign statewide."

Former NCTA president Allen

Successful Campaign
The cover of the case statement for the North Carolina Tennis Foundation Campaign.

L. RICHARDSON AND EMILY PREYER

Greensboro residents, L. Richardson Preyer and his wife Emily were among the state's greatest tennis supporters and patrons for a generation. Though serving as a Congressman and Federal Judge, he always found time to play. She was widely known for her gracious personality and love of the game, whether by playing, organizing tennis events or hosting players in her home. She was famous for her ability to remember everyone's name from the youngest junior to the oldest senior. All of their children were excellent tennis players, including Jane who played professionally.

Richardson and Emily Preyer

A New Home
The Harold T. & Mildred F. Southern North Carolina Tennis Center is the first home the NCTA and the Hall of Fame has had on its own.

Morris, one of many who pitched in, noted how volunteers worked their connections. "We were pretty successful getting money. I was able to go to a lot of the guys I had played tennis with way back and got some fairly substantial gifts."

"The campaign was a dedicated effort of many people, and particularly John Peddycord," added Richard Holderness of Greensboro, who has served as NCTF Treasurer for over 20 years. "Truly, the state has been blessed with great and faithful leaders who have ensured that excellence will be sustained for decades to come."

The leading benefactors of this effort were the Southerns of Winston-Salem, whose generous donation is memorialized by the name of the building, and the Richardson Preyer family of Greensboro, who provided the substantial seed money for the endowment in honor of their mother, Emily Preyer. Significant funds were generated through donations made for naming rights for various awards and naming rights throughout the building. Everybody was involved in some way.

When the USTA committed to spend $31.4 million dollars in the late 1990s over the next five years to bring 800,000 new players to the game, it was clear that the game's growth would continue.

The Building and the Endowment

Today, the Harold T. & Mildred F. Southern North Carolina Tennis Center is owned by the charitable Foundation, which leases space to the Association. The relationship has worked well for all. "We could never have meetings in our old office because there was nowhere to have them," said Hale. "Now we

The History is Here
The displays in the Hall of Fame tell the rich history of tennis in North Carolina.

have a training center where we can bring in new coordinators and we can bring in small groups for whatever the staff or committees need to do there."

The Hall of Fame, with images of and memorabilia from its inductees, serves as the focal point, and is surrounded by NCTA offices and meeting rooms.

Thanks to the Preyer family and the overall success of the fundraising efforts, the Foundation's Emily H. Preyer Family Endowment Fund is able to give away significant funds annually for one of four charitable purposes: junior development scholarships for kids needing assistance; new programs involving outreach, inclusion and adaptive programming; camp scholarships for deserving kids; and college assistance for kids needing such help.

"We distribute on an annual basis," said Andrews. "A certain percentage of those funds go towards whatever we deem necessary that year. Kids in need get lessons and equipment. Kids who can't afford tennis camps get to go. Kids that might not be getting a tennis scholarship to play tennis are able to go to college. The great thing about the endowment is that these kids' parents can't make but so much money. They've got to write a letter. It's pretty cool."

NORTH CAROLINA TENNIS ASSOCIATION

Long-Range Plan

When the USTA committed to spend $31.4 million dollars in the late 1990s over the next five years to bring 800,000 new players to the game, it was clear that the game's growth would continue. In anticipation, NCTA executive director Kelly Gaines brought members of the management committee, past presidents, and staff together for two days of strategic planning to prepare, and in so doing, dramatically changed, deepened, and coordinated the administrative structure of tennis in North Carolina.

The resulting long-range plan determined that the game had to be nourished and managed at regional levels, and established area advisory councils, with area directors, to work with the NCTA, community tennis associations, parks and recreation associations,

schools, volunteers, and anyone else to promote the game. This decentralized administrative structure would provide a framework for growth in the first decade of the 21st century.

In the 1980s, before the major money started flowing, programs and funding to stimulate the game were modest. "The USTA would throw out a program here or there, but really wouldn't train you or fund you completely to get it done," said Kelly Gaines. "The STA had a staff person who did all the schools for nine states. That person would travel to all the states. One person. It was just hard for one person to be effective among nine states."

By veining management deep into regional and even local levels, in the late 1990s the NCTA was able to use the money coming from the USTA to increase these grass-roots programs. Today the NCTA's

US Open in the Ball Park

The Greensboro Grasshoppers made way for tennis as part of one of NCTA's marketing programs.

programs to stimulate tennis are too varied to list, and run the gamut from local events to school programs to age-group events. Gaines has assembled a highly professional staff, and the NCTA Board has an active Management Committee consisting of persons highly knowledgeable as to tennis matters. For example, Winston-Salem accountant Teresa Lindsay, who serves as treasurer of the Board, is one of the many capable volunteers who give greatly of their time and professional expertise.

"The big change," says Gaines, "is that we are trying to involve non-tennis people and children in simple programs. We explore different approaches and utilize many venues to raise awareness of tennis." School programs are one example. "We go into a school and teach the teachers how to teach. We provide a curriculum guide with lesson plans, and we provide equipment. We are trying to work with the after-school directors to actually do a little bit more in their after-school program. Some of those kids are there for three hours every afternoon. They do homework, then they play. We want them to rotate tennis into that curriculum. We have been in almost all 100 counties."

It doesn't stop with high school. In order to keep players who played in high school involved in the game, the NCTA sponsored a survey to 53 colleges to find out what tennis is available on their campus or in their area, and then informed college players of these opportunities.

During the 2009 US Open, the NCTA, led by the efforts of Mary

Lloyd Barbera, NCTA's director of marketing and special events, worked with a local television station, WFMY-TV, the local CBS affiliate in Greensboro, to present the "US Open in the Ballpark" at New Bridge Bank Park, home of the Greensboro Grasshoppers. A pregame tennis carnival was held for the fans to raise awareness of tennis and the NCTA with a larger audience in the community. More than 1,000 enthusiastic tennis fans showed up at the ballpark.

Over the past decade, the NCTA, with Barbera leading the effort, has also seized the opportunity at professional and charity events to sponsor a variety of on-site youth activities, including inviting children to participate in a carnival, clinic, or high-performance workout each day prior to the matches. Often the NCTA coordinates the activities with the local school children. Local pros, city officials and celebrities are all involved. In short, NCTA programs and promotions in 2012 are now limited only by imagination.

POCKETS OF THE GAME

Local Tennis
In the 1990s, and particularly since the beginning of the 21st century, community

Forty Years of Service
Four longtime USTA North Carolina staff members with more than 10 years of service top to bottom, Mary Lloyd Barbera, Chris Bryce, Amy Franklin, and Jane Scott.

tennis associations have increasingly served as clearinghouses for all local organized tennis activities. Amy Franklin, the NCTA's director of community development, outreach, and training, notes that, "as a result of US Open profits, our push is to do more locally, and with the help of area directors, we have seen greatly increased community activity and funding." This funding is based on the number of members, programs, and activities.

For instance, the NCTA and the STA awarded a total of over $75,000 to community tennis associations in North Carolina to support USTA programs on the local level. The NCTA matched $1 for every $2 approved and distributed by the STA. Amounts awarded were based on the USTA membership in each local association's area. In 2011, that same award totaled over $100,000 for community tennis.

As the role of CTAs grew and local USTA Leagues continued to expand, the fact that the two were operating independently became a topic of discussion. After much effort, the local league coordinators joined forces with the CTAs to the mutual satisfaction of both. Long independent, the transition was sometimes slow but today is an example of USTA program and community teamwork.

Much of this activity on the local level has been driven by dedicated individuals such as Greater Wilmington Tennis Association's past president, Yona Bar-Zeev. "He does an incredible amount of work," said Amy Franklin. "Yona is a classic example like many

other community leaders who forge outstanding relationships amongst the different tennis community stakeholders to grow tennis at the local level."

Similarly dedicated people

The development of league tennis led the charge for larger public facilities, and North Carolina has become a destination for national and sectional events because its large tennis centers can accommodate them.

work in various capacities all across the state. In addition to high-profile volunteers such as Mildred Southern, there are people like Randy Pate, owner of the Randy Pate Tennis Academy, who has consistently produced highly ranked players for years. Bobby Taylor from Snow Hill has generated a higher percentage of USTA members than just about anywhere in the South with his clubs and tournaments. Kathy Kim has been influencing kids in Hickory to play tennis for 40 years. In Greensboro, Mike Belangia has taken the State Closed Adult Championship to a new level with prize money and sponsorship. Buster Brown, former owner of the Asheville Racquet Club, and former parks and recreation executive Jeff Joyce have long fostered tennis in western North Carolina, just as Henry Hostetler has done in the eastern part of the state. The list is a long and distinguished one.

Public Courts

In most communities in North Carolina, public parks are the

Downeast Tennis Czar
Bobby Taylor from Snow Hill has created a competitive atmosphere in eastern North Carolina.

backbone of tennis activity. Over 70 percent of all tennis is played in public venues. Today, most public venues have paid tennis directors who have provided a hub for organization and community involvement.

The development of league tennis led the charge for larger public facilities, and North Carolina has become a destination for national and sectional events because its large tennis centers can accommodate them. Those events in turn justify the expenditure of public money because they support local restaurants, hotels, and tourism.

No better example can be found than the Cary Tennis Park, which was built on 24 rolling acres with 30 courts, and in 2006 won both the USTA Outstanding Tennis Facility Award and the Racquet Sports Industry Facility of the Year Award. In 2011, it is the only facility in North Carolina with four permanent 36-foot courts

and two 60-foot courts lined on a normal 78-foot court. Smaller rackets, smaller courts, and low-compression balls—the new way to learn tennis for the next generation of young players—are used for play on these smaller courts. Due to the strength of the public facilities in Cary, Raleigh, Durham, and Chapel Hill, plus the surrounding communities, the USTA in 2011 has chosen the Triangle area as a pilot for an early development center in which facilities and programs are geared toward children.

In 1997 Burlington opened a 12-court complex at the downtown City Park. "There were a lot of people who didn't even know the facility was open at first," said city tennis director John Walton, who doubled as women's tennis coach at Elon College. Activity quickly picked up, however.

In 2004, Goldsboro dedicated ten lighted tennis courts at Herman Park in honor of local

Brown Supports Western North Carolina Tennis
Buster Brown, a national age group champion, owned the Asheville Racquet Club and supported many competitions and programs in the Asheville area.

Cary Park
QuickStart 36′ courts at Cary Tennnis Park.

Isenhour Dedication
Naming the NC State courts after J.W. Isenhour was a popular move.

tennis organizer John Allen Farfour.

In 2006 Asheville's Aston Tennis Center was refurbished, and the new Covington Clubhouse was dedicated in memory of longtime Asheville son Dick Covington. And

Today, most public venues have paid tennis directors who have provided a hub for organization and community involvement.

though it's not entirely public, the owner of the Crowne Plaza in Asheville built an indoor facility and four new outdoor courts.

"We've been really lucky in North Carolina with public tennis systems," said Herman Enochs, past NCTA and Southern President. "Latham Park and J. Spencer Love Tennis Center in Greensboro, Millbrook Exchange Tennis Center in Raleigh, Cary Tennis Park, River Birch in Greenville...we've really got

some nice public tennis centers, and for a pretty good while there have been tennis directors there full-time. What that did was really open up tennis to the masses."

This was community-wide tennis as opposed to just club tennis. Ted Reese, NCTA President, points out that "with the projected growth of tennis it will be necessary to rely on public facilities to meet the demands." To this end, the NCTA formed a facility task force under Anna Martin to provide matching grants to facilities seeking USTA facility funding.

Colleges Expand As Well

Major universities also added new facilities or expanded old ones at an unprecedented rate in the 21st century.

In 2004 NC State dedicated the 30,000-square-foot J.W. Isenhour Tennis Center on West Campus near Doak Field for use by the men's and women's tennis programs, and immediately won the USTA's Outstanding Facility Award, one of only four collegiate complexes to receive the honor. The main advantage for Wolfpack tennis is the four indoor courts.

"Nobody at NC State had ever raised money for an indoor center," said Andy Andrews, who only agreed to chair the effort if the entire Wolfpack complex was named in honor of his coach and mentor, J.W. Isenhour. The indoor courts are named after Andrews.

In 2005, Appalachian State University dedicated a new tennis center in honor of former men's tennis and basketball coach Bob Light. In 2011 the Wake Forest Tennis

Center was built at a cost of nearly $3 million. The 13-court facility next to Bridger Field House at BB&T Field was built through the efforts of Don Flow and Winston-Salem Professional Tennis, Inc. to host a professional tennis tournament, the ATP's Winston-Salem Open, each summer, which is part of the US Open Tennis Series. Flow, a tireless promoter of tennis events, had led the successful efforts of Winston-Salem in 2001, 2007, and 2008 to host US Davis Cup home ties—assisted by the supportive cast of Harold Pollard, Doug Roberts, Gray Smith, Rich Keshian, and others.

In 2011, NC State renovated its facilities. The refurbished Curtis & Jacqueline Dail Outdoor Tennis Stadium is one of the premiere outdoor tennis complexes in the country, and includes an entrance plaza, grandstand, and new scoreboard.

Juniors

In the years between 1993 and 2011, Junior Team Tennis continued to grow and blossom. The foundation had been laid over the years with many local junior leagues throughout the state. The nationalization of the program in 1993 provided a common organizational structure with a consistent play format and rules throughout the local, state, section, and national levels. Under the leadership of Charlotte's Carla O'Connor and the NCTA staff, Junior

Honored by the Mountaineers
Bob LIght, Appalcahian State's longtime coach, was recognized for his service when the school named the new tennis center after him in 2005.

Team Tennis has provided players with a team experience unlike any they previously received in tournaments. O'Connor noted that, "Junior Team Tennis provides the same team format for kids that became so popular with adults when the USTA League was added in the 1980s."

Junior Team Tennis play enabled competition to expand with competitive play for all age and ability levels. After several years of statewide jamborees, the first state championship was held in 2000 with winning teams facing league winners from other cities. As with adult leagues, this competition expanded to eventually include southern and national playoffs.

"It has been exciting to watch participation grow year after year," said O'Connor. "Junior Team Tennis has clearly become an important component of youth tennis programming in public and private venues across the state. Tennis professionals recognize the value of providing organized local match play opportunity for children, and parents and players are

Next Pages →
Eight and under participants from the 2012 USTA North Carolina Jr. Team Tennis State Championships in Greenville, NC.

Kids Programs
North Carolina has produced many outstanding players who got their start in local grassroots clinics and programs. Ten and under tennis using the Quickstart format is a recent innovation that has taken hold across North Carolina and should bring thousands of kids into the game. This enthusiastic competitor is using QuickStart racquets and multi-colored, low compression balls.

Boosting QuickStart at the Grassroots.
Durham's Anna Mercer-McLean, a longtime tennis player and volunteer, has been instrumental in Durham's QuickStart program.

attracted to the team format where children have the opportunity to play with and against other children of similar age and ability level. Ultimately, program delivery is possible through the dedication of enthusiastic local league coordinators and supportive community tennis associations and park and recreation agencies."

Individual volunteers such as Hendersonville's Ralph Wingerter have been equally critical in fostering youth programs throughout the state. Wingerter began giving tennis lessons to children at a local park in 1989, and eventually started a Junior Team Tennis League for Hendersonville. His efforts expanded geographically to include children from Henderson County and the Henderson County YMCA.

Junior Tennis Leader
Carla O'Connor of Charlotte has been tireless in support of junior tennis.

The biggest innovation relating to kids' tennis came from the USTA with the development and promotion of QuickStart, a play format in which the youngest kids play with reduced-pressure balls using smaller rackets on smaller courts. "We started QuickStart in Chapel Hill," said Durham's Anna Mercer-McLean. "We had 100 participants the first time, and 100 the second time. We did it with Chapel Hill Parks and Recreation with Patti Fox, our community tennis coordinator, and went out to the schools, and to the parks by Hargrave Center, Cedar Falls, and Ephesus. We're hoping to grow QuickStart in Durham just as fast."

The QuickStart format also made inroads at private clubs. In terms of raising junior participation throughout the country, the QuickStart format has become the key component of the 10 and Under Tennis initiative in 2011; the potential impact on the growth of tennis with younger players both in exposing them to the game and in retaining them for a lifetime is tremendous. Junior Team Tennis could well cause an explosion in participation unlike anything tennis has seen since the tennis boom in the 1970s. The ability to compete more effectively with other youth sports in attracting participants at an earlier age than ever before, and also hopefully attracting superior athletes, is exciting both in increasing participation but also in grooming future champions. It will create the need for new courts and facilities, but that is a good problem to have. The future looks bright.

Colleges and Schools

Tennis in North Carolina's schools and colleges was healthy as the turn of the century approached. Today, over 300 high schools in North Carolina support tennis teams. For years, the NCTA worked with NCHSAA head Charlie Adams to promote the sport for the mutual benefit of both organizations, and for the past 15 years the NCTF, as part of its educational mission, has helped fund state championships, currently held in Burlington. In the

Wildcat Coach
Jeff Frank coached many outstanding teams at Davidson from 1972 to 2006, and became the winningest coach at any sport in Davidson history.

2000s the coaches came together under the leadership of Greene Central's girls' coach Donald Clark and created a coaches association, which convenes at UNC-G each summer for a workshop.

High school players who want to play at the next level in North Carolina have long had a wealth of opportunities. At Elon, for example, in 1996 Coach Tom Parham recorded his 500th win after 30 years of coaching. In 1997, along with High Point, Elon moved up to the Big South conference of Division I, although they had to forego postseason play until 2000.

ACC tennis is stronger than ever—as strong as any conference in the nation. In 2002 the ACC celebrated 50 years of men's and women's tennis with a list of the 50 greatest players in which North Carolina products figured prominently. The Duke women have

registered the most consistent success of any of North Carolina's ACC teams in garnering 12 straight ACC titles from 1988 through 2001. They won the NCAA team championship in 2009.

The state of North Carolina is fortunate to be the home of an unusually large number of great colleges and universities, and these institutions have had the good fortune to have top-flight pros coaching their teams. Many of these coaches bring in top tennis talent from around the world and run excellent summer camps at their institutions. At Duke, Jay Lapidus's men's teams have won 11 ACC championships and have consistently achieved national prominence, and the Blue Devils' women's coach, Jamie Ashworth, has coached teams to numerous titles, including the 2009 NCAA championship. At UNC, Sam Paul

National Champions, 2009
In a period between 1988 and 2001, spanning four different coaches, the Duke's women's tennis team garnered 12 ACC titles in a row. They reached the pinnacle by winning the national championship in 2009, and were led in that effort by Fayetteville's Reka Zsilinszka, seen above in white cap, who was named the tournament MVP.

has continued the university's successful tennis tradition for over 20 years, and Brian Kalbas is achieving similar success with the women's program. At NC State, Jon Choboy and Hans Olsen are producing a series of very successful teams. At Wake Forest, Jeff Zinn led the men's teams to success for over 15 years.

Most pros don't focus on elite protégés, but rather teach recreational tennis at parks and clubs to beginners and players who have no aspirations beyond fun and improving their game.

There have been just as many highly successful college coaches in recent decades outside of the ACC arena. At Davidson, Jeff Frank led the Wildcats to great success over several decades. A few of the many other long-serving coaches include Bob Lake at Appalachian, Jeff Trivette at UNC-G, Tom Morris at ECU, and Jenny Garrity at UNC-W. These and many other coaches and assistant coaches make the rigors of college tennis a rewarding experience that provides great life lessons to their student athletes.

Teaching Pros
As tennis blossomed and matured in the decades surrounding the turn of the 21st century, teaching pros had become the face of the game at the local level. The proliferation of teaching pros was both a cause and effect of the growth in tennis in general. From only a handful of pros prior to the tennis boom, there are an estimated 650 teaching pros in the state in 2011.

A few pros have chosen the "high performance" route and have catered to aspiring juniors. Pros such as Chris Cagle, Shane Wells, Michael Leonard, Bill Schillings, Calvin Davis, Randy Pate, and Oscar Blacutt, just to name a few, followed in the paths blazed by predecessors such as J.W. Isenhour and Woody Blocher. They spend countless hours in junior development. They accompany their players to tournaments on the weekends and teach them life skills as well as tennis strategies. Their presence in the state provides a much less expensive alternative to the out-of-state tennis academies that aggressively seek to recruit the state's top juniors. These pros have been hugely important in the success of North Carolina juniors on the national level.

Most pros don't focus on elite protégés, but rather teach recreational tennis at parks and clubs to beginners and players who have no aspirations beyond fun and improving their game. They teach a lifetime sport with enthusiasm and a love of the game, offering free clinics, recruiting teams, arranging league matches and mediating disputes between different tennis interests. They get kids off the

No Clean Shirts
Pinehurst and Wilmington Landfall pro Charlie Owens was one of the most colorful players in the game, diving and rolling all over the court, and laughing all the way to many titles.

couch and improve our country's public health. They develop top players from time to time when the opportunity arises, but they never lose sight of the broad recreational base of the sport.

Some of these pros, like Tom Cascarano, Bill Francis, Laird Dunlop, and Dan Weant, have served at large country clubs for several decades. Others, such as Tommy Dixon, Jack Blankenhorn, Karen Rembert, and Mike Zaluski, have served for decades at clubs that are more focused on tennis. Still others, including Mike Belangia, Chris Henson, and Junie Chatman, have worked primarily at public parks. Many of these pros, too numerous to mention, have spent a lifetime successfully promoting the sport they love and have affected the lives of thousands of people in a positive way.

While it is not necessary for a top teaching pro to have been a great player, some top teaching pros also have played adult tournaments very successfully when they could find the time. Skilled players such as Charlie Owens, Bobby Heald, and Wayne Hearn occasionally managed to get time off from their teaching jobs to play tournaments. Other teaching pros, like Adam Thomson, Cliff Skakle, Todd Upchurch, and Derek Gamble, have volunteered their time serving their fellow professionals through organizations such as the USPTA that strive to improve the competence and success of tennis pros across the state.

Other pros—Ted Reese, Henry Hostetler, and Cy King—have given huge amounts of their valuable time to the statewide administrative work of the NCTA and NCTF, all while running a full range of programming from grassroots initiatives to high-performance coaching. The good work of these and other pros who have volunteered their time will improve the lives of thousands of future tennis players who will never even know their names.

COMPETITIVE TENNIS

In 2011, more than 100 adult and NTRP tournaments offer opportunities for North Carolina adults who relish competitive tennis. The state's top players often succeed in USTA national and international events, regularly winning "gold balls" signifying national championships.

No current tournament has a longer history than the very popular Asheville City Open. "The Open has retained its vitality for several reasons," said Jeff Joyce. "One, the STA designates it as a 200-point tournament and that continues to keep the top players coming. Second, the players know that the city of Asheville runs quality events on good courts. Third, there are good social gatherings during the tournament. And fourth, while it's still in the South, it is probably an average of ten to 15 degrees cooler than the rest of the South. Later in the summer, the Yonahlossee tournament near Boone also allows players to escape the heat."

The Carolina Cup represents an innovative approach developed

TOP OF THE GAME

Fred Robinson from Charlotte and Marianna Routh Hollman from Greensboro know how to win national championships and represent the U.S. in team competition. Marianna has won over 20 gold balls in USTA championships in age groupings from 30 and over to 45 and over. Fred has 13 gold balls for age division championships for ages 45 to 55.

Both Marianna and Fred have represented the U.S. in international competition on numerous occasions, including the 2011 ITF Senior World Championships in New Zealand. They were there when the devastating earthquake struck Christchurch on the south island on February 22, 2011, preventing the completion of the tournament. Both players returned home safely.

**Iron Man
Fred Robinson**

Friendly Competitors
Led by captains Lesley McIver and Debbie Carmazzi, North Carolina's western region managed to wrangle the Carolina Cup away from the team from the Triangle.

Home Grown Champ
The Winston-Salem Open, held at the new Wake Forest Tennis Center for the first time in 2011, has drawn a world class field and big crowds, who were thrilled to watch North Carolina's John Isner walk away with the trophy in both 2011 and 2012.

by Sanford Senior Player Peggy Golden in the 1990s that combines team and individual competition. The format divides top players from across the state into four regions: East, Triangle, Piedmont, and West. Each region fields a team in age groups 30-70 for men and women, singles and doubles. Though the Triangle area has dominated, the other areas have strongly challenged as competition has moved to different locations around the state.

North Carolina has also continued to be a leader in the Southern section with its Southern Senior Cup team. The Southern Senior Cup is a competition between the nine southern states, with men and women competing in singles and doubles in age groups 35s through 75s. Vicki Everette, North Carolina's captain for many years, has championed this event, and in 2010 the STA gave her special recognition for her tireless efforts. Mildred Southern was instrumental in the success of the Southern Senior Cup, and the men's and women's point winners award carries her name.

Professional Tennis in North Carolina

Professional tennis continues to make appearances in North Carolina. In 1995 the US Men's Clay Court Championships, previously held in Charlotte, returned to North

Vicki Everette
Vicki Everette has been a volunteer and North Carolina's Southern Cup captain for many years.

Fed Cup
The Fed Cup was played at Charlotte's Olde Providence Racquet Club in 2002 against Austria.

Carolina for two years in Pinehurst before leaving for a long stretch in Houston, Texas.

In 1999 the Fed Cup returned to the Raleigh Racquet Club, with Monica Seles and Chanda Rubin leading the USA to a 5-0 victory over Croatia. In 2001 Winston-Salem began a successful career as a Davis Cup city, hosting a qualifying match in which the USA defeated India 4-1 to stay in the world group. UNC's Don Johnson, who won 24 ATP doubles titles, including Wimbledon in 2001 with Jared Palmer, played the doubles rubber.

In 2002 Olde Providence

Racquet Club hosted the Fed Cup when the USA team under captain Billie Jean King proved victorious against Austria.

The Davis Cup returned to Winston-Salem twice more when the U.S. defeated Spain 4-1 in 2007 and France 4-1 in 2008, both times being led by Andy Roddick, James Blake, and the Bryan brothers, Mike and Bob.

Winston-Salem continued to burnish its reputation as an international tennis city in 2011, hosting the first Winston-Salem Open, an ATP 250-level event, which was played for the first time at Wake Forest's new stadium. A special bonus for North Carolina fans, former state high school champion from Greensboro Page High School, John Isner, perhaps the best singles player to emerge from North Carolina since Tim Wilkison and John Sadri 30 years before, captured his third title in a five-year career that has seen him rise to a top-20 world ranking. The owner of three singles titles and three doubles titles, Isner went on to the quarterfinals of the US Open a month later.

JOHN ISNER'S RECORD MATCH

Greensboro's John Isner played the longest match in tennis history with his first-round opponent, Nicolas Mahut, at Wimbledon in 2010.

A veteran of tiebreakers because of his massive serve, which he delivers from his 6'-9" height, Isner prevailed over Mahut in a match spanning 11 hours over three days, 70-68 in the fifth set, the long set a result of Wimbledon's policy of eschewing tiebreakers in the fifth set.

"It's something I'll get asked about for the rest of my career, but that's fine," he said. "It doesn't get old. I hear it a lot. But what we did for those three days was pretty extraordinary."

There is a plaque at Wimbledon to commemorate this feat, and Isner and Mahut's racquets from the match are in the Tennis Hall of Fame in Newport, R.I.

World Champs Hold Forth at the Davis Cup
Mike and Bob Bryan anchored the U.S. Davis Cup teams that played in Winston-Salem in 2007 and 2008.

North Carolina Players on the Tour

Beginning in the 1970s, with the confluence of full-time teaching pros, year-round play in indoor facilities, and sponsorship from the NCTA, North Carolina began to produce outstanding players who compete on the WTA and the ATP professional circuits.

Laura Dupont from Charlotte reached a career-high ranking of number 10 in singles, and reached the quarterfinals at the US Open; Jane Preyer of Greensboro reached number 32 with a win over former world number one Evonne Goolagong Cawley; Louise Allen from Winston-Salem won the Broderick Award for the best collegiate player in women's tennis and was later ranked number 65; Sarah Taylor from Raleigh reached a singles ranking of 68. Ally Baker of Raleigh and Cory Anne Avants of Gastonia have also played on the professional tour.

On the men's side, John Sadri of Charlotte achieved a singles ranking of 14 and reached the finals of the Australian Open; Tim Wilkison of Shelby reached number 23 and won six singles titles; Don Johnson, who played and coached at UNC, achieved a world number one ranking

Laura!
Charlotte's Laura DuPont, who played her college tennis at UNC, cracked the top ten in the 1970s.

in doubles and won Wimbledon doubles with Jared Palmer; Tripp Phillips from Charlotte reached a ranking of 29 in doubles and won two ATP doubles titles; Lawson Duncan from Asheville achieved a ranking of 47 in singles and reached the quarterfinals of the 1989 French Open; and Andy Andrews was 1983 runner-up with Sadri in the Australian Open doubles. Other ATP players with a North Carolina pedigree have included Keith Richardson, Pender Murphy, Chris Kennedy, Wayne Hearn, Matt McDonald, Gene Hamilton, Cliff Skakle, Robbie Smith, Stephen Enochs, Sammy Martin, and John Lucas.

It's Official!

As in the rest of the country, officiating in North Carolina was basically performed by untrained

Top Tenner
Greensboro's John Isner's towering serve, delivered from his 6'-9" height, led the 2012 U.S. Davis Cup team to upsets of Switzerland, with Roger Federer, and France. Later that spring he became the first North Carolina-born player to crack the world's top ten.

Jane Preyer
A top-50 player on tour, Jane Preyer took the Duke coaching job in 1985 and coached the Blue Devils to the top of the ACC.

volunteers until the 1970s. Even after national certification and training programs were begun, most officiating was still handled by unpaid volunteers well into the 1980s.

Floyd Willis of Charlotte, whose career started in 1972, was probably the state's first official certified as a chair umpire, receiving his card from what was then the USLTA in 1975, and he was still working a full schedule of amateur, collegiate, and professional events four decades later.

In the early 1980s, Mont Graham of Reidsville and Dougald MacMillan of Fayetteville brought more structure and training to the process. They became USTA-certified trainers and conducted classes for prospective officials throughout the state.

Along with Jim Horton of Cullowhee, they were also instrumental in forming the North Carolina Professional Tennis Umpires Association, a separate organization working on behalf of officials. Graham was inducted into the North Carolina Tennis Hall of Fame in 1992.

In the mid-1980s, as tennis was experiencing a national boom, an increase in tournaments across North Carolina led to a rapid expansion of the state's officiating corps. Ron Violette of Concord and Rebel Good of Elkin joined Willis, Graham, MacMillan, and Horton in being selected to work the US Open.

Over the years the state's cadre of officials at the Open grew, reaching as many as 11 several times. Among those selected to

Rebel Good
One of North Carolina's many officials, pictured here at the 2012 US Open.

work men's or women's singles finals at the Open were Susan Cooper of Greenville, Diane Spangler of Cary, David Giltz of Greensboro, Al Klassen of Holly Springs, Tracy Crossland, an Elkin native, and Good. The state's officials were also working in the NCAA Championships, the Olympics, Davis Cup, and Fed Cup, in addition to Grand Slam and professional events both national and international.

In 1991, Good became the state's first International Bronze Badge Chair Umpire certified by the International Tennis Federation; he also was the first to simultaneously hold Professional Line and Professional Chair certifications from the USTA. He became a trainer/evaluator on the sectional and national level, and taught rules and procedures to officials across the country for more than 20 years. Spangler was the first North Carolinian certified by the ITF as a Chief Umpire, and Lindsay Pratt of Southern Pines as an ITF Referee.

By the turn of the 21st century, the state boasted a corps of officials that

Golden Girl
Peggy Golden of Sanford discovered tennis at age 49. She made up for lost time as one of North Carolina's most active volunteers and senior players.

numbered close to 200, spurred by the NCTA's leadership in requiring more and better-trained officials for its sanctioned events, and by the growth in collegiate tennis.

LEAGUES

The rise of league tennis that began in the 1980s gained even more speed in the late 1990s and early 2000s.

Nationally, sponsorship passed between Volvo, Heineken, Citizen Watch, Infiniti, and Lincoln, and the USTA changed the name in 1990 to the USTA League Tennis Program, again in 1999 to USA League Tennis, and back to USTA League Tennis in 2006.

In 1996 North Carolina teamed up with South Carolina to pilot a Super Senior league and championship. The two states joined to hold the Carolina Challenge. The event was so successful that Georgia wanted to participate, and in 1997 the Tri-State Challenge was held. Word spread and in 1998 Kentucky and Tennessee joined and the first Southern Championship for Super Seniors was held. In two years, 7 of the 9 southern states were participating and other sections became interested in this new Super Senior program idea. Super Seniors became a national program in 2005 for the 60s and 70s, with the first official National Championship in 2007.

Once again, North Carolina embraced the USTA League program and continued to be one of the most active USTA League Tennis states in the entire country, sponsoring not only all available versions of league play, but numerous state championships for teams at straight or combined NTRP levels from the coast to the mountains. For instance, because of growth in the Adult and Senior divisions, in 2000 North Carolina USTA League Tennis spread its state championships between Wilmington, which hosted the Seniors, 2.5s, and 5.0, and Pinehurst, which held the Adults 3.0-5.0s. Some divisions, such as Seniors and Mixed, were experiencing 15 percent increases annually at the turn of the century. Overall the NCTA in 2011 runs seven events covering championships for five leagues (Adult/Senior, Super Senior, Mixed Doubles, Combo Doubles, Singles), with a total state championship participation of nearly 6,000 players.

Much of this growth was cultured by money provided by the USTA to bring in state coordinators for training and collaboration at an annual workshop in Atlanta. NCTA supported a similar training for local coordinators. This investment in training provided a comprehensive approach at all levels, leading to consistency of administration. "If the leagues were going to grow," said Judy Utley of the early days, "it was going to be because of the efforts of the coordinators." In North Carolina, the state coordinator served as the glue that tied all the local coordinators together to form the team effort required to support league administration.

Continued growth in the USTA League program with all its divisions,[12] in addition to the Southern Combo Doubles, led to an expansion in the number of local leagues. More divisions meant more opportunities and ultimately more players. According to Henry Hostetler, "the eastern part of North Carolina is one of the busiest areas. Just last year the Downeast USTA League, long covering one large area, split into three different leagues: Coastal Plain, Neuse, and Albemarle. And each league has its own local coordinator now." As of 2011, there are 14 USTA Leagues[13] in North Carolina, with over 56,000 players.[14]

The USTA provided the backdrop to North Carolina embarking on a long diversification program. By the end of the 1990s, the senior league, launched in 1991, had

As in the rest of the country, officiating in North Carolina was basically performed by untrained volunteers until the 1970s.

48,711 players, and mixed doubles boasted 59,028 players. All divisions together combined for over 350,000 participants at the end of 2000. In 2007, the first Super Senior National Championship was held. By the end of 2010, USTA League Tennis reached almost 780,000 participants. All-time participation grows to over 8.6 million individuals playing in USTA League over the years—quite an achievement from its early pilot programs in two sections.

With such great numbers, the USTA in 2001 approved TennisLink, an online system to register players, report scores, and provide standings on the World Wide Web—quite an improvement from the old days of mailing paper rosters and scorecards. The next year, the Dynamic NTRP rating system was introduced to allow for ease of

HEALING LEAGUES

North Carolinians Peggy Rinaldi, Donna Buchman, Mary Beth Poncin, and Pam Olsen are all avid tennis players. In 2011 all four women played on a team from Lake Norman in the USTA League 4.0 Senior National Championships.

The four had a tighter bond than most teammates: Rinaldi, Buchman, and Poncin are breast cancer survivors, Poncin also beat thyroid cancer

and Olsen recovered from melanoma.

"We're a very close team. All of this has brought us together," said Sheila Reitler, the team captain. "We're not only tennis players and a team, but we're friends. We enjoy each other's company and we're there for each other every step of the way."

Reitler, who describes the trip to the Nationals as "a once-in-a-lifetime thing," added, "We've all

been praying. God has blessed us. He has the answer to our prayers. We all feel really blessed to be together and have each other."

Rinaldi says playing tennis has played a key role in her recovery. "My oncologist says the best thing you can do is to keep exercising and keep busy because otherwise you just fade away and [cancer] could come out somewhere else. She's encouraging me to

keep as active as I can."

Playing at the Nationals has been a special experience for the team. Eight of the ten team members were accompanied by their husbands. "We feel dually blessed to have them here supporting us," Rinaldi said. When asked to summarize her team's season, Rinaldi responded, "We bonded as a team because of the pain we've endured. We are so thankful we can still play tennis."

Nice Match!
Left to right, Robert Fox, Greensboro and Mark Troutman, High Point congratulate Mike Foster, Pinehurst and Mike Criscoe, Biscoe on a match well played at the 2012 State Senior 4.5 League Tournament in Asheville.

and over Adult and Mixed divisions."

When asked what caused the phenomenal success of USTA League tennis, Bonnie Vandergrift, 2011-2012 chair of the Southern Adult League Committee, responded, "It was not the millions of dollars in advertising but word of mouth from the players who just had fun while satisfying their competitive spirit. It was the combined effort of many volunteers and staff from the national to the local level working together to ensure a quality program year after year."

The Sport for a Lifetime

For almost a century and a quarter, from the time a UNC chemistry professor dug out a sand court in Chapel Hill, the game of tennis has proved its popularity in North Carolina. A dozen courts soon appeared around campus, and then started popping up in Asheville and Pinehurst and other corners of the Old North State. Originally an upper-class pastime for resort guests and those with private courts, today tennis is a game of the people, and still growing.

In 2011, there are over 35,000 NCTA members, up from about 15,000 just 15 years before, and these 36,000 represent only a small fraction of total tennis players who compete on public and private courts. There are more than 100 adult and NTRP tournaments and well over a dozen different league divisions for all ages from juniors to super seniors.

The North Carolina Tennis Foundation, just past its half-centennial, continues to seed the game with funding and other kinds

entry for new players entering the program. The system included a self-rating component to complement the online system. Gone were the days of Verification Clinics!

Chris Bryce, NCTA State League Coordinator, explains that growth in this program has far exceeded early expectations. "With programs in place, the shift has been to utilize technology to enhance the USTA League experience. Online tools to manage teams using cell phones or other devices have been added. Beginning in 2013, USTA League tennis will once again reinvent itself by restructuring the age divisions with the goal of retaining existing players and increasing the number of play opportunities and thus participation. The Adult, Senior, and Mixed divisions will be replaced by an 18 and over, 40 and over, and 55

of support, and the dynamic North Carolina Tennis Association, with a staff ten strong, sponsors programs, events, tournaments, leagues, clinics, and every other form of activity to bring the game to every corner of the state.

The real heroes, however, have been the individual volunteers who have labored ceaselessly in small towns and large, public courts and private, working with seniors and juniors, in tournaments, clinics, and leagues, to foster the game they love. The Dick Covingtons, Henry Clarks, Henry Hostetlers, Jeff Joyces, Cy Kings, Judy Utleys, and John Allen Farfours have been mentioned, but the list goes on and on.

The success of tennis today can often be traced back in time to the efforts of volunteers several generations ago. In the northeastern area of the state, leaders such as Tom Norfleet of Roxobel,

Kelly Abeounis of Bethel and Tom Ward of Robersonville promoted the sport in their sparsely populated areas, and helped produce a surprising number of good players, like Maurice Everette of Robersonville. Everette, in turn, taught many juniors in the state. In Wilmington, Dr. Eaton had to fight on multiple fronts to propel Althea Gibson to international fame and to help assure that tennis reflected the many faces of North Carolina. In Kinston, the Skillman family promoted tennis tirelessly and fueled the interest of Marshall Happer, whose significant success as a player was far eclipsed by his founding of tennis facilities in the state and his subsequent prominence as the top administrator on the world stage of tennis. In Laurinburg, enthusiasts such as Tony Leonard and Dr. M.E. Johnson promoted the sport and

LADY UTLEY
As a former English teacher Judy Utley brought her considerable organizational skills and eye for detail to the many tasks that she took on in serving tennis at all levels of the USTA from administering leagues to serving as President of the Southern Tennis Association. Her style and grace earned her the affectionate title of "Lady Utley" from all who had the opportunity to work with her. Over the years she has been recognized and has received awards for her contributions at the N.C., Southern and National level.

League Leader
As league administrator, Judy Utley oversaw almost exponential growth in league tennis in North Carolina.

All Together Now!
League teams who travel together win together. This group made it all the way to the Senior State League Championships 2012.

CHANGE IS HARD!

One of the most significant changes in USTA League tennis was the approval of using the tiebreak in lieu of a third set at the national championship level in 1999.

This change was met by no small amount of kicking and screaming but eventually the scoring method filtered down to the local leagues. USTA League tennis was the first to implement this innovative scoring method that has since been adopted by other levels of competition, including professional doubles.

It Starts Here...
An enthusiastic young player gives it his all.

produced very successful players who today coach other successful players. In Shelby, J. L. Suttle, Dick LeGrand, and Buck Archer tirelessly promoted the game and brought in college players to teach every summer to teach rising juniors. Eventually their efforts helped produce players of prominence such as Jim Corn, Belinda Vaughn, Sally Schweppe, the Cloningers, and, most notably, Tim Wilkison.

Whole families did their part. In the major cities of the Piedmont, benefactors such as the Southerns and the Preyers committed both their time and their resources to promote the

...And Continues Here
Dave Carey of Asheville has won over 20 national titles after the age of 85.

future and sustain the history of the game they love. Their contributions will inure to the benefit of tennis players for generations to come. In Lenoir, Hickory, and other areas in the western part of the state, families such as the Bernhardts, the Shufords, and the Armfields promoted tennis for many years. In the Piedmont towns of Burlington and Graham, the Vernon, Koury, Goode, and Powell families did the same thing, producing players such as Robert and Tom Register, Jay Pulliam, Eddie Stewart, Jim Latham, John Walton, Bobby Andrews, and Kelly Key Gaines, who today travels the state tirelessly as the highly successful executive director of the NCTA. In Lexington, the Bingham family promoted tennis and produced many good tennis players. In Goldsboro the Pratt and Stallings families housed and fed players, while

the Weil family provided great support, including donating a sportsmanship trophy.

With advanced equipment that reduces that vibration on a player's arm, and courts that better cushion the pounding on the feet, the sport of a lifetime becomes even more accessible to those at advanced stages of life, like Raleigh's Jim Chavasse and Asheville's David Carey, who has won over 20 national titles in his 80s and 90s. On the other end, the five- and six-year-olds are for the first time capable of playing out points because of the new technology and will be ensuring that tennis will only continue to grow in the 21st century. ॐ

Appendix

NCTA PRESIDENTS

Hughes Davis 1949
Emery Green 1950
1951–52 no record
Whit Cobb 1953–56
Francis J. Fitzjohn 1957–59
Henry Clark 1960
Carlyle B. Lewis 1961–62
Gilbert T. Stacy 1963
David Morgan, Jr. 1964
John Allen Farfour 1965
Cliff Turner 1966
Allen Morris 1967–68
Bob Light 1969–70
Semi Mintz 1971–72
Marshall Happer 1973–74
Mildred Southern 1975–76
William Blackburn 1977–78
John Peddycord 1979–80
Jim Haslam 1981–82
Sam Woods 1983–84
Neill R. McGeachy 1985–86
Herman Enochs 1987–88
Cy King 1989–90
Art Rondeau 1991
Art Kiser 1992–93
Dru Michaels 1994–95
Vicki Everette 1996–97
Herb Bolick 1998–99
Judy Utley 2000–01
Paula Hale 2002–03
Henry Hostetler 2004–05
Jeff Joyce 2006–07
Bonnie Vandergrift 2008–09
Ted Reese 2010–11
Alex Rucker 2012–13

NCTF PRESIDENTS

J. Spencer Love 1961
Dave Morgan Sr. 1962-63
L. Richardson Preyer 1964-67
J.M. Leighton 1968-70
John A. Farfour 1971-73
Herbert H. Browne, Jr, 1974
M. Marshall Happer 1975-76
Mildred Southern, 1977-78

Beginning in 1979, each NCTA President has followed his or her tenure with two years as NCTF President. There have just been three exceptions—Sam Woods, Art Rondeau, and Art Kiser—when life circumstances prevented that service.

NCTA STAFF SINCE 1974

Sally Wendt
Nancy Cirvello
Dru Michaels
Mary Milam
Ellen Drake
Jonelle Todd
Karen Peatross
Ellen Lyon
Nell Barksdale
Sue Catherine
Kin Roseboro
Kelly Key Gaines
Amy Franklin
Alice Heidgerd Buckner
Jeff Gagnon
Karen Welch
Mary Lloyd Barbera
Jane Scott
Chris Bryce
Cookie Guarini
Francie Barragan
Billy Price
Amy Thomas
Liliana Camara
Marianna Dunn Bryce
Gwenda Priest
Marusa Pogacnik
Jenny Phelps
Tyson Thompson
Caroline Downs
Matt Gottfried
Dan Holman

NORTH CAROLINA TENNIS HALL OF FAME MEMBERS

Established in 1975, the North Carolina Tennis Hall of Fame has been created to honor those persons who by excellence of their activities in or connected with North Carolina Tennis have brought substantial recognition and esteem to themselves and to the State.

1975
John Kenfield, Chapel Hill*
Ann Martindale, Greensboro*
Bo Roddey, Charlotte
Archibald Henderson, Houston*

1976
Allen Morris, Greensboro
Teddy Burwell, Charlotte*

1977
Dick Covington, Asheville*
Laura DuPont, Charlotte*
Buck Archer, Shelby*

1978
Eliza Coxe Jackson, Asheville*
Carlyle Lewis, Lexington*

1979
Mary Lou Jones, Sanford
Robert Crosland, Charlotte*
John Allen Farfour, Goldsboro*

1980
John Vernon, Burlington*
Julia Anne Holt, Greensboro
Dr. Henry Clark, Chapel Hill*

1981
Marshall Happer, North Venice, FL
C.R. Council, Raleigh*

1982
Herb Browne, Charlotte
Jim Leighton, Winston-Salem*

1983
Mildred Southern, Winston–Salem
Bev Earle, Charlotte

1984
Dr. Hubert Eaton, Wilmington*
Jack Warmath, Greensboro

1985
Whit Cobb, Durham*
Bob Spurrier, Charlotte*

1986
Don Skakle, Chapel Hill*
Grady Elmore, Raleigh*

1987
Tim Wilkison, Charlotte
Norman Chambers, Raleigh

1988
Frances Hogan, Chapel Hill*
Maurice Everette, Winston-Salem

1989
Gene Hamilton, Candler
Mary Garber, Winston-Salem*

1990
Tom Parham, Emerald Isle
John Peddycord, Winston–Salem

1991
John Sadri, Charlotte
Jane Preyer, Chapel Hill

1992
Mont Graham, Reidsville
Jim Winstead, Greensboro

1993
Herb Bolick, High Point
Charles Morris, Raleigh*

1994
Jerry Robinson, Raleigh*
Cliff Turner, Charlotte*

1995
J.W. Isenhour, Jr., Raleigh
Audrey Brown Johnson, Goldsboro

1996
Elbert (Buster) Brown, Asheville
Jeff Frank, Davidson*

1997
David L. Lash, Winston-Salem*
Robert (Bob) Light, Boone

1998
John Lucas, Houston, TX
Bill Weathers, Whispering Pines

1999
Robert Vincent Connerat, Charlotte*
Neill R. McGeachy, Jr., Hickory

2000
Camey Timberlake Dillon, Greensboro
Peggy Clemmer Golden, Sanford

200
Vicki Everette, Winston–Salem
Keith Richardson, Rock Hill, SC

2002
Sam B. Woods, Jr., Charlotte
2003
Louise Allen, Austin, TX
Alex B. (Andy) Andrews, Raleigh

2004
Dave Carey, Asheville
Kitty Harrison, Chapel Hill

2005
Cy King, Raleigh
Susan McDanald Love, Charlotte

2006
Tal Henry, III, Charlotte*
Don Johnson, Chapel Hill
Jim Jones, Boone

2007
Tommy Dixon, Raleigh
Sharron Frahm, Greensboro
Dr. Fred West, Misenheimer*

2008
Bobby Heald, Holly Springs
Pender Murphy, Charlotte

2009
Jim Corn, Shelby
Susan (Susie) Black Wall, Burlington

2010
Tom Morris, Blount's Creek
Tom Willson, Cashier

2011
Judy Utley, Greensboro
Lendward Simpson, Jr., Knoxville

2012
Ron Smarr, Pamplico, SC
Keith Stoneman, Charlotte

*deceased

USTA LEAGUE NATIONAL CHAMPIONS FROM NORTH CAROLINA

1997
Sr M 3.5 Downeast (Washington): Tom Richter, Fred Austin, Ray Sullivan, John Blount, Lee Knott, Gil Davis, Mike Gray, Bill Outland

2005
W 2.5 Cary: Tamra Aguilar

2005
Sr W 3.0 Downeast (Goldsboro): Sharon Crawford

2006
Sr W 4.5 Charlotte: Marla Figard, Dona Bowland, Debbie Carmazzi, JoAnn Crolley, Saundra Denny, Sharron Frahm, Sharon Greene, Miriam Morey, Faye Thomas, Gwynn Sasser

2006
Super Senior M 4.0: Klaus Sabert

2009
M 5.0 Greensboro: Derek Gamble, Matt Rowe, Dipesh Rao, Toby Curtis, Tony Mule, Damon Martin, Mike Weidl

2009
Super Senior W 4.5 Charlotte: Caroline Kenning

2011
Men's 5.5 (Greensboro): Damon Martin, Matthew G. Rowe, Susheel Narla, Toby Curtis, Dispesh Rao, Tanner Haddon, Captain Derek Gamble, Tony Mule, Michael Weidl, Christopher Cagle, Mike Murray, Oscar Blacutt

2011
USTA Jr. Team Tennis 14 & Under Intermediate National Champions (Weddington Racquets, Charlotte): Coach Dwayne Thomas, Nathaniel Bryson, Carra Clemons, Caytie Clemons, William Hatt, Cameron Hobson, Jackson Plyler, Kennedy Schmitt, Sahil Vasa, Woody Watson

Tal Henry

ACC 50TH ANNIVERSARY: TOP 50 PLAYERS PLAYERS WITH NORTH CAROLINA CONNECTIONS

MEN

Andy Andrews
(Raleigh), NC State (1978–1981). All-American in 1980 and 1981. No. 1 doubles championship. Helped lead team to ACC Championships.

Peter Ayers
(Charlotte), Duke (1993–1996). All-ACC in 1993 and '94 and All-America in 1995. Seventh all-time in singles wins and first in doubles wins at Duke.

Lawson Duncan
(Asheville), Clemson (1984). All American in 1984. ACC Champion at No. 1 singles. Finalist at NCAA Tournament. Second in Clemson winning percentage.

Bryan Jones
(Kings Mountain), North Carolina (1989–1992). ACC Player of the Year and All-American in 1992. Helped lead the team to the 1992 ACC Tournament Championship.

John Lucas
(Durham), Maryland (1973–1976). All-American and ACC No. 1 singles champion in 1974 and 1976. Played NBA basketball.

Matt McDonald
(Charlotte), NC State (1977–1980). All-American in doubles in 1980. ACC No. 1 doubles champion in 1980 and ACC No. 2 doubles champion in 1979.

Huntley Montgomery
(Chapel Hill), Virginia (1997–2000). Three-time All-ACC. 1998 ACC doubles champion. Ranked No. 2 nationally in doubles, reaching NCAA semifinals.

Pender Murphy

(Charlotte), Clemson (1978–1981). Four-time All-American. High on Clemson career list for most singles and doubles wins.

Tripp Phillips

(Chapel Hill), North Carolina (1996–2000). All-American. NCAA quarterfinalist and ranked 12 nationally. First player since Vic Seixas to receive UNC's Patterson Medal.

John Sadri

(Charlotte), NC State (1975–1978). All-American and ACC No. 1 winner in 1977 and 1978, leading team to ACC Championships. Runner-up in "best ever" NCAA singles finals to John McEnroe in 1978. Good pro career.

Bobby Heald

(Cary), South Carolina (1966–1968). All-American, ACC Player of the Year and ACC Champion in 1968.

Don Johnson

(Chapel Hill), North Carolina (1987–1990). All-ACC, and later coached at UNC. Wimbledon mixed doubles champion in 2000, doubles champion in 2001 and runner-up at the US Open. Played Davis Cup doubles in Winston-Salem.

WOMEN

Laura DuPont

(Charlotte), North Carolina (1967–1970). Collegiate singles champion in 1970. Played on pro tour for 12 years and was ranked ninth in the world. Inducted into Intercollegiate Tennis Association's Women's Collegiate Tennis Hall of Fame in 2002. Won 1984 and 1985 US Open Championship for women over 35.

Bobbi Guthrie

(Raleigh), Georgia Tech (1997–2001). All-ACC in 1998. Set four Georgia Tech records, including singles wins in a season, doubles wins in a season, single-season winning percentage, and doubles wins in a career.

Jenny Sell

NC State (1989–1992). All-ACC and team MVP award. Ranked 64th in the Volvo/ITCA rankings, becoming the first nationally ranked player from NC State. Succeeded Kelly Key as NCSU head coach in 1996. Currently coaches at UNC Wilmington.

COLLEGIATE ALL-AMERICANS FROM NORTH CAROLINA

DIVISION I

NC State

MEN
John Sadri, Charlotte (s,d) 1977–8
Andy Andrews, Raleigh (s,d) 1980–81
Matt McDonald, Charlotte (d) 1980
Mark Dillon, Charlotte (d) 1981

UNC

MEN
Brian Jones, Kings Mt (s) 1992
Tripp Phillips, Charlotte (s) 2000
Brad Pomeroy, Asheville (d) 2006

WOMEN
Laura DuPont (s,d) 1970
Cinda Gurney, Asheville (s) 1992, (s,d) 1993

Duke

MEN
Peter Ayers, Charlotte (d) 1995
Jonathan Stokke, Durham (d) 2006

WOMEN
Reka Zsilinszka, Fayetteville (s) 2008–9

Maryland

MEN
John Lucas, Durham (s) 1976
Andy Orban, Fayetteville (d) 2008

Clemson

MEN
Lawson Duncan, Asheville (s) 1984
Pender Murphy, Charlotte (s,d) 1980–81

Virginia

MEN
Huntley Montgomery, Chapel Hill (d) 2001

Florida State

MEN
Matt Cloer, Hendersonville (s) 2005

Georgia

MEN
Stephen Enochs, Greensboro (s) 1987 & 1989
John Isner, Greensboro (s,d) 2004–2007

WOMEN
Stacey Schefflin, Matthews (s,d) 1990

Trinity

MEN
Chris Kennedy, Cary (s,d) 1984–85

WOMEN
Louise Allen, Winston–Salem (s,d) 1981–1984

Kentucky

MEN
John Yancey, Morganton (d) 1990–91

Southwest Louisiana

MEN
Ashley Rhoney, Hickory (d) 1987–88

NAIA

Elon

Michael Leonard, Laurinburg (d) 1990–91
Danny Colangelo. Raleigh (s,d) 1994–95
Duane Johnson, Graham (d) 1988

North Florida

Diane Pensabene, Charlotte (d) 1991

Keith Richardson

DIVISION II

Elon

Danny Colangelo, Raleigh (s) 1996

DIVISION III

Williams College

Dan Greenberg, Chapel Hill (s) 2006 & 2008

Kenyon College

Mike Greenberg, Chapel Hill (s,d) 2008–2010

Mary Washington

Evan Goff, Cary (d) 2010

Methodist College

Chip Collins, Fayetteville (d) 1992
Chris Collins, Fayetteville (d) 1992

JUNIOR COLLEGE

Peace College

Leslie Lewis, Fayetteville (s) 1981
Mary Lloyd Hodges Barbera, Henderson (s) 1984
Bonnie Johnson, Cary (d) 1989
Susan Stanley, Charlotte (d) 1989
Diane Pensabene, Charlotte (s) 1989
Nicole Nissley, Brevard (s) 1989

MEN'S INTERCOLLEGIATE TENNIS ASSOCIATION HALL OF FAME

2010
Jay Lapidus, Duke Coach

2008
Don Johnson, UNC Player

2007
Tom Parham, Elon College Coach

2005
John Sadri, NC State Player

2001
Fred McNair, UNC Player

1993
Allen Morris, Presbyterian Player

1991
Don Skakle, UNC Coach

1986
John Kenfield, UNC Coach

1986
Jim Leighton, Wake Forest Coach

1985
Bitsy Grant, UNC Player

1984
Vic Seixas, UNC Player

WOMEN'S INTERCOLLEGIATE TENNIS ASSOCIATION HALL OF FAME

2002
Laura DuPont, UNC Player

PROFESSIONAL TENNIS PLAYERS FROM NORTH CAROLINA

MEN

Don Johnson
Chapel Hill 1989–1999, singles: World #194, doubles: World #1, Wimbledon doubles champion

John Sadri
Charlotte 1976–1987, singles: World #14, doubles: World #16, Australian Open runner-up

John Isner
Greensboro 2007 to present, singles: World #18, doubles: World #27, 3 titles (as of October 2011)

Tim Wilkison
Shelby 1976–1993, singles: World #23, doubles: World #21, 6 titles

Andy Andrews
Raleigh 1979–1985, singles: World #78, doubles: World #37, Australian Open doubles runner-up

Lawson Duncan
Hickory 1984–1991, singles: World #47, doubles: World #182, French Open quarterfinalist.

Keith Richardson
Rocky Mount 1976–79, singles: World #74

Pender Murhpy
Charlotte, singles: World #102, doubles: World #322

Chris Kennedy
Cary 1985–1988, singles: World #305, doubles: World #144

Wayne Hearn
Charlotte 1986–1988, singles: World #247, doubles: World #423

Cliff Skakle
Chapel Hill 1981–1983, singles: World #266

Matt McDonald
Charlotte 1979–1984, singles: World #273, doubles: World #337

Gene Hamilton
Asheville 1978–1979, singles: World #279

Robbie Smith
Asheville 1978–1986, singles: World #324, doubles: World #773

Stephen Enochs
Greensboro 1989, singles: World #367

Sammy Martin
Raleigh 1978–79, singles: World #436

John Lucas
Durham 1979, singles: World #579

Tripp Phillips
Charlotte 1997–2004, singles: World #343, doubles: World #29

WOMEN

Laura DuPont
Charlotte, singles: World #10, first woman to win a national title in any sport for the University of North Carolina, first female All-American at the school, won the Canadian (1979), Argentine, New Zealand (singles as well as doubles), and German, South African doubles champion, US Clay Courts singles in 1977, US Open 35 and over singles, US Open quarterfinalist

Louise Allen
Winston–Salem 1984–1993 singles: World #65, 5 Titles

Jane Preyer
Greensboro 1980–1983, singles: World #32

Ally Baker
Raleigh 2000–2003, singles: World #295

Sarah Taylor
Raleigh 2001–2005, singles: World #68

Cory Ann Avants
Gastonia 2004–2005, singles: World #264

Bonnie Logan
Durham 1972–73, First African-American woman on the Virginia Slims tour

ALL RANKINGS DRAWN FROM OFFICIAL LISTINGS BY ATP AND WTA.

NORTH CAROLINIANS WINNING USTA NATIONAL CHAMPIONSHIPS (GOLD BALL)

Louise Allen
1980 Girls' 18s doubles (with Marian Kremer), USTA National Championships; 1983 Women's doubles (with Gretchen Rush), NCAA Championships

Andy Andrews
1977 Boys' 18s doubles (with Lever Stewart), USTA Interscholastic Championships

Buck Archer
1977 Men's 55s singles, USTA Clay Court Championships; 1977 Men's 55s doubles (with John Rogers), USTA Clay Court Championships; 1978 Men's 55s singles, USTA Clay Court Championships; 1979 Men's 55s doubles (with Tom Falkenberg), USTA Clay Court Championships; 1980 Men's 55s doubles (with Tom Falkenberg), USTA Grass Court Championships; 1982 Men's 60s singles, USTA Clay Court Championships; 1982 Men's 60s doubles (with Bobby Riggs), USTA Clay Court Championships; 1982 Men's 60s doubles (with Bobby Riggs), USTA Clay Court Championships; 1983 Men's 60s doubles (wth Bobby Riggs), USTA Grass Court Championships; 1984 Men's 60s doubles (with Bobby Riggs), USTA Grass Court Championships; 1989 Men's 65s doubles (with Towson Ellis), USTA Clay Court Championships

Bill Ashley
2011 Men's 55s doubles (with Fred Robinson), USTA National Hard Court Championships

Cory Ann Avants
2000 Girls' 18s singles, USTA Super National Clay Court; 2000 Girls' 18s doubles (with Kristina Stastry), USTA Super National Clay Court

Peter Ayers
1989 Boys' 16s doubles (with Rob Givone), USTA Indoor Championships; 1990 Boys' 18s doubles (with Craig Baskin), USTA Interscholastic Championships; 1991 Boys' 18s doubles (with Craig Baskin), USTA Interscholastic Championships

Ally Baker
1999 Girls' 14s singles, USTA National Championships; 1999 Girls' 14s singles, Easter Bowl; 1999 Girls' 14s doubles (with Alexis Prousis), Easter Bowl; 2000 Girls' 16s singles, USTA Super National Clay Court; 2000 Girls' 16s doubles (with Shadisha Robinson), USTA Super National Clay Court

Aaron Barrick
1997 Men's 25s doubles (with Derek Brooks), USTA Indoor Championships; 1997 Men's 25s doubles (with Derek Brooks), USTA Hard Court Championships; 2001 Men's 30s doubles (with Derek Brooks), USTA Grass Courts

Marshall Burroughs
1992 Men's singles, USTA Hard Court Championships

Clayton Burwell
1965 Men's 55s doubles (with Alphonso Smith), USTA Hard Court Championships

David Carey
1998 Men's 85s singles, USTA Clay Court Championships; 1998 Men's 85s doubles (with Edward Baumer), USTA Clay Court Championships; 1998 Men's 85s singles, USTA Hard Court Championships; 1999 Men's 85s singles, USTA Clay Court Championships; 2000 Men's 85s doubles (with Gardner Mulloy), USTA Clay Court Championships; 2001 Men's 85s doubles (with Gardner Mulloy), USTA Grass Court Championships; 2002 Men's 85s doubles (with Gardner Mulloy), USTA Grass Court Championships;

2003 Men's 90s singles, USTA Grass Court Championships; 2003 Men's 90s doubles (with Gardner Mulloy), USTA Grass Court Championships; 2003 Men's 90s singles, USTA Clay Court Championships; 2003 Men's 90s doubles (with Whitelaw Reid), USTA Clay Court Championships; 2003 Men's 90s singles, USTA Hard Court Championships; 2003 Men's 90s doubles (with Vern Hughs), USTA Hard Court Championships; 2004 Men's 90s doubles (with Gardner Mulloy), USTA Grass Court Championships; 2004 Men's 90s doubles (with Edgar Kendall), USTA Indoor Championships; 2004 Men's 90s doubles (with Ted Zoob), USTA Clay Court Championships; 2004 Men's 90s singles, USTA Hard Court Championships; 2005 Men's 90s singles, USTA Clay Court Championships; 2005 Men's 90s doubles (with William Lurie), USTA Clay Court Championships; 2005 Men's 90s doubles (with Tracy Strong), USTA Hard Court Championships

Jim Chavasse
2004 Men's 85s doubles (with Wade MacDonald), USTA Clay Court Championships; 2009 Men's 90s doubles (with Wade MacDonald), USTA Clay Court Championships

Stan Cocke
1992 Men's doubles (with Mike Weidl), USTA Indoor Championships

Vince Connerat
1995 Men's 85s doubles (with Herman Ratcliff), USTA Grass Court Championships; 1995 Men's 85s doubles (with Herman Ratcliff), USTA Clay Court Championships; 1995 Men's 85s doubles (with Herman Ratcliff), USTA Indoor Championships; 1995 Men's 85s doubles (with Herman Ratcliff), USTA Hard Court Championships; 1996 Men's 85s doubles (with Herman Ratcliff), USTA Grass Court Championships; 1996 Men's

NORTH CAROLINIANS WINNING USTA NATIONAL CHAMPIONSHIPS (GOLD BALL)
(CONTINUED)

85s doubles (with Herman Ratcliff), USTA Clay Court Championships; 1996 Men's 85s doubles (with Herman Ratcliff), USTA Hard Court Championships; 1997 Men's 85s doubles (with Herman Ratcliff), USTA Indoor Championships; 1997 Men's 85s doubles (with Herman Ratcliff), USTA Grass Court Championships; 2000 Men's 90s doubles (with Herman Ratcliff), USTA Indoor Championships; 2001 Men's 95s singles, USTA Clay Court Championships

Kayla Duncan
2009 Girls' 18s doubles (with Allison Falkin), USTA Clay Court Championships

Lawson Duncan
1982 Boys' 18s doubles (with Eric Rosenfeld), USTA Jr. International Championships

Laura DuPont
1970 Women's singles, NCAA Championships

Stephen Enochs
1980 Boys' 12s singles, USTA Clay Court Championships; 1980 Boys' 12s doubles (with John Boytim), USTA Clay Court Championships; 1985 Boys' 18s doubles (with Jim Childs), USTA Interscholastic Championships; 1987 Mixed doubles (with Lisa Apanay), USTA Amateur Championships

Meg Fanjoy
1999 Girls' 12s doubles (with Melissa Mang), USTA National Championships; 2002 Girls' 14s doubles (with Brintne Larson), Easter Bowl

Albert Gaskill
2001 Men's 90s doubles (with Emil Johnson), USTA Clay Court Championships

Max Hilkey
1994 Boys' 14s singles, Easter Bowl

John Haywood
2005 Men's doubles (with Rob Haywood), USTA Clay Court Championships

Rob Haywood
2005 Men's doubles (with John Haywood), USTA Clay Court Championships

Chase Helpingstine
2009 Grandfather Grandson doubles, USTA Grass Court Championships

Lauren Herring
2005 Girls' 12s doubles (with Grace Min), USTA Hard Court Championships; 2005 Girls' 12s doubles (with Erin Stephens), USTA Clay Court Championships; 2005 Girls' 12s singles, USTA Winter National; 2005 Girls' 12s doubles (with Chanelle Van Nguyen), USTA Winter National; 2008 Girls' 18s doubles (with Grace Min), USTA National Spring

Mariana Routh Hollman
1992 Women's 30s doubles (with Sue Rasmussen), USTA Hard Court Championships; 1993 Women's 30s singles, USTA Clay Court Championships; 1994 Women's doubles (with Rosie Bareis), USTA Clay Court Championships; 1995 Women's 30s singles, USTA Clay Court Championships; 1995 Women's 30s doubles (with Susan Carver), USTA Clay Court Championships; 1996 Women's 30s singles, USTA Clay Court Championships; 1997 Women's 30s singles, USTA Indoor Championships; 1997 Women's 35s doubles (with Rosie Bareis), USTA Grass Court Championships; 1997 Women's 35s doubles (with Ellie Compton), USTA Clay Court Championships; 1998 Women's 35s doubles (with Ellie Compton), USTA Clay Court Championships; 2001 Women's 30s doubles (with Patricia Riddell), USTA Indoor Championships; 2001 Women's 35s doubles (with Joni Hannah), USTA Grass Court Championships; 2002 Women's 40s doubles (with Joni Hannah), USTA Indoor Championships; 2004 Women's 40s doubles (with Joni Hannah), USTA Grass Court Championships; 2004 Women's 40s singles, USTA Indoor Championships; 2004 Women's 40s doubles (with Stacey Williams), USTA Indoor Championships; 2004 Women's 40s singles, USTA Clay Court Championships; 2004 Women's 40s doubles (with Joanne Hannah), USTA Clay Court Championships; 2005 Women's 40s doubles (with Anna Zimmermann), USTA Indoor Championships; 2006 Women's 40s singles, USTA Clay Court Championships; 2008 Women's 45s doubles (with Susan Wright), USTA Grass Court Championships; 2008 Women's 45s doubles (with Susan Wright), USTA Hard Court Championships; 2009 Women's 45s singles, USTA Hard Court Championships; 2010 Women's 45s doubles (with Susan Wright), USTA Grass Court Championships; 2010 Women's 45s doubles (with Shelly Works), USTA Hard Court Championships

Zach Hunter
2004 Boys' 14s doubles (with Brennan Boyajian), USTA Clay Court Championships

John Isner
2001 Boys' 16s doubles (with Sukhwa Young), USTA Super National Hard Court; 2001 Boys' 16s doubles (with Sukhwa Young), USTA Super National Clay Court; 2003 Boys' 18s doubles (with Pramod Dabir), USTA Super National Hard Courts

Vicki Everette (seated at right) and her 2012 Southern Senior Cup Team.

J.J. Jackson
1988 Boys' 14s doubles (with Tom Shimada), USTA National Championships; 1989 Boys' 14s singles, USTA Indoor Championships; 1991 Boys' 16s singles, USTA National Championships; 1991 Boys' 16s doubles (with Eric Taino), USTA Clay Court Championships; 1992 Boys' 18s doubles (with Eric Taino), USTA Clay Court Championships; 1992 Boys' 18s singles, USTA Junior International Championships

Don Johnson
1988 Men's doubles (with David Pollack), USTA Clay Court Championships; 1988 Men's doubles (with David Pollack), USTA Hard Court Championships

Anudeep Kodali
2010 Boys' 12s singles, USTA Clay Court Championships

Chris Kennedy
1981 Boys' 18s doubles (with Rick Leach), USTA Clay Court Championships; 1981 Boys' 18s singles, USTA Interscholastic Championships

Kimberly Kessaris
1985 Girls' 12s singles, USTA National Championships; 1985 Girls' 12s doubles (with Spencer Shelfer), USTA National Championships; 1985 Girls' 12s singles, USTA Clay Court Championships; 1986 Girls' 14s doubles (with Patricia Miller), USTA Clay Court Championships

Thad Langford
1988 Mixed doubles (with Shannan McCarthy), USTA Clay Court Championships

Bonnie Logan
1966 Girls' 18s doubles (with Evelyn Haase), USTA Indoor Championships

Wade MacDonald
2004 Men's 85s doubles (with Jim Chavasse), USTA Clay Court Championships; 2009 Men's 90s doubles (with Jim Chavasse), USTA Clay Court Championships

Susan McDanald Love
1992 Women's 30s doubles (with Lisa Seeman), USTA Clay Court Championships

Sammy Martin
1999 Men's 45s singles, USTA Clay Court Championships; 2001 Men's 45s doubles (with Cliff Skakle), USTA Clay Court Championships

Huntley Montgomery
1999 Men's singles, USTA National Adult Championships; 1999 Men's doubles (with Edward Carter), USTA Clay Court Championships

Allen Morris
1977 Men's 45s singles, USTA Clay Court Championships; 1978 Men's 45s singles, USTA Clay Court Championships; 1978 Men's 45s doubles (with John Powless), USTA Clay Court Championships; 1979 Men's 45s singles, USTA Clay Court Championships; 1979 Men's 45s doubles (with John Powless), USTA Clay Court Championships

Catherine Newman
2004 Girls' 16s singles, USTA Super National Hard Courts

Ryan Noble
2005 Boys' 14s doubles (with James Seal), USTA National Hard Courts; 2007 Boys' 16s doubles (with James Seal), USTA National Winter; 2008

NORTH CAROLINIANS WINNING USTA NATIONAL CHAMPIONSHIPS (GOLD BALL)
(CONTINUED)

Boys' 18s doubles (with James Seal), USTA Clay Court Championships

Andy Orban
1999 Boys' 12s singles, USTA Clay Court Championships; 2001 Boys' 14s doubles (with Brian Hartness), USTA Super National Hard Courts; 2003 Boys' 16s doubles (with Christian Welte), USTA Super National Clay Courts; 2004 Boys' 18s doubles (with Eric Riley), USTA Super National Clay Courts; 2005 Boys' 18s doubles (with Michael Venus), USTA Clay Court Championships

Charlie Owens
1966 Boys' 16s singles, Orange Bowl; 1968 Boys' 18s singles, USTA Interscholastic Championships; 1985 Men's 35s singles, USTA Clay Courts Championships; 1985 Mens' 35s doubles (with Armistead Neely), USTA Clay Courts Championships; 1986 Mens' 35s singles, USTA Clay Courts Championships; 1986 Mens' 35s doubles (with Armistead Neely), USTA Clay Courts Championships; 1987 Mens' 35s singles, USTA Clay Courts Championships; 1987 Mens' 35s doubles (with Armistead Neely), USTA Clay Courts Championships

Tommy Paul
2009 Boys' 12s singles, USTA Clay Court Championships; 2009 Boys' 12s doubles (with Henrik Wiersholm), USTA Clay Court Championships

Ashley Rhoney
1983 Boys' 18s doubles (with Jimmy Weilbacher), USTA Interscholastic Championships; 1984 Boys' 18s singles, USTA Inter. Championships

Fred Robinson
1998 Men's 45s singles, USTA Grass Court Championships; 2001 Men's 45s doubles (with Tom Smith), USTA Grass Court Championships; 2003 Men's 50s doubles (with Tom Smith), USTA Grass Court Championships; 2003 Men's 50s doubles (with Tom Smith), USTA Indoor Championships; 2003 Men's 50s singles, USTA Indoor Championships; 2004 Men's 50s singles, USTA Clay Court Championships; 2005 Men's 50s singles, USTA Grass Court Championships; 2005 Men's 50s singles, USTA Hard Court Championships; 2005 Men's 50s doubles (with Tom Smith), USTA Hard Court Championships; 2006 Men's 50s singles, USTA Grass Court Championships; 2006 Men's 50s doubles (with Tom Smith), USTA Indoor Championships; 2009 Men's 55s doubles (with Tom Smith), USTA Grass Court Championships; 2009 Men's 55s singles, USTA Hard Court Championships; 2010 Men's 55s singles, USTA Clay Court Championships; 2010 Men's 55s doubles (with Zan Guerry), USTA Clay Court Championships; 2010 Men's 55s singles, USTA Hard Court Championships; 2011 Men's 55s doubles (with Bill Ashley), USTA Hard Court Championships;
Jim Rogerson; 1988 Boys' 18s doubles (with John Yancey), USTA Interscholastic Championships

John Sadri
1978 Men's singles, USTA Hard Court Championships; 1978 Men's doubles (with Tony Graham), USTA Hard Court Championships; 1991 Men's singles, USTA Indoor Championships

Jim Schaefer
1997 Men's 40s doubles (with Tom Smith), USTA Clay Court Championships; 1998 Men's 40s doubles (with Tom Smith), USTA Clay Courts Championships

Stacey Schefflin
1987 Women's doubles (with Lisa Apanay), USTA Clay Courts; 1987 Women's doubles (with Diana Merrett), USTA Hard Court Championships

Cliff Skakle
2001 Men's 40s doubles (with John Chatlak), USTA Grass Court Championships; 2001 Men's 45s doubles (with Sammy Martin), USTA Clay Court Championships
Jane & Tory Schroeder
1991 Mother Daughter doubles, USTA Hard Court Championships; 1992 Mother Daughter doubles, USTA Hard Court Championships; 1992 Mother Daughter doubles, USTA Grass Court Championships; 1993 Mother Daughter doubles, USTA Grass Court Championships

Dell Sylva
1975 Men's 45s singles, USTA Grass Court Championships; 1976 Men's 45s doubles (with Bill Davis), USTA Indoor Championships; 1982 Men's 50s doubles (with Bill Bonham), USTA Clay Court Championships; 1982 Men's 55s doubles (with Bill Davis), USTA Grass Court Championships; 1983 Men's 50s singles, USTA Clay Court Championships; 1983 Men's 50s doubles (with Bill Bonham), USTA Clay Court Championships; 1985 Men's 55s doubles (with Bill Davis), USTA Clay Court Championships

Debbie Southern
2002 Senior Mother Daughter doubles (with Mildred Southern), USTA Hard Court Championships

Mildred Southern
1996 Women's 75s singles, USTA Grass Court Championships; 2001 Women's 80s singles, USTA Clay Court Championships; 2001 Women's 80s doubles (with Mary Mentzer), USTA Clay Court Championships; 2002 Senior Mother Daughter doubles (with Debbie Southern), USTA Hard Court Championships

Sammy Stinnett
1988 Men's doubles (with Ian Skidmore), USTA National Amateur Championships

Jonathan Stokke
1999 Boys' 16s doubles (with Rajeev Ram), USTA Clay Court Championships; 2000 Boys' 16s doubles (with Rajeev Ram), USTA Super National Hard Courts; 2000 Boys' 16s doubles (with Rylan Rizza), USTA Super National Clay Courts; 2000 Boys' 16s doubles (with Brian Baker); Easter Bowl; 2001 Boys' 18s doubles (with Rajeev Ram), USTA Super National Hard Courts; 2002 Boys' 18s doubles (with Rajeev Ram), USTA Super National Hard Courts; 2002 Boys' 18s doubles (with James Pade), USTA Super National Clay Courts

J.L. Suttle
1996 Men's 85s singles, USTA Indoor Championships; 1997 Men's 85s doubles (with Herman Ratcliffe), USTA Hard Court Championships

Kathryn Talbert
2003 Girls' 12s doubles (with Ebie Wilson), USTA National Spring Championships; 2003 Girls' 12s doubles 9with Ebie Wilson), USTA National Winter Championships; 2004 Girls' 12s doubles (with Ebie Wilson), USTA National Spring Championships

Thomas Tanner
1989 Mixed doubles (with Kelly Erven), USTA Clay Court Championships

Sarah Taylor
1995 Girls' 14s singles, Easter Bowl

Faye & Scotti Thomas
1995 Mother–Daughter doubles, USTA Grass Court Championships; 1995 Mother–Daughter doubles, USTA Clay Court Championships

Katrina Tsang
2002 Girls' 16s singles, USTA Super National Clay Courts; 2003 Girls' 16s doubles (with Liberty Sveke), Easter Bowl

Woody Webb
1989 Boys' 18s singles, USTA Interscholastic Championships; 1990 Men's singles, USTA Clay Court Championships

Mike Weidl
1992 Men's singles, USTA Indoor Championships; 1992 Men's doubles (with Stan Cocke), USTA Amateur Championships

Jimmy Weilbacher
1983 Boys' 18s doubles (with Ashely Rhoney), USTA Interscholastic Championships

Tim Wilkison
1976 Boys' 16s singles, USTA National Championships; 1976 Boys' 16s doubles (with Murray Robinson),

USTA National Championships; 1976 Boys' 16s singles, USTA Clay Court Championships

Douglas Wink
2002 Girls' 18s doubles (with Melisssa Applebaum), Easter Bowl

John Yancey
1987 Boys' 18s doubles (with Michael Watson), USTA Interscholastic Championships; 1988 Boys' 18s doubles (with Andy Potter), USTA Clay Court Championships; 1988 Boys' 18s singles, USTA Interscholastic Championships; 1988 Boys' 18s doubles (with Jim Rogerson), USTA Interscholastic Championships

Reka Zsilinszka
2003 Girls' 14s singles, USTA Super National Hard Courts; 2006 Girls' 18s singles, USTA National Spring

NORTH CAROLINA JUNIOR STATE CLOSED CHAMPIONS

BOYS' 10S

1967
Singles: Bill Stephanz (Burlington)
Doubles: Allen Farfour (Goldsboro),
Dee Keesler (Charlotte)

1968
Singles: Carlton Harris (Greensboro)
Doubles: Carlton Harris
(Greensboro), Allen Farfour
(Goldsboro)

1969
Singles: Allen Farfour (Goldsboro)
Doubles: Allen Farfour (Goldsboro),
John Perkinson (Winston-Salem)

1970
Singles: Andy Avram (Winston-
Salem)
Doubles: rained out

1971
Singles: Don Gilliam (Raleigh)
Doubles: Don Gilliam (Raleigh),
Andy Wilkison (Shelby)

1972
Singles: Jeff Farfour (Goldsboro)
Doubles: Jeff Farfour (Goldsboro),
Jim Hamm (Hickory)

1973
Singles: Chris Kennedy (Cary)
Doubles: Chris Kennedy (Cary), Paul
Bitler (Raleigh)

1974
Singles: Laneal Vaughn (Asheville)
Doubles: Bill Venable (Raleigh), Mike
Corthum (Greensboro)

1975
Singles: Mike Corthum (Greensboro)
Doubles: Phil Payne (Greensboro),
Trip Caldwell (Hickory)

1976
Singles: Eric Little (Charlotte)
Doubles: Mike Corthum
(Greensboro), Ken Skillman
(Wilmington)

1977
Singles: Stephen Enochs
(Greensboro)
Doubles: Stephen Enochs
(Greensboro), Jeff Raper
(Greensboro)

1978
Singles: Bev Tucker (Henderson)
Doubles: Rod McGeachy (Winston-
Salem), John Morris (Winston-
Salem)

1979
Singles: Michael Leonard
(Laurinburg)
Doubles: Michael Leonard
(Laurinburg), Victor Meir (Raleigh)

1980
Singles: Victor Meir (Raleigh)
Doubles: Willie Ellison (Laurinburg),
Scott Fligel (Charlotte)

1981
Singles: John Moody (Greensboro)
Doubles: John Moody (Greensboro),
Jon Hodges (Henderson)

1982
Singles: Chad Alala (Hickory)
Doubles: Chad Alala (Hickory),
Marshall Burroughs (Raleigh)

1983
Singles: Peter Ayers (Charlotte)
Doubles: Matt Rogers (High Point),
Robert Wein (Greensboro)

1984
Singles: Stuart Sherrill (Charlotte)
Doubles: Stuart Sherill (Charlotte),
Chris Hill (Chapel Hill)

1985
Singles: Jimmy Jackson (Chapel Hill)
Doubles: Chris Menocal
(Wilmington), Dan Parham (Wilson)

1986
Singles: David Britt (Charlotte)
Doubles: David Britt (Charlotte),
Rashad Simpson (Greensboro)

1987
Singles: Rashad Simpson
(Greensboro)
Doubles: Fritz Gildemeister
(Durham), Greg Hill (Hendersonville)

1988–2004
No State Chps. for 10-year-olds

2005
Singles: Josh Du Toit (Charlotte)
Doubles: Gregory & Matthew
Galush (Cary)

2006
Singles: Marshall Parker (Shelby)
Doubles: Eban Wells (Kitty Hawk),
Tommy Paul (Greenville)

2007
Singles: Anudeep Kodali (Raleigh)
Doubles: Blain Boyden (Raleigh),
John Karlawish (Raleigh)

2008
Singles: Patrick Kypson (Greenville)
Doubles: Sean Ross (Chapel Hill),
Thomas Wang (Chapel Hill)

2009
Singles: Drew Baird (Raleigh)
Doubles: Mazen Kuseybi
(Summerfield), Blake Hardwick
(Raleigh)

2010
Singles, Spring Closed: Michael
Ogundele (Raleigh)
Singles, Summer Closed: Charlie
Schuls (Gastonia)
Doubles, Spring Closed: Donovan
Lilov (Mooresville), Michael
Ogundele (Raleigh)
Doubles, Summer Closed: Priyan
Desilva (Chapel Hill), Kevin Huang
(Chapel Hill)

2011
Singles, Spring Closed: Banks Evans
(Clayton)
Singles, Summer Closed: Mark
Dillon (Charlotte)
Doubles: Banks Evans (Clayton),
Foster Evans (Clayton)
Doubles: Banks Evans (Clayton),
Foster Evans (Clayton)

BOYS' 12S

1963
Singles: Bobby Koury (Burlington)

1965
Doubles: Randy Merritt (Lexington),
Arthur Bingham (Lexington)

1967
Singles: Chuck Cloninger (Shelby)
Doubles: Chuck Cloninger (Shelby),
Joe Merritt (Lexington)

1968
Singles: Bill Stephanz (Greensboro)
Doubles: Sprock Leitner (Charlotte),
Greg Sanders (Charlotte)

1969
Singles: Bill Stephanz (Greensboro)
Doubles: Bill Stephanz (Greensboro),
Carlton Harris (Greensboro)

1970
Singles: Carlton Harris (Greensboro)
Doubles: Allen Farfour (Goldsboro),
Carlton Harris (Greensboro)

1971
Singles: Andy Andrews (Raleigh)
Doubles: Andy Andrews (Raleigh),
Allen Farfour (Goldsboro)

1972
Singles: Ed Hamm (Hickory)
Doubles: Ed Hamm (Hickory), Jim
Latham (Burlington)

1973
Singles: Jim Latham (Burlington)
Doubles: Jim Latham (Burlington),
John Hogan (Raleigh)

1974
Singles: Fred Rosenkampff (Shelby)
Doubles: Don Gilliam (Raleigh), Fred
Rosenkampff (Shelby)

1975
Singles: Doug Maynard (Asheville)
Doubles: Matt Chandler (Durham),
Chris Kennedy (Cary)

1976
Singles: Craig Hall (Asheville)
Doubles: Craig Hall (Asheville), Eric
Arkin (Gastonia)

1977
Singles: Lawson Duncan (Cullowhee)
Doubles: Lawson Duncan
(Cullowhee), Phil Payne
(Greensboro)

1978
Singles: Mike Corthum (Greensboro)
Doubles: Mike Corthum (Greensboro),
Brad Rosenkampff (Shelby)

1979
Singles: Bev Tucker (Henderson)
Doubles: Bev Tucker (Henderson),
Brian Burchfield (Concord)

1980
Singles: Scott Tredennick (Winston–
Salem)
Doubles: Bev Tucker (Henderson),
Thomas Tanner (Rocky Mount)

1981
Singles: John Bristow
(Hendersonville)
Doubles: Michael Leonard
(Laurinburg), Taft Mills (Monroe)

1982
Singles: Victor Meir (Raleigh)
Doubles: Kevin Grotsky (Wilson), Jim
Rogerson (Wilson)

1983
Singles: John Moody (Greensboro)
Doubles: John Moody (Greensboro),
Woody Webb (Chapel Hill)

1984
Singles: Marshall Burroughs (Raleigh)
Doubles: Doug Burleson
(Lumberton), Vivek Tandon
(Rowland)

1985
Singles: Miles Highsmith (Charlotte)
Doubles: Miles Highsmith (Charlotte),
Robert Wein (Greensboro)

1986
Singles: Jimmy Jackson (Chapel Hill)
Doubles: Chris Hill (Chapel Hill),
Jimmy Jackson (Chapel Hill)

NORTH CAROLINA JUNIOR STATE CLOSED CHAMPIONS
(CONTINUED)

1987
Singles: Quentin Huff (Winston-Salem)
Doubles: Scott Huie (Greensboro), Andy Sands (Reidsville)

1988
Singles: Chad Copenhaver (Shelby)
Doubles: Chad Copenhaver (Shelby), John Stubbs (New Bern)

1989
Singles: Shaun Thomas (Charlotte)
Doubles: Jeffrey Smith (Charlotte), Shaun Thomas (Charlotte)

1990
Singles: Brian Cowman (Charlotte)
Doubles: David Cheatwood (Fayetteville), Robert Taylor (Raleigh)

1991
Singles: Jason Kang (Raleigh)
Doubles: Max Hilkey (Chapel Hill), Jason Kang (Raleigh)

1992
Singles: Jeff Goins (Hickory)
Doubles: Deval Desai (Greensboro), Jeff Goins (Hickory)

1993
Singles: Allen Gowin (Gibsonville)
Doubles: Drew Sandri (Raleigh), Paxton Badham (Raleigh)

1994
Singles: Patrick Kennedy (Belmont)
Doubles: Paxton Badham (Raleigh), Dash Pierce (Farmville)

1995
Singles: Jonathan Janda (Shelby)
Doubles: Nicolas Rose (Raleigh), Jonathan Stokke (Chapel Hill)

1996
Singles: Trevor Johnson (Gastonia)
Doubles: Tyler Hager (Charlotte), Andy Orban (Fayetteville)

1997
Singles: William Noblitt (Shelby)
Doubles: Mark Brodie (Greensboro), David Stone (Greensboro)

1998
Singles: David Stone (Greensboro)
Doubles: David Stone (Greensboro), Mason Schermerhorn (Colfax)

1999
Singles: Clay Weller (High Point)
Doubles: Kevin Fussell (Raleigh), Kevin Logan (Goldsboro)

2000
Singles: Chris Carlton (Gastonia)
Doubles: Chris Carlton (Gastonia), Matthew Rorech (Raleigh)

2001
Singles: Preston Spencer (Statesville)
Doubles: Sam Mason (Raleigh), Bill Bobbitt (Raleigh)

2002
Singles: Ryan Noble (Fayetteville)
Doubles: Ryan Noble (Fayetteville), William Parker (Shelby)

2003
Singles: Thomas Fanjoy (Statesville)
Doubles: Thomas Fanjoy (Statesville), Robbie Mudge (Huntersville)

2004
Singles: Robbie Mudge (Huntersville)
Doubles: None

2005
Singles: Will Suk (Raleigh)
Doubles: Will Suk (Raleigh), Austin Ansari (Greensboro)

2006
Singles: Alex Gaines (Wilmington)
Doubles: Kassim Alani (Chapel Hill), Strong Kirchheimer (Cary)

2007
Singles: Josh Du Toit (Charlotte)
Doubles: Josh Du Toit (Charlotte), Marshall Parker (Shelby)

2008
Singles: Eben Wells (Kitty Hawk)
Doubles: Tommy Paul (Greenville), Eben Wells (Kitty Hawk)

2009
Singles: Anudeep Kodali (Raleigh)
Doubles: Harrison Kent (Wrightsville Beach), Nick Stachowiak (Cary)

2010
Singles, Spring Closed: Nick Stachowiak (Cary)
Singles, Summer Closed: Nick Stachowiak (Cary)
Doubles: Nick Stachowiak (Cary), Harrison Kent (Wrightsville Beach)
Doubles: Austin Cobb (Raleigh), Klein Evans (Clayton)

2011
Singles, Spring Closed: Grant Stuckey (Charlotte)
Singles, Summer Closed: Blake Hardwick (Raleigh)
Doubles, Spring Closed: Andrew Redding (Concord), Grant Stuckey (Charlotte)
Doubles, Summer Closed: Daniel Crossin (Huntersville), Max Vicario (Mooresville)

BOYS' 14S

1963
Singles: Fenton Winstead (Roxboro)
Doubles: Fenton Winstead (Roxboro), Jim Corn (Shelby)

1965
Doubles: Richard McKee (Charlotte), Bob Koury (Charlotte)

1967
Singles: John Lucas (Durham)
Doubles: Artie Small (Charlotte), Tommy Dixon (Raleigh)

1968
Singles: Bruce Von Cannon (Asheboro)
Doubles: Arthur Bingham (Lexington), Phil Head (Lexington)

1969
Singles: Chuck Cloninger (Shelby)
Doubles: Chuck Cloninger (Shelby), Joe Merritt (Lexington)

1970
Singles: Jimmy Neal (Greensboro)
Doubles: Rained Out

1971
Singles: Bill Stephanz (Greensboro)
Doubles: Bill Stephanz (Greensboro),
Tal Henry (Charlotte)

1972
Singles: Carlton Harris (Greensboro)
Doubles: Carlton Harris
(Greensboro), Tal Henry (Charlotte)

1973
Singles: Tim Wilkison (Shelby)
Doubles: Tim Wilkison (Shelby),
Allen Farfour (Raleigh)

1974
Singles: Andy Avram (Winston-
Salem)
Doubles: Andy Avram (Winston-
Salem), Jim Latham (Burlington)

1975
Singles: Jim Latham (Burlington)
Doubles: Don Gilliam (Raleigh),
Freddie Rosenkampff (Shelby)

1976
Singles: Andy Wilkison (Shelby)
Doubles: Robbie Bach (Winston-
Salem), Mark Nottingham (Fort
Bragg)

1977
Singles: Chris Kennedy (Cary)
Doubles: Craig Hall (Asheville), Chris
Kennedy (Cary)

1978
Singles: Hayes Dallas (High Point)
Doubles: Lawson Duncan
(Cullowhee), Craig Hall (Asheville)

1979
Singles: Koley Keel (Fayetteville)
Doubles: Mike Corthum
(Greensboro), Brad Rosenkampff
(Shelby)

1980
Singles: Ashley Rhoney (Hickory)
Doubles: Ashley Rhoney (Hickory),
Eric Little (Charlotte)

1981
Singles: Brian Burchfield (Concord)
Doubles: Brian Burchfield (Concord),
Bev Tucker (Henderson)

1982
Singles: Charles Hoots (Clemmons)
Doubles: Derek Weilbacher
(Asheville), Aaron Barrick (Charlotte)

1983
Singles: Jim Rogerson (Wilson)
Doubles: Joel Adelman (Greensboro),
Kent Lovett (Raleigh)

1984
Singles: Thad Langford (Lexington)
Doubles: Peter Ayers (Charlotte),
Thad Langford (Lexington)

1985
Singles: John Moody (Greensboro)
Doubles: John Moody (Greensboro),
Joey Sie (Charlotte)

1986
Singles: Bert Bolick (High Point)
Doubles: Bert Bolick (High Point),
Marshall Burroughs (Raleigh)

1987
Singles: Robert Wein (Greensboro)
Doubles: Sammy Ortiz (Chapel Hill),
Robert Wein (Greensboro)

1988
Singles: Chris Hill (Chapel Hill)
Doubles: Scott Huie (Greensboro),
Andy Sands (Reidsville)

1989
Singles: Chad Copenhaver (Shelby)
Doubles: Chad Copenhaver (Shelby),
John Stubbs (New Bern)

1990
Singles: Jeffrey Smith (Charlotte)
Doubles: David Bolick (Elon College),
Ryan Fleming (Asheville)

1991
Singles: Shaun Thomas (Charlotte)
Doubles: Jeffrey Smith (Charlotte),
Shaun Thomas (Charlotte)

1992
Singles: Jason Kang (Raleigh)
Doubles: Brian Cowman (Charlotte),
Brandon Brookshire (Charlotte)

NORTH CAROLINA JUNIOR STATE CLOSED CHAMPIONS
(CONTINUED)

1993
Singles: Jason Kang (Raleigh)
Doubles: Edward Easton (Charlotte), Matt Lucas (Boone)

1994
Singles: Billy Wilkinson (Charlotte)
Doubles: Tony Ro (Raleigh), Judson Williams (Raleigh)

1995
Singles: Allen Gowin (Gibsonville)
Doubles: Allen Gowin (Gibsonville), Casey Hansen (Charlotte)

1996
Singles: Jordan Isner (Greensboro)
Doubles: Nicholas Rose (Raleigh), Andrew Simpson (Raleigh)

1997
Singles: Matt Cloer (Linville)
Doubles: Matt Cloer (Linville), Nicholas Rose (Raleigh)

1998
Singles: Will Plyler (Raleigh)
Doubles: Brad Pomeroy (Asheville), David Gora (Boone)

1999
Singles: Brooks Weller (High Point)
Doubles: Jay Chitty (Shelby), Will Plyer (Raleigh)

2000
Singles: Tyler Fleming (Boone)
Doubles: Michael Kociecki (Raleigh), Kenneth Warner (Fayetteville)

2001
Singles: Kevin Galloway (Charlotte)
Doubles: Kevin Fleck (Statesville), Jonathan Staton (Greensboro)

2002
Singles: Andrew Crone (Hickory)
Doubles: Andrew Crone (Hickory), Trip Johnson (Hickory)

2003
Singles: Ryan Noble (Fayetteville)
Doubles: Chase Helpingstine (Chapel Hill), Parker Preyer (Hillsborough)

2004
Singles: Harrison Holbrook (Greensboro)
Doubles: None

2005
Singles: Thomas Fanjoy (Statesville)
Doubles: Thomas Fanjoy (Statesville), Pierce Hoover (Durham)

2006
Singles: Austin Ansari (Greensboro)
Doubles: Michael Allan (Raleigh), Gregory Patterson (Elon)

2007
Singles: Strong Kirchheimer (Cary)
Doubles: Kassim Alani (Chapel Hill), Strong Kirchheimer (Cary)

2008
Singles: Alex Gaines (Wilmington)
Doubles: Benjamin Kelley (Weaverville), Kevin Le (Raleigh)

2009
Singles: Josh Du Toit (Charlotte)
Doubles: Josh Du Toit (Charlotte), Eric Greene (Elon)

2010
Singles, Spring Closed: Oliver Otero (Winston-Salem)
Singles, Summer Closed: Blaine Boyden (Raleigh)
Doubles: Oliver Otero (Winston-Salem), Bradley Schneider (Winston-Salem)
Daniel Belsito (Charlotte), Kendall Stephens (Matthews)

2011
Singles, Spring Closed: Nick Stachowiak (Cary)
Singles, Summer Closed: Daniel Belsito (Charlotte)
Doubles: Matthew Galush (Cary), Harrison Kent (Wrightsville Beach)
Danel Belsito (Charlotte), Louis Rico (Cary)

BOYS' 16S

1942
Singles: Bo Roddey (Charlotte)

1943
Singles: Bo Roddey (Charlotte)

1944
Singles: Whit Cobb (Durham)

1945
Singles: Tommy Southerland (Durham)

1946
Singles: Bob Spurrier (Charlotte)
Doubles: Dick Stover (Durham), Bob Patterson (Asheboro)

1947
Singles: Lacy Keesler (Charlotte)
Doubles: Dick Radford (Greensboro), Jack Hurd (Greensboro)

1949
Singles: Cutler Ham (Greensboro)
Doubles: Cutler Ham (Greensboro), Ed Hudgins, Jr. (Greensboro)

1950
Singles: Ed Hudgins, Jr. (Greensboro)
Doubles: Ed Hudgins, Jr. (Greensboro), Tommy Holder (Charlotte)

1954
Singles: Finley Lee (Charlotte)

1955
Singles: Jack Hepting (Asheville)
Doubles: Jack Hepting (Asheville), Stan Cocke (Asheville)

1956
Singles: Jack Hepting (Asheville)

1962
Singles: Gene Hamilton (Asheville)

1963
Singles: Mark Griffin (Asheville)

1965
Singles: Jim Corn (Shelby)

1966
Singles: Robert Tate (Greensboro)

1967
Singles: Bob Koury (Burlington)
Doubles: John Lucas (Durham), Artie Small (Charlotte)

1968
Singles: John Lucas (Durham)
Doubles: Roger Kavanaugh (Greensboro), Randy Merritt (Lexington)

1969
Singles: John Lucas (Durham)
Doubles: Tommy Dixon (Raleigh), Artie Small (Charlotte)

1970
Singles: Bruce Von Cannon (Asheboro)
Doubles: Rained Out

1971
Singles: Chip Koury (Burlington)
Doubles: Chip Koury (Burlington), Chuck Cloninger (Shelby)

1972
Singles: Hap Core (Charlotte)
Doubles: Bill Stephanz (Greensboro), Drew Lewis (Charlotte)

1973
Singles: Hap Core (Charlotte)
Doubles: Hap Core (Charlotte), Bill Stephanz (Greensboro)

1974
Singles: Tim Wilkison (Shelby)
Doubles: Allen Farfour (Goldsboro), Carlton Harris (Greensboro)

1975
Singles: Pender Murphy (Charlotte)
Doubles: Allen Farfour (Goldsboro), Joseph Meir (Raleigh)

1976
Singles: Jim Latham (Burlington)
Doubles: Gray Yancey (Oxford), Mark Dillon (Charlotte)

1977
Singles: Phil Raiford (Chapel Hill)
Doubles: Phil Raiford (Chapel Hill), Ken Ludwig (Chapel Hill)

1978
Singles: Wayne Hearn (Charlotte)
Doubles: Robbie Bach (Winston-Salem), Freddie Rosenkampff (Shelby)

1979
Singles: Chris Kennedy (Cary)
Doubles: Jamie Langford (Charlotte), Shep Robinson (Charlotte)

1980
Singles: Andy Putnam (Bessemer City)
Doubles: David Creech (New Bern), Raymond Thomas (New Bern)

1981
Singles: Koley Keel (Fayetteville)
Doubles: Oscar Kranz (Charlotte), Koley Keel (Fayetteville)

1982
Singles: Koley Keel (Fayetteville)
Doubles: Oscar Kranz (Charlotte), Koley Keel (Fayetteville)

1983
Singles: Brian Burchfield (Concord)
Doubles: Charles Hoots (Clemmons), Brad Hubbard (Asheville)

1984
Singles: Rod McGeachey (Winston-Salem)
Doubles: Eric Abrams (Charlotte), Van Brockwell (Wilson)

1985
Singles: Kent Lovett (Raleigh)
Doubles: Chip Collins (Fayetteville), Chris Collins (Fayetteville)

1986
Singles: Warren Rand (Goldsboro)
Doubles: John Beyer (Fayetteville), Jon Hodges (Henderson)

1987
Singles: Wells Brabham (Greensboro)
Doubles: Andrew Randle (Charlotte), Brian Rudisill (Charlotte)

1988
Singles: Marshall Burroughs (Raleigh)
Doubles: Walt Kennedy (Charlotte), Ashley Shaw (Charlotte)

1989
Singles: Zack Bolen (Chapel Hill)
Doubles: Zack Bolen (Chapel Hill), Chris Hill (Chapel Hill)

1990
Singles: Danny Colangelo (Raleigh)
Doubles: Danny Colangelo (Raleigh), Chris Hill (Chapel Hill)

1991
Singles: Jeffrey Taylor (Raleigh)
Doubles: Chris Menocal (Wilmington), Dan Parham (Burlington)

1992
Singles: Reagan Crabtree (Raleigh)
Doubles: Shaun Thomas (Charlotte), Reagan Crabtree (Raleigh)

1993
Singles: Robert Williams (Charlotte)
Doubles: Max Hilkey (Chapel Hill), Robert Taylor (Raleigh)

1994
Singles: Jason Kang (Raleigh)
Doubles: Blair Easton (Charlotte), Zane Sharpe (Advance)

1995
Singles: Matt Lucas (Boone)
Doubles: Matt Lucas (Boone), Zane Sharpe (Advance)

1996
Singles: Adam Greiner (Rocky Mount)
Doubles: Deval Desai (Greensboro), Adam Greiner

1997
Singles: Jonathan Britt (Charlotte)
Doubles: Jonathan Parks (Matthews), Michael Sutcliffe (Charlotte)

1998
Singles: Ronnie Orban (Fayetteville)
Doubles: Jon Davis (Southern Pines), Brian Patnode (Southern Pines)

1999
Singles: Jonathan Walker (Burlington)
Doubles: Jonathan Walker (Burlington), Matthew Walton (Elon)

NORTH CAROLINA JUNIOR STATE CLOSED CHAMPIONS
(CONTINUED)

2000
Singles: Ryan Criscoe (Southern Pines)
Doubles: Drew Befus (Raleigh), Bryant Tran (Fayetteville)

2001
Singles: Mark Brodie (Greensboro)
Doubles: Drew Befus (Raleigh), Mark Brodie (Greensboro)

2002
Singles: Matt Stein (Raleigh)
Doubles: Tyler Fleming (Boone), Mason Moseley (Boone)

2003
Singles: Andrew Crone (Hickory)
Doubles: Eric & Ryan Noble (Fayetteville)

2004
Singles: Parker Preyer (Hillsborough)
Doubles: None

2005
Singles: Taylor Meyer (Raleigh)
Doubles: Michael Pereira (Fayetteville), Christopher Toussaint (Charlotte)

2006
Singles: John Schmitt (Raleigh)
Doubles: Timmy Bayus (Chapel Hill), John Runge (Chapel Hill)

2007
Singles: Thomas Fanjoy (Statesville)
Doubles: Steed Johnson (Ahoskie), Michael Reilly (Raleigh)

2008
Singles: Austin Ansari (Greensboro)
Doubles: Chad Hoskins (Spencer), Dillon Segur (Mooresville)

2009
Singles: Charles Depaolo (Asheville)
Doubles: Matt Stachowiak (Cary), AJ Stilwell (Wilmington)

2010
Singles, Spring Closed: Joshua Swindler (Clemmons)
Singles, Summer Closed: Alex Gaines (Wilmington)
Doubles: Kevin Le (Winston-Salem), Parks Thompson (Statesville)
Alex Gaines (Wilmington), Eric Greene (Elon)

2011
Singles, Spring Closed: Eric Greene (Elon)
Singles, Summer Closed: Eric Greene (Elon)
Doubles: Josh Du Toit (Charlotte), Eric Greene (Elon)
Doubles: Josh Du Toit (Charlotte), Eric Greene (Elon)

BOYS' 18S

1935
Singles: Mebane Croom (Winston-Salem)

1936
Singles: Bill Rawlings (Winston-Salem)
Doubles: Bill Rawlings (Winston-Salem), Melville Jordan (Chapel Hill)

1937
Singles: Melville Jordan (Chapel Hill)
Doubles: Bill Rawlings (Winston-Salem), John Henderson (Chapel Hill)

1938
Singles: Moyer Hendrix (Winston-Salem)
Doubles: Melville Jordan (Chapel Hill), Hunt Hobbs (Chapel Hill)

1939
Singles: Bob Spurrier (Charlotte)
Doubles: Jack Markham (Durham), Tom Wadden (Raleigh)

1940
Singles: Stokes Rawlings (Greensboro)
Doubles: Stokes Rawlings (Greensboro), John Tate (Greensboro)

1941
Singles: Bob Haltiwanger (Winston-Salem)
Doubles: Rob Robinson (Charlotte), Ted Keesler (Charlotte)

1942
Singles: Teddy Keesler (Charlotte)
Doubles: Teddy Keesler (Charlotte), Bob Spurrier (Charlotte)

1943
Singles: Bo Roddey (Charlotte)

1944
Singles: Bo Roddey (Charlotte)

1945
Singles: Bo Roddey (Charlotte)
Doubles: Whit Cobb (Durham), Jimmy Baynes (Durham)

1946
Singles: Bo Roddey (Charlotte)
Doubles: Bo Roddey (Charlotte), Bob Chapman (Charlotte)

1947
Singles: Jack Warmath (Greensboro)
Doubles: Dewey Keesler (Charlotte), Hubert Mosley (Charlotte)

1948
Singles: Allen Strand (Greensboro)
Doubles: Ray Herbin (Greensboro), Curtis Laughlin (Greensboro)

1949
Singles: Hal Furr (Charlotte)
Doubles: John Bremer (Wilmington), Hal Furr (Charlotte)

1950
Singles: Ed Hudgins, Jr. (Greensboro)
Doubles: Ed Hudgins, Jr. (Greensboro), Jack Hurd (Greensboro)

1951
Singles: Lacy Keesler (Charlotte)

1954
Singles: Ed Hudgins, Jr. (Greensboro)
Doubles: Ed Hudgins, Jr. (Greensboro), Dave Pearsall (Charlotte)

1955
Singles: Marshall Happer (Kinston)
Doubles: John West (Durham), Bill Weaver (Durham)

1956
Singles: Marshall Happer (Kinston)

1962
Singles: Gene Hamilton (Asheville)
Doubles: Gene Hamilton (Asheville),
Ken Oettinger (Chapel Hill)

1963
Singles: Gene Hamilton (Asheville)
Doubles: Billy Trott (Raleigh), Ed
Parker (Raleigh)

1964
Singles: Gene Hamilton (Asheville)

1965
Singles: Fred Rawlings (Durham)
Doubles: Fred Rawlings (Durham),
Rich Preyer (Greensboro)

1966
Singles: Allen Lassiter (Winston-
Salem)

1967
Singles: Jim Corn (Shelby)
Doubles: Jim Corn (Shelby), Robert
Tate (Greensboro)

1968
Singles: Jim Corn (Shelby)

1969
Singles: Bobby Koury (Burlington)
Doubles: Bobby Koury (Burlington),
John Lucas (Durham)

1970
Singles: Tommy Dixon (Raleigh)
Doubles: Rained Out

1971
Singles: Tommy Dixon (Raleigh)
Doubles: Tommy Dixon (Raleigh),
Bruce Von Cannon (Asheboro)

1972
Singles: Chip Koury (Burlington)
Doubles: Joe Merritt (Lexington),
Mike Owen (Boone)

1973
Singles: Chip Koury (Burlington)
Doubles: Chip Koury (Burlington),
Chuck Cloninger (Shelby)

1974
Singles: John Sadri (Charlotte)
Doubles: Davis Babb (Charlotte),
Carl Bumgardner (Raleigh)

1975
Singles: Cliff Skakle (Chapel Hill)
Doubles: Cliff Skakle (Chapel Hill),
Rick Lovett (Raleigh)

1976
Singles: Karl Johnston (Asheville)
Doubles: Hines, Pender Murphy
(Charlotte)

1977
Singles: Mark Dillon (Charlotte)
Doubles: Lewis Coppedge
(Charlotte), Billy Cruise
(Wilmington)

1978
Singles: John Grigg (Charlotte)
Doubles: John Grigg (Charlotte),
Norman Schellenger, Jr. (Charlotte)

1979
Singles: Wayne Hearn (Charlotte)
Doubles: Phil Raiford (Chapel Hill),
Ken Ludwig (Chapel Hill)

1980
Singles: Chris Kennedy (Cary)
Doubles: Chris Kennedy (Cary), Jay
Pulliam (Burlington)

1981
Singles: Clint Weathers (Southern
Pines)
Doubles: Mark Featherston
(Charlotte), Shep Robinson
(Charlotte)

1982
Singles: Ashley Rhoney (Hickory)
Doubles: Phil Payne (Greensboro),
Rusty Woy (Shelby)

1983
Singles: Michael White (Chapel Hill)
Doubles: Mike Corthum
(Greensboro), Brad Rosenkampff
(Shelby)

1984
Singles: Brian Burchfield (Concord)
Doubles: John Morris (Chapel Hill),
Brad Winslow (Chapel Hill)

1985
Singles: Aaron Barrick (Charlotte)
Doubles: Brian Burchfield (Charlotte),
Peter Sweitzer (Chapel Hill)

1986
Singles: James Krege (Greensboro)
Doubles: James Krege (Greensboro),
Thomas Tanner (Rocky Mount)

1987
Singles: Darren Harper (Brevard)
Doubles: Marshall Burroughs
(Raleigh), Darren Harper (Brevard)

1988
Singles: Wells Brabham (Greensboro)
Doubles: Lee Dunn (Wilson), Jim
Rogerson (Wilson)

1989
Singles: Marshall Burroughs (Raleigh)
Doubles: Jason Abhau (Raleigh), Paul
Goebel (Hendersonville)

1990
Singles: Tee Parham (Burlington)
Doubles: Jason Abhau (Raleigh),
Ashley Shaw (Charlotte)

1991
Singles: Chris Hill (Chapel Hill)
Doubles: Danny Colangelo (Raleigh),
Chris Hill (Chapel Hill)

1992
Singles: Jeff Taylor (Raleigh)
Doubles: David Britt (Charlotte),
Eric Saunders (Salisbury)

1993
Singles: Kenny Kirby (Wilmington)
Doubles: Chase Hodges (Raleigh),
Scott Sink (Boone)

1994
Singles: Eric Joffe (Raleigh)
Doubles: Eric Joffe (Raleigh), Kenny
Kirby (Wilmington)

1995
Singles: Jason Kang (Raleigh)
Doubles: Ahad Athar (Mount Airy),
Billy Boykin (Davidson)

1996
Singles: Billy Boykin (Davidson)
Doubles: David Boyer (Winston-
Salem), Billy Boykin (Davidson)

1997
Singles: Charlie Briggs (Huntersville)
Doubles: Patrick Hauser (Conover),
Robert Kurrle (Statesville)

NORTH CAROLINA JUNIOR STATE CLOSED CHAMPIONS
(CONTINUED)

1998
Singles: Doug Ormsby (Laurinburg)
Doubles: Lee Bailey (Greenville), Richard Dutton (Elon College)

1999
Singles: Jonathan Parks (Matthews)
Doubles: Jon Davis (Southern Pines), Charles Patnode (Southern Pines)

2000
Singles: Bryant Tran (Fayetteville)
Doubles: Steven Mantzouris (Southern Pines), Charles Patnode (Southern Pines)

2001
Singles: Will Plyler (Raleigh)
Doubles: Keith Criscoe (Biscoe), Jonathan Walker (Burlington)

2002
Singles: William Noblitt (Shelby)
Doubles: Jay Chitty (Shelby), William Noblitt (Shelby)

2003
Singles: Joe Cariello (Chapel Hill)
Doubles: Joe Cariello (Chapel Hill), Mark Eagan (Chapel Hill)

2004
Singles: Michael Kociecki (Raleigh)
Doubles: None

2005
Singles: Bill Bobbitt (Raleigh)
Doubles: Chris Carlton (Gastonia), David Hannon (Gastonia)

2006
Singles: Paul Bartholomy (Charlotte)
Doubles: David Chermak (Raleigh), Alan Donald (Wilmington)

2007
Singles: Alan Donald (Wilmington)
Doubles: Sam Funkhouser (Raleigh), Ely Khoury (Greenville)

2008
Singles: Andrew Bock (Fayetteville)
Doubles: Wesley Barrett (Cary), Christopher Mauch (Durham)

2009
Singles: John Banks (Charlotte)
Doubles: Peter McDonald (Chapel Hill), Sean Weber (Raleigh)

2010
Singles, Spring Closed: Peter McDonald (Chapel Hill)
Singles, Summer Closed: Dana Parziale (Pinehurst)
Doubles: John Banks (Charlotte), Roman Cacha (Cary)
Doubles: Graham Duncan (Cary), Wesley Barrett (Cary)

2011
Singles, Spring Closed: Robbie Mudge (Winston–Salem)
Singles, Summer Closed: Chad Hoskins (Spencer)
Doubles: William Kent (Wrightsville Beach), Woravin Kumthonkittikul (Wilmington)
Doubles: James Alex Gaines (Wilmington), Chad Hoskins (Spencer)

GIRLS' 10S

1967
Singles: Ann Dortch (Greensboro)
Doubles: Meg Elmore (Raleigh), Ann Yarbrough (Durham)

1968
Singles: Ann Dortch (Greensboro)
Doubles: Ann Dortch (Greensboro), Meg Elmore (Raleigh)

1969
Singles: Ellen Easter (Lexington)
Doubles: Debbie Southern (Winston–Salem), Beth Cloninger (Shelby)

1970
Singles: Elizabeth Tolson (New Bern)
Doubles: Elizabeth Tolson (New Bern), Carolyn Walser (Lexington)

1971
Singles: Mary Shuford (Hickory)
Doubles: Mary Shuford (Hickory), Nita Gilley (Winston–Salem)

1972
Singles: Elizabeth Tolson (New Bern)
Doubles: Katherine Tolson (New Bern), Betsy Carlson (Greensboro)

1973
Singles: Katherine Tolson (New Bern)
Doubles: Helen Graham (Reidsville), Katherine Tolson (New Bern)

1974
Singles: Francis Taylor (Wilmington)
Doubles: Margaret Hogan (Raleigh), Frances Taylor (Wilmington)

1975
Singles: Kathy Caldwell (Winston–Salem)
Doubles: Mary Lloyd Hodges (Henderson), Ann Vaughan (Greensboro)

1976
Singles: Miriam Crosland (Concord)
Doubles: Kim Vaughn (Greensboro), Angela Featherstone (Charlotte)

1977
Singles: Kim Vaughn (Greensboro)

1978
Singles: Christie Overton (Greensboro)
Doubles: Christie Overton (Greensboro), Stacy Schefflin (Charlotte)

1979
Singles: Susan Stanley (Charlotte)
Doubles: Susan Stanley (Charlotte), Amy Mullis (Charlotte)

1980
Singles: Susan Saunders (Salisbury)
Doubles: Nicole Main (Salisbury), Susan Saunders (Salisbury)

1981
Singles: Lisa Adelman (Greensboro)
Doubles: Ashley McGeachy (Winston–Salem), Andrea Rogers (High Point)

1982
Singles: Christy Hedgpeth (Thomasville)
Doubles: Vidhya Basham (Raleigh), Ashley Moser (Laurinburg)

1983
Singles: DeeAnn Busey (Winston–Salem)
Doubles: Andrea Burns (Kinston), Cara White (Henderson)

1984
Singles: Tory Schroeder (Carrboro)
Doubles: Tory Schroeder (Carrboro), Jane Stubbs (New Bern)

1985
Singles: Tory Schroeder (Carrboro)
Doubles: Kristen Franus (Matthews), Jennifer Sopel (Charlotte)

1986
Singles: Blair Sutton (Fayetteville)
Doubles: Cathy Callahan, Elizabeth Williams (Fayetteville)

1987
Singles: Roulhac Clark (Fayetteville)
Doubles: Carey Causway (Wilson), Neiko Riggsbee (Carrboro)

1988–2004
Singles: No State Championships for 10-year-olds

2005
Singles: Olivia King (Raleigh)
Doubles: Jasmine Gabriel (Charlotte), Olivia King (Raleigh)

2006
Singles: Jasmine Gabriel (Charlotte)
Doubles: Jasmine Gabriel (Charlotte), Saisanjana Vattigunta (Charlotte)

2007
Singles: Nancy Bridges (Shelby)
Doubles: Nancy Bridges (Shelby), Hannah Templeton (Greensboro)

2008
Singles: Susanne Boyden (Raleigh)
Doubles: Susanne Boyden (Raleigh), Gianna Democko (Goldsboro)

2009
Singles: Tiffany Pyritz (Wake Forest)
Doubles: Abigail Markel (Charlotte), Tiffany Pyritz (Wake Forest)

2010
Singles, Spring Closed: Abigail Markel (Charlotte)
Singles, Summer Closed: Jenna Stachowiak (Cary)
Doubles: Abigail Markel (Charlotte), Tiffany Pyritz (Wake Forest)
Doubles: Abigail Forbes (Raleigh), Jenna Knors (Raleigh)

2011
Singles, Spring Closed: Natalie Lutz (Kings Mountain)
Singles, Summer Closed: Jenna Thompson (Charlotte)
Doubles: Emma Bixler (Charlotte), Kathryne Garrido (Gastonia)
Doubles: Karen Galush (Cary), Jenna Thompson (Charlotte)

GIRLS' 12S

1963
Singles: Carol Davenport (Greensboro)

1967
Singles: Emily Yarbrough (Durham)
Doubles: Emily Yarbrough (Durham), Julie Andrews (Greensboro)

1968
Singles: Patsy Millar (Winston–Salem)
Doubles: Julie Andrews (Greensboro), Margie Hartley (High Point)

1969
Singles: Lee Young (Shelby)
Doubles: Ann Dortch (Greensboro), Nanny Andrews (Greensboro)

1970
Singles: Ann Dortch (Greensboro)
Doubles: Ann Dortch (Greensboro), Meg Elmore (Madison)

1971
Singles: Cindy Corey (Chapel Hill)
Doubles: Cindy Corey (Chapel Hill), Debbie Southern (Winston–Salem)

NORTH CAROLINA JUNIOR STATE CLOSED CHAMPIONS
(CONTINUED)

1972
Singles: Wendy Corey (Chapel Hill)
Doubles: Elizabeth Hutchins (High Point), Elizabeth Tolson (New Bern)

1973
Singles: Wendy Corey (Chapel Hill)
Doubles: Dorothy Hamrick (Shelby), Nita Gilley (Winston–Salem)

1974
Singles: Amy Barnette (Charlotte)
Doubles: Starla Bunker, Liza Sharpless (Greensboro)

1975
Singles: Katherine Tolson (New Bern)
Doubles: Katherine Tolson (New Bern), Kelly Kavanaugh (Winston–Salem)

1976
Singles: Margaret Hogan (Raleigh)
Doubles: Margaret Hogan (Raleigh), Frannie Taylor (Winston–Salem)

1977
Singles: Mary Lloyd Hodges (Henderson)
Doubles: Laura Balentine (Charlotte), Mary Lloyd Hodges (Henderson)

1978
Singles: Vijatha Vijava (Henderson)
Doubles: Kim Vaughn (Greensboro), Kristin Rosenkampff (Shelby)

1979
Singles: Anna Coleman (Lexington)
Doubles: Fiz Anderson (Charlotte), Kristin Rosenkampff (Shelby)

1980
Singles: Susan Stanley (Charlotte)
Doubles: Saundra Davis, Kandi O'Connor (Thomasville)

1981
Singles: Jenee Cross (Winston–Salem)
Doubles: Jenee Cross (Winston–Salem), Tonya Damon (Salisbury)

1982
Singles: Susan Saunders (Salisbury)
Doubles: Beth Choate (Morganton), Carol Hancock (Hickory)

1983
Singles: Renika Shaw (Greensboro)
Doubles: Lisa Adelman (Greensboro), Beth Choate (Morganton)

1984
Singles: Wendy Thompson (Linville)
Doubles: Susannah Cobb (Thomasville), Jennifer Thomas (Chapel Hill)

1985
Singles: Margaret Kenny (Greensboro)
Doubles: Daniella Marx (Goldsboro), Lee Worrell (Goldsboro)

1986
Singles: Tory Schroeder (Carrboro)
Doubles: Dana Allen (Greensboro), Erin Smith (Greensboro)

1987
Singles: Tory Schroeder (Carrboro)
Doubles: Tory Schroeder (Carrboro), Blair Sutton (Fayetteville)

1988
Singles: Alexandra LaGrange (Horseshoe)
Doubles: Carey Causway (Wilson), Gina MacDonald (Raleigh)

1989
Singles: Gina MacDonald (Raleigh)
Doubles: Carey Causway (Wilson), Gina MacDonald (Raleigh)

1990
Singles: Francie Barragan (Fayetteville)
Doubles: Monika Jandera (Charlotte), Marissa Gildemeister (Durham)

1991
Singles: Jackie Houston (Kings Mountain)
Doubles: Christina Causway (Wilson), Sarah Taylor (Raleigh)

1992
Singles: Haley Chitty (Shelby)
Doubles: Christina Causway (Wilson), Sarah Taylor (Raleigh)

1993
Singles: Kendrick Bunn (Wilson)
Doubles: Haley Chitty (Shelby), Loni Worsley (Winston–Salem)

1994
Singles: Cory Ann Avants (Gastonia)
Doubles: Cory Ann Avants (Gastonia), Rankin Williams (Raleigh)

1995
Singles: Rankin Williams (Raleigh)
Doubles: Erin Logan (Goldsboro), Lauren Sears (Goldsboro)

1996
Singles: Bonnie Baird (Raleigh)
Doubles: Bonnie Baird (Raleigh), Ally Baker (Raleigh)

1997
Singles: Ally Baker (Raleigh)
Doubles: Katherine O'Herron (Raleigh), Christine Simpson (Raleigh)

1998
Singles: Meg Fanjoy (Statesville)
Doubles: Hanes Harris (Wilmington), Hannah Priest (Carthage)

1999
Singles: Kara Worsley (Winston–Salem)
Doubles: Ashley Bratton (Winston–Salem), Kara Worsley (Winston–Salem)

2000
Singles: Kasey Ellis (Charlotte)
Doubles: Jennifer Stone (Greensboro), Brooke Walter (Brown Summit)

2001
Singles: Winnie Quick (Greensboro)
Doubles: Kathryn Talbert (Mooresville), Stephanie Teague (Hickory)

2002
Singles: Megan Mariano (Huntersville)
Doubles: Maggie Dickens (Fayetteville), Lauren Sessoms (Belmont)

2003
Singles: Kathleen Elkins (Davidson)
Doubles: Christian Love (Rocky Mount), Lauren Herring (Greenville)

2004
Singles: Jenny Falcone (Davidson)
Doubles: None

2005
Singles: Alexandra Burgiss (Statesville)
Doubles: Alexandra Burgiss (Statesville), Taylor Davidson (Statesville)

2006
Singles: Madison Walters (Raleigh)
Doubles: Clare Cox (Greensboro), Brooke McAmis (Greensboro)

2007
Singles: Jessie Lynn Paul (Greenville)
Doubles: Jasmine Gabriel (Charlotte), Lauren Brooker (Wake Forest)

2008
Singles: Jasmine Gabriel (Charlotte)
Doubles: Nancy Bridges (Shelby), Kirsten Ward (Statesville)

2009
Singles: Elizabeth Ansari (Greensboro)
Doubles: Supriya Narisetti (Cary), Heidi Swope (Weddington)

2010
Singles, Spring Closed: Morgan Ingram (Charlotte)
Singles, Summer Closed: Abigail Markel (Charlotte)
Doubles: Morgan Ingram (Charlotte), Kennedy Wicker (Charlotte)
Doubles: Susanne Boyden (Raleigh), Gianna Democko (Goldsboro)

2011
Singles, Spring Closed: Abigail Markel (Charlotte)
Singles, Summer Closed: Tiffany Pyritz (Wake Forest)
Doubles, Spring Closed: Ann Taylor Hinton (Raleigh), Sophia Patel (Cary)
Doubles, Summer Closed: Meredith Krege (Greensboro), Sarah Pittard (Whitsett)

GIRLS' 14S

1963
Singles: Carol Davenport (Greensboro)

1964
Singles: Elizabeth Sloan (Winston-Salem)

1965
Singles: Carol Davenport (Greensboro)

1967
Singles: Stewart Smith (Winston-Salem)
Doubles: Stewart Smith (Winston-Salem), Sally Miller (Winston-Salem)

1968
Singles: Margaret Newbold (Raleigh)
Doubles: Margaret Newbold (Raleigh), Sally Schweppe (Shelby)

1969
Singles: Sally Schweppe (Shelby)
Doubles: Sally Schweppe (Shelby), Emily Yarbrough (Durham)

1970
Singles: Camey Timberlake (Lexington)
Doubles: Julie Andrews (Greensboro), Margie Hartley (High Point)

1971
Singles: Lee Young (Shelby)
Doubles: Lee Young (Shelby), Abbie Dowd (Matthews)

1972
Singles: Cindy Corey (Chapel Hill)
Doubles: Wendy Corey (Chapel Hill), Debbie Southern (Winston-Salem)

1973
Singles: Cindy Corey (Chapel Hill)
Doubles: Cindy Corey (Chapel Hill), Debbie Southern (Winston-Salem)

1974
Singles: Katherine Hogan (Raleigh)
Doubles: Jane Dudley (Winston-Salem), Beth Harrison (High Point)

1975
Singles: Wendy Corey (Chapel Hill)
Doubles: Starla Bunker, Amy Barnette (Charlotte)

1976
Singles: Kelly Cavanagh (Winston-Salem)
Doubles: Louise Allen (Winston-Salem), Eva Redfield (Asheville)

1977
Singles: Katherine Tolson (New Bern)
Doubles: Holly Mills (Hendersonville), Katherine Tolson (New Bern)

1978
Singles: Mary Lloyd Hodges (Henderson)
Doubles: Mary Lloyd Hodges (Henderson), Meg Callas (High Point)

1979
Singles: Meg Callas (High Point)
Doubles: Kim Lash (Winston-Salem), Laura Ballentine (Charlotte)

1980
Singles: Fiz Anderson (Charlotte)
Doubles: Vijitha Vijaya (Raleigh), Josie Ward (Greensboro)

NORTH CAROLINA JUNIOR STATE CLOSED CHAMPIONS
(CONTINUED)

1981
Singles: Anna Coleman (Lexington)
Doubles: Fiz Anderson (Charlotte), Spencer Barnes (Winston–Salem)

1982
Singles: Susan Stanley (Charlotte)
Doubles: Karen John (High Point), Becky Kopack (High Point)

1983
Singles: Susan Saunders (Salisbury)
Doubles: Becky Kopack (High Point), Alice Martin (Greensboro)

1984
Singles: Susan Saunders (Salisbury)
Doubles: Cacy Kinney (High Point), Susan Saunders (Salisbury)

1985
Singles: Jenny Boone (Raleigh)
Doubles: Jenny Boone (Raleigh), Christy Hedgpeth (Thomasville)

1986
Singles: Scotti Thomas (Durham)
Doubles: Vidhya Bashyam (Raleigh), Christy Hedgpeth (Thomasville)

1987
Singles: Daniella Marx (Goldsboro)
Doubles: Daniella Marx (Goldsboro), Lee Worrell (Goldsboro)

1988
Singles: Paige Powell (Greenville)
Doubles: Elizabeth Megorden (Charlotte), Jamie Miyares (High Point)

1989
Singles: Laura Cowman (Charlotte)
Doubles: Elizabeth Donovan (Hickory), Elizabeth Tuttle (Hickory)

1990
Singles: Hesta Fleming (Winston–Salem)
Doubles: Hesta Fleming (Winston–Salem), Somer Khanlarian (Greensboro)

1991
Singles: Francie Barragan (Fayetteville)
Doubles: Marissa Gildemeister (Durham), Beth Schroeder (Raleigh)

1992
Singles: Jackie Houston (Kings Mountain)
Doubles: Katrina Gildemeister (Durham), Marissa Gildemeister (Durham)

1993
Singles: Jackie Houston (Kings Mountain)
Doubles: Katrina Gildemeister (Durham), Caroline Hill (Chapel Hill)

1994
Singles: Caroline Hill (Chapel Hill)
Doubles: Katrina Gildemeister (Durham), Caroline Hill (Chapel Hill)

1995
Singles: Kendrick Bunn (Wilson)
Doubles: Lori Beth Walters (Lexington), Loni Worsley (Winston–Salem)

1996
Singles: Cory Ann Avants (Gastonia)
Doubles: Natalie Cherry (Washington), Lauren Williams (Chapel Hill)

1997
Singles: Rankin Williams (Raleigh)
Doubles: Kate LaCoste (Charlotte), Lauren Williams (Chapel Hill)

1998
Singles: Marilyn Clark (Chapel Hill)
Doubles: Marilyn Clark (Chapel Hill), Erin Logan (Goldsboro)

1999
Singles: Katherine O'Herron (Raleigh)
Doubles: Mary Cartner (Statesville), Laura Fanjoy (Statesville)

2000
Singles: Meg Fanjoy (Statesville)
Doubles: Laura Fanjoy (Statesville), Meg Fanjoy (Statesville)

2001
Singles: Catherine Newman (Greensboro)
Doubles: Logan Beam (Shelby), Kasey Ellis (Charlotte)

2002
Singles: Jennifer Stone (Greensboro)
Doubles: Kathryn Talbert (Mooresville), Jennifer Stone (Greensboro)

2003
Singles: Kathryn Talbert (Mooresville)
Doubles: Caroline Mauch (Durham), Heather Prior (Raleigh)

2004
Singles: Kayla Duncan (Winston–Salem)
Doubles: None

2005
Singles: Lauren Herring (Greenville)
Doubles: Jennifer Ansari (Greensboro), Lauren Herring (Greenville)

2006
Singles: Madeleine Hamilton (Greensboro)
Doubles: Madeleine Hamilton (Greensboro), Sarah Thomas (Wilson)

2007
Singles: Gabby Gabriel (Charlotte)
Doubles: Chloe Willetts (Winston–Salem), Sarah King (Raleigh)

2008
Singles: Jamie Rogers (Cary)
Doubles: Olivia King (Raleigh), Jessie Lynn Paul (Greenville)

2009
Singles: Jamie Rogers (Cary)
Doubles: Jennifer Moores (Wilmington), Jamie Rogers (Cary)

2010
Singles, Spring Closed: Jasmine Gabriel (Weddington)
Singles, Summer Closed: Hannah Templeton (Greensboro)

Doubles: Maggie Kane (Raleigh), Jamie Rogers (Cary)
Doubles: Samantha Smith (Cary), Hannah Templeton (Greensboro)

2011
Singles, Spring Closed: Kimberly Schubel (Cary)
Singles, Summer Closed: Susanne Boyden (Raleigh)
Doubles: Kara Summerford (Raleigh), Caroline Utt (Raleigh)
Doubles: Morgan Valentine (Waxaw), Karena Zhang (Cary)

GIRLS' 16S

1963
Singles: Ann Bingham (Lexington)

1964
Singles: Elizabeth Sloan (Winston–Salem)
Doubles: Elizabeth Sloan (Winston–Salem), Carol Davenport (Greensboro)

1965
Singles: Laura DuPont (Charlotte)

1966
Singles: Belinda Vaughn (Shelby)

1967
Singles: Donna Hartley (High Point)
Doubles: Donna Hartley (High Point), Carol Davenport (Greensboro)

1968
Singles: Stewart Smith (Winston–Salem)
Doubles: Stewart Smith (Winston–Salem), Jane Preyer (Greensboro)

1969
Singles: Stewart Smith (Winston–Salem)
Doubles: Stewart Smith (Winston–Salem), Jane Preyer (Greensboro)

1970
Singles: Sally Schweppe (Shelby)
Doubles: Sally Schweppe (Shelby), Margaret Newbold (Raleigh)

1971
Singles: Nina Cloaninger (Charlotte)
Doubles: Nina Cloaninger (Charlotte), Camey Timberlake (Lexington)

1972
Singles: Camey Timberlake (Lexington)
Doubles: Camey Timberlake (Lexington), Lee Young (Shelby)

1973
Singles: Lee Young (Shelby)
Doubles: Ann Dortch (Greensboro), Basye Hendrix (Greensboro)

1974
Singles: Ava Watkins (Raleigh)
Doubles: Margaret Scott (Wilmington), Donna Snipes (Goldsboro)

1975
Singles: Margaret Scott (Wilmington)
Doubles: Debbie Southern (Winston–Salem), Cindy Corey (Chapel Hill)

1976
Singles: Elizabeth Tolson (New Bern)
Doubles: Wendy Corey (Chapel Hill), Elizabeth Tolson (New Bern)

1977
Singles: Amy Barnette (Charlotte)
Doubles: Wendy Corey (Chapel Hill), Carola Hertle (Greensboro)

1978
Singles: Holly Mills (Hendersonville)

1979
Singles: Marshall Graham (Reidsville)
Doubles: Lisa Monaco (Fayetteville), Margit Monaco (Fayetteville)

1980
Singles: Meg Callas (High Point)
Doubles: Sara Turner (Raleigh), Donna Scheltinga (Raleigh)

1981
Singles: Spencer Barnes (Winston–Salem)
Doubles: Landis Cox (Greensboro), Meg Callas (High Point)

1982
Singles: Stacy Schefflin (Charlotte)
Doubles: Elizabeth Anderson (Charlotte), Spencer Barnes (Winston–Salem)

1983
Singles: Stacy Schefflin (Charlotte)

Doubles: Katie Boyer (Charlotte), Marion Stone (Greensboro)

1984
Singles: Jenee Cross (Winston–Salem)
Doubles: Diane Pensabene (Charlotte), Hani Sie (Charlotte)

1985
Singles: Jenee Cross (Winston–Salem)
Doubles: Cacy Kinney (High Point), Susan Saunders (Salisbury)

1986
Singles: Michelle Frye (Chapel Hill)
Doubles: Cacy Kinney (High Point), Susan Saunders (Salisbury)

1987
Singles: Scotti Thomas (Durham)
Doubles: Helen Spencer (Burlington), Scotti Thomas (Durham)

1988
Singles: Scotti Thomas (Durham)
Doubles: Scotti Thomas (Durham), Helen Spencer (Burlington)

1989
Singles: Shannon Clement (Southern Pines)
Doubles: Daniella Marx (Goldsboro), Lee Worrell (Goldsboro)

1990
Singles: Tory Schroeder (Chapel Hill)
Doubles: Elizabeth Donovan (Hickory), Natalie Teague (Hickory)

1991
Singles: Elizabeth Williams (Fayetteville)
Doubles: Natalie Teague (Hickory),

NORTH CAROLINA JUNIOR STATE CLOSED CHAMPIONS
(CONTINUED)

Elizabeth Tuttle (Hickory)

1992
Singles: Katherine Hilkey (Chapel Hill)
Doubles: Jeni Burnette (Raleigh), Claire Cheatwood (Fayetteville)

1993
Singles: Katrina Gildemeister (Durham)
Doubles: Jeni Burnette (Raleigh), Claire Cheatwood (Fayetteville)

1994
Singles: Elizabeth Haney (Durham)
Doubles: Blair Adams (Wilson), Kathryn Brown (Statesville)

1995
Singles: Dora Vastag (Chapel Hill)
Doubles: Holly Ann McFarland

(Statesville), Tiffany Speas (Winston–Salem)

1996
Singles: Christine Orban (Fayetteville)
Doubles: Katrina Gildemeister (Durham), Caroline Hill (Chapel Hill)

1997
Singles: Kendrick Bunn (Wilson)
Doubles: Amanda Devore (Fayetteville), Ja'net McWillis (Winston–Salem)

1998
Singles: Catherine Craven (Charlotte)
Doubles: Natalie Cherry (Washington), Elisha Mabe (Eden)

1999
Singles: Jessica Kesler (Wilmington)
Doubles: Amanda Paluch (Chapel Hill), Marilyn Clark (Chapel Hill)

2000
Singles: Neils T. Barringer (Durham)
Doubles: Marilyn Clark (Chapel Hill), Salem Kirven (Greensboro)

2001
Singles: Meredith Skeeters (Greensboro)
Doubles: Frances Blanton (Raleigh), Lisa Suggs (Fayetteville)

2002
Singles: Lindsey Stuckey (Greensboro)
Doubles: Mary Ford (Charlotte), Stephanie Goss (Charlotte)

2003
Singles: Melissa Wolf (Greensboro)
Doubles: Kelly Gillis (Statesville), Kathryn Talbert (Mooresville)

2004
Singles: Emily Mauser (Hickory)
Doubles: None

2005
Singles: Jennifer Ansari (Greensboro)
Doubles: Amber Arciero (Matthews), Mary Pate (Matthews)

2006
Singles: Kaitlin Burns (Wilmington)
Doubles: Emily Graybeal (Cary), Kirsten Kohagen (Raleigh)

Wake Forest Women's Team.

2007
Singles: Kathleen Elkins (Davidson)
Doubles: Lauren Frazier (Greenville), Kristen Joyner (Greenville)

2008
Singles: Taylor Davidson (Statesville)
Doubles: Taylor Davidson (Statesville), Brianna Norris (Charlotte)

2009
Singles: Smith Hinton (Raleigh)
Doubles: Smith Hinton (Raleigh), Chloe Willetts (Winston–Salem)

2010
Singles, Spring Closed: Smith Hinton (Raleigh)
Singles, Summer Closed: Mary Lee (Charlotte)
Doubles: Gabby Gabriel (Weddington), Jasmine Gabriel (Weddington)
Doubles: Maggie Kane (Raleigh), Jamie Rogers (Cary)

2011
Singles, Spring Closed: Kaitlyn McCarthy (Cary)
Singles, Summer Closed: Maggie Kane (Raleigh)
Doubles: Maggie Kane (Raleigh), Jamie Rogers (Cary)
Doubles: Kalli Karas (Waxhaw), Mary Lee (Charlotte)

GIRLS' 18S

1946
Singles: Nancy Burton (Greensboro)
Doubles: Nancy Burton (Greensboro), Julia Anne Olgetree (Greensboro)

1947
Singles: Julia Anne Ogletree (Greensboro)

1948
Singles: Pat Pinyan (Greensboro)
Doubles: Pat Pinyan (Greensboro), Janice Richmond (Greensboro)

1949
Singles: Mary Lou Jones (Sanford)

1950
Singles: Ann Carlson (Greensboro)
Doubles: Ann Carlson (Greensboro), Mary Lou Jones (Sanford)

1955
Singles: Kitty Dixon (Asheville)
Doubles: Pat Henry (Thomasville), Lillian Bullock (Southern Pines)

1956
Singles: Lillian Bullock (Southern Pines)

1962
Singles: Sally O'Rourke (Charlotte)

1963
Singles: Jane Davenport (Greensboro)

1965
Singles: Laura DuPont (Charlotte)

1966
Singles: Laura DuPont (Charlotte)
Doubles: Elizabeth Sloan (Winston–Salem), Belinda Vaughn (Shelby)

1967
Singles: Elizabeth Sloan (Winston–Salem)

1968
Singles: Belinda Vaughn (Shelby)
Doubles: Belinda Vaughn (Shelby), Suzanne Meads (Winston–Salem)

1969
Singles: Jo Ann Peacock (Goldsboro)
Doubles: Donna Hartley (High Point), Carol Davenport (Greensboro)

1970
Singles: Beth Hamilton (Cullowhee)

1971
Singles: Jane Preyer (Greensboro)
Doubles: Jane Preyer (Greensboro), Stewart Smith (Winston–Salem)

1972
Singles: Sally Schweppe (Shelby)
Doubles: Sally Schweppe (Shelby), Nina Cloaninger (Charlotte)

1973
Singles: Camey Timberlake (Lexington)

Doubles: Camey Timberlake (Lexington), Nina Cloaninger (Charlotte)

1974
Singles: Camey Timberlake (Lexington)
Doubles: Linda Matthews, Sydney Swain

1975
Singles: Susie Black (Greensboro)
Doubles: Hunter Dortch (Greensboro), Ava Watkins (Raleigh)

1976
Singles: Hunter Dortch (Greensboro)
Doubles: Hunter Dortch (Greensboro), Kim Clarke (Kernersville)

1977
Singles: Louise Allen (Winston–Salem)
Doubles: Ann Frautschi (Chapel Hill), Hope McArn (Laurinburg)

1978
Singles: Louise Allen (Winston–Salem)
Doubles: Louise Allen (Winston–Salem), Mary Hutson (Arden)

1979
Singles: Louise Allen (Winston–Salem)
Doubles: Louise Allen (Winston–Salem), Marshall Graham (Reidsville)

1980
Singles: Stephanie Rauch (Gastonia)
Doubles: Starla Bunker (Salisbury), Katherine Tolson (New Bern)

1981
Singles: Kim Lash (Winston–Salem)
Doubles: Laura Barnett, Laura Ballentine (Charlotte)

1982
Singles: Marshall Graham (Reidsville)
Doubles: Laura Balentine (Charlotte), Kim Lash (Winston–Salem)

1983
Singles: Mary Lloyd Hodges (Henderson)
Doubles: Landis Cox (Greensboro),

NORTH CAROLINA JUNIOR STATE CLOSED CHAMPIONS (CONTINUED)

Josie Ward (Greensboro)

1984
Singles: Katie Boyer (Charlotte)
Doubles: Elizabeth Anderson (Charlotte), Spencer Barnes (Winston–Salem)

1985
Singles: Paige Fisher (Battleboro)
Doubles: Diane Pensabene (Charlotte), Nori Sie (Charlotte)

1986
Singles: Renika Shaw (Greensboro)
Doubles: Kari Howe (Raleigh), Barbara Johnson (Cary)

1987
Singles: Lisa Adelman (Greensboro)
Doubles: Kari Howe (Raleigh), Bonnie Johnson (Cary)

1988
Singles: Bonnie Johnson (Cary)
Doubles: Jenny Boone, Margaret Bridger (Raleigh)

1989
Singles: Helen Spencer (Burlington)
Doubles: Susannah Cobb (Chapel Hill), Christy Hedgpeth (Thomasville)

1990
Singles: Helen Spencer (Burlington)
Doubles: Helen Spencer (Burlington), Scotti Thomas (Durham)

1991
Singles: Cara White (Henderson)
Doubles: Shannon Clement (Southern Pines), Cara White (Henderson)

1992
Singles: Elizabeth Megordon (Charlotte)
Doubles: Angie Roberts (Chapel Hill), Elizabeth Tuttle (Hickory)

1993
Singles: Elizabeth Williams (Fayetteville)
Doubles: Hesta Fleming (Winston–Salem), Wendy Kulp (Winston–Salem)

1994
Singles: Jeni Burnette (Raleigh)
Doubles: Jeni Burnette (Raleigh), Claire Cheatwood (Fayetteville)

1995
Singles: Caroline Hill (Chapel Hill)
Doubles: Katherine Annas (Charlotte), Rebecca Weeks (Charlotte)

1996
Singles: Dora Vastag (Chapel Hill)
Doubles: Bobbi Guthrie (Raleigh), Brooke Skeen (Burlington)

1997
Singles: Kealy Carter (Thomasville)
Doubles: Carla Simpson (Cameron), Charlene Figgins (Wilmington)

1998
Singles: Loni Worsley (Winston–Salem)
Doubles: Kelly Cantrell (Greensboro), Lauren Burrow (Charlotte)

1999
Singles: Loni Worsley (Winston–Salem)
Doubles: Natalie Cherry (Washington), Elisha Mabe (Eden)

2000
Singles: Jessica Kesler (Wilmington)
Doubles: Jessica Kesler (Wilmington), Alena Simmonds (Raleigh)

2001
Singles: Kelly Fleck (Statesville)
Doubles: Kelly Fleck (Statesville), Elizabeth Kernodle (Burlington)

2002
Singles: Emily Wade (Raleigh)
Doubles: Katherine Marshall (Raleigh), Joanie Winter (Raleigh)

2003
Singles: Amanda Taillfer (Raleigh)
Doubles: Amanda Taillfer (Raleigh), Rhodes Proctor (Raleigh)

2004
Singles: Hanes Harris (Wilmington)
Doubles: None

2005
Singles: Alexa Ely (Asheville)
Doubles: Alexa Ely (Asheville), Anna Lee Evans (Vilas)

2006
Singles: Jenny Falcone (Davidson)
Doubles: Winnie Quick (Greensboro), Stephanie Teague (Hickory)

2007
Singles: Aleah Marrow (Durham)
Doubles: Aleah Marrow (Durham), Amanda Marrow (Durham)

2008
Singles: Kirsten Kohagen (Raleigh)
Doubles: Kirsten Kohagen (Raleigh), Abby Richmond (Edenton)

2009
Singles: Brooke McAmis (Greensboro)
Doubles: Grace Baker (Charlotte), Neena Wanko (Southern Pines)

2010
Singles, Spring Closed: Taylor Davidson (Statesville)
Singles, Summer Closed: Taylor Davidson (Statesville)
Doubles: Taylor Davidson (Statesville), Brooke McAmis (Greensboro)
Doubles: Lauren Frazier (Greenville), Hamilton Lovett (Raleigh)

2011
Singles, Spring Closed: Taylor Davidson (Statesville)
Singles, Summer Closed: Katherine Butler (Charlotte)
Doubles: Taylor Davidson (Statesville), Brooke McAmis (Greensboro)
Doubles: Clare Cox (Greensboro), Brooke McAmis (Greensboro)

ADULT STATE CLOSED CHAMPIONS HISTORY

1927
Men's singles: Bob Crosland; Women's (s): Mrs. G. Ward Finley; Mixed: Mr. and Mrs. G. Ward Finley

1928
Men's (s): Bob Elliott; Women's (s): Mrs. D.H. Butner; Mixed: Not Held

1929
Men's (s): Grady Frank; Women's (s): Not Held; Mixed: Not Held

1930–1934
Not Held

1935
Men's (s): John Vernon; Mens's (d): John Vernon, Carlyle Lewis; Women's (s): Anne Martindale; Womens's (d): Not Held; Mixed: Not Held

1936
Men's (s): Archie Henderson; Mens's (d): Archie Henderson, Byron Abels; Women's (s): Anne Martindale; Womens's (d): Not Held; Mixed: Not Held

1937
Men's (s): Clayton Burwell; Mens's (d): Archie Henderson, Byron Abels; Women's (s): Anne Martindale; Womens's (d): Not Held; Mixed: Not Held

1938
Men's (s): Clayton Burwell; Mens's (d): Robert Lovill, Eugene Goodes; Women's (s): Mary M. Binford; Womens's (d): Not Held; Mixed: Not Held

1939
Men's (s): Eugene Goodes; Mens's (d): Robert Lovill, Eugene Goodes; Women's (s): Mrs. C.B. Hall; Womens's (d): Mrs. James Kelly, Rhoda Widery; Mixed: Not Held

1940
Men's (s): Clayton Burwell; Mens's (d): Grady Frank, Bob Spurrier; Women's (s): Anne Martindale; Womens's (d): Anne Martindale, Eloise McLean; Mixed: Not Held

1941
Men's (s): Hughes Davis; Mens's (d): Byron Abels, Eugene Goodes; Women's (s): Ethel Norton; Womens's (d): Ethel Norton, Mrs. C.B. Hall; Mixed: Not Held

1942
Men's (s): Bob Spurrier; Mens's (d): Bob Spurrier, Teddy Keesler; Women's (s): Frances Boyd; Womens's (d): Frances Boyd, Barbara Strongmiller; Mixed: Not Held

1943
Men's (s): Hubert Barrier; Mens's (d): Carlyle Lewis, Tom Gold; Women's (s): Elizabeth Hardin; Womens's (d): Not Held; Mixed: Not Held

1944
Men's (s): Barney Welsh; Mens's (d): Jimmy Trotter, Joe Lee; Women's (s): Frances Boyd; Womens's (d): Not Held; Mixed: Not Held

1945
Men's (s): Tom Chambers; Mens's (d): Tom Chambers, Hubert Barrier; Women's (s): Virginia Ketner; Womens's (d): Gertrude Archer, Virginia Ketner; Mixed: Not Held

1946
Men's (s): Hughes Davis; Mens's (d): Eddie DeGray, Lenoir Wright; Women's (s): Anne Martindale; Womens's (d): Gertrude Archer, Leone Bell; Mixed: Not Held

1947
Men's (s): Bo Roddey; Mens's (d): Carlyle Lewis, Eugune Goodes; Women's (s): Anne Martindale; Womens's (d): Anne Martindale, Leone Bell; Mixed: Not Held

1948
Men's (s): Teddy Keesler; Mens's (d): Teddy Keesler, Heath Alexander; Women's (s): Anne Martindale; Womens's (d): Audrey Brown, Mary Ruth Davis; Mixed: Not Held

ADULT STATE CLOSED CHAMPIONS HISTORY (CONTINUED)

1949
Men's (s): Bo Roddey; Mens's (d): Bo Roddey, Whit Cobb; Women's (s): Anne Martindale; Womens's (d): Audrey Brown, Mary Ruth Davis; Mixed: Not Held

1950
Men's (s): Buddy Ager; Mens's (d): Buddy Ager, Maurice Fincher; Women's (s): Audrey Brown; Womens's (d): Audrey Brown, Mary Ruth Davis; Mixed: Not Held

1951
Men's (s): Bo Roddey; Mens's (d): Bo Roddey, Heath Alexander; Women's (s): Audrey Brown; Womens's (d): Audrey Brown, Mary Ruth Davis; Mixed: Audrey Brown, Charles Morris

1952
Men's (s): Bo Roddey; Mens's (d): Bo Roddey, Heath Alexander; Women's (s): Audrey Brown; Womens's (d): Audrey Brown, Mary Ruth Davis; Mixed: Canceled—rain

1953
Men's (s): Frank Keister; Mens's (d): Lou Faquin, Whit Cobb; Women's (s): Sarah Walters; Womens's (d): Sarah Walters, Mary Lou Jones; Mixed: Canceled—rain

1954
Men's Open (s): Lacy Keesler; Men's Open (d): Lacy Keesler, Dewey Keesler; Men's 40s (s): Bill Carrigan; Men's 40s (d): Dudley Cowden, H.S. McGinty; Women's Open (s): Audrey Brown; Women's Open (d): Audrey Brown, Mary Lou Jones; Mixed: Julia Anne Holt, Dewey Keesler

1955
Men's Open (s): Sam Daniel; Men's Open (d): Sam Daniel, Jack Warmath; Men's 40s (s): Bill Carrigan; Men's 40s (d): Sam Ravenel, H.S. McGinty; Women's Open (s): Frances Hogan; Women's Open (d): Rosalie Bryant, Mary Lou Jones; Mixed: Frances Hogan, Norm Jarrard

1956
Men's Open (s): Sam Daniel; Men's Open (d): Sam Daniel, Jack Warmath; Men's 40s (s): Bill Carrigan; Men's 40s (d): Carlyle Lewis, Ed Armfield; Women's Open (s): Sarah Walters; Women's Open (d): Julia Anne Holt, Mary Lou Jones; Mixed: Mary Lou Jones, Sam Daniel

1957
Men's Open (s): Sam Daniel; Men's Open (d): Herb Browne, Ed Hudgins; Men's 40s (s): Fred West; Men's 40s (d): Fred West, H.S. McGinty; Women's Open (s): Sarah Walters; Women's Open (d): Julia Anne Holt, Mary Lou Jones; Mixed: Sara Walter, Herb Browne

1958
Men's Open (s): Allen Morris; Men's Open (d): Sam Daniel, Jack Warmath; Men's 40s (s): Gil Stacy; Men's 40s (d): Carlyle Lewis, Bill Carrigan; Women's Open (s): Sarah Walters; Women's Open (d): Julia Anne Holt, Joanne Cooper; Mixed: Julia Anne Holt, Allen Morris

1959
Men's Open (s): Sam Daniel; Men's Open (d): Ted Keelser, Tommy Holder Men's 40s (s): Gil Stacy; Men's 40s (d): Carlyle Lewis, Bill Carrigan; Women's Open (s): Raymonde Jones; Women's Open (d): Raymonde Jones, Mrs Burke Davis; Mixed: Julia Anne Holt, Ted Keesler

1960
Men's Open (s): Sam Daniel; Men's Open (d): Malcom Clark, Charles Shaffer; Men's 45s (s): Gil Stacy; Men's 45s (d): Gil Stacy, C.R. Council; Women's Open (s): Joanne Cooper; Women's Open (d): Carol Craver, Joanne Cooper; Mixed: Joanne Cooper, Malcom Clark

1961
Men's Open (s): Allen Morris; Men's Open (d): Bo Roddey, Jack Warmath; Men's 45s (s): Fred West; Men's 45s (d): Carlyle Lewis, Bill Carrigan; Women's Open (s): Sarah Walters; Women's Open (d): Sarah Walters, Helen Mayer; Mixed: Carol Craver, Semi Mintz

1962
Men's Open (s): Allen Morris; Men's Open (d): Allen Morris, Jack Warmath; Men's 45s (s): Fred West; Men's 45s (d): Ed Armfield, Bob Edmunds; Women's Open (s): Joanne Cooper; Women's Open (d): Joanne Cooper, Julia Anne Holt; Mixed: Emily Preyer, Bo Roddey

1963
Men's Open (s): Allen Morris; Men's Open (d): Allen Morris, Jack Warmath; Men's 45s (s): Fred West; Men's 45s (d): Ed Armfield, Bob Edmunds; Women's Open (s): Alicia Smythe; Women's Open (d): Alicia Smythe, Betty Brown; Mixed: Julia Anne Holt, Ted Keesler

1964
Men's Open (s): Allen Morris; Men's Open (d): Allen Morris, Jack Warmath; Men's 45s (s): Fred West; Men's 45s (d): Ed Armfield, Bob Edmunds; Women's Open (s): Alicia Smythe; Women's Open (d): Alicia Smythe, Betty Brown; Mixed: Betty Brown, Jack Warmath; Father–Son: Fred West, Ken West

1965
Men's Open (s): Allen Morris; Men's Open (d): Norman Chambers, Bob Light; Men's 45s (s): Fred West; Men's 45s (d): John A. Farfour, Henry Clark; Women's Open (s): Bonnie Logan; Women's Open (d): Julia Anne Holt, Helen Mayer; Mixed:

Julia Anne Holt, Paul Caldwell; Father–Son: Jim Hamiltion, Gene Hamilton

1966
Men's Open (s): Gene Hamilton; Men's Open (d): Jim Kyle, Marshall Happer; Men's 45s (s): Jim Hamilton; Men's 45s (d): Bob Edmunds, Ed Armfield; Women's Open (s): Julia Anne Holt; Women's Open (d): Julia Anne Holt, Laura DuPont; Mixed: Julia Anne Holt, Paul Caldwell; Father–Son: Jim Hamilton, Gene Hamilton

1967
Men's Open (s): Allen Morris Men's Open (d): Gene Hamilton, Marshall Happer; Men's 35s (s): Sam Woods; Men's 35s (d): Sam Woods, Dewey Keesler; Men's 45s (s): Buck Archer; Men's 45s (d): Buck Archer, Bob Spurrier; Men's 55s (s): William Powell; Men's 55s (d): Paul Jones, Vince Meunier; Women's Open (s): Laura DuPont; Women's Open (d): Julia Anne Holt, Laura DuPont; Women's 35s (s): Julia Anne Holt; Women's 35s (d): none; Mixed: Laura DuPont, Jack Lowe; Father–Son: Jim Hamilton, Gene Hamilton

1968
Men's Open (s): Mike Green; Men's Open (d): Mike Green, Herb Browne; Men's 35s: Herb Browne; Men's 35s (d): Sam Woods, Herb Browne; Men's 45s (s): Buck Archer; Men's 45s (d): Buck Archer, Bob Spurrier; Men's 55s (s): Vince Connerat; Men's 55s (d): Vince Connerat, Allen Smith; Women's Open (s): Julia Anne Holt; Women's Open (d): Mary Lou Jones, Nancy deGrummond; Women's 35s (s): Julia Anne Holt; Women's 35s (d): Julia Anne Holt, Helen Meyer; Mixed: Bonnie Logan, Lenward Simpson; Father–Son: Fred and Ken West

1969
Men's Open (s): Gene Hamilton; Men's Open (d): Gene Hamilton, Norman Chambers; Men's 35s: Herb Browne; Men's 35s (d): Lacy

Keesler, Dewey Keesler; Men's 45s (s): Buck Archer; Men's 45s (d): Buck Archer, Bob Spurrier; Men's 55s (s): Vince Connerat; Men's 55s (d): Vince Connerat, Allen Smith; Women's Open (s): Laura DuPont; Women's Open (d): Betty Brown, Bonnie Logan; Women's 35s (s): Mary Lou Jones; Women's 35s (d): none; Mixed: Bonnie Logan, Lenward Simpson; Father–Son: Fred and Ken West

1970
Men's Open (s): Gene Hamilton; Men's Open (d): Jim Donnan, Sanji Arisawa; Men's 35s: Norman Schellenger; Men's 35s (d): Norman Schellenger, Bill Long; Men's 45s (s): Buck Archer; Men's 45s (d): Buck Archer, Bob Spurrier; Men's 55s (s): Vince Connerat; Men's 55s (d): Vince Connerat, Claude Brown; Women's Open (s): Bonnie Logan; Women's Open (d): Betty Brown, Bonnie Logan; Women's 35s (s): Julia Anne Holt; Women's 35s (d): Mary Lou Jones, Loa Morris; Mixed: Unknown; Father–Son: Fred and Ken West

1971
Men's Open (s): Keith Stoneman; Men's Open (d): Gene Hamilton, Jim Corn; Men's 35s (s): Norman Schellenger; Men's 35s (d): Norman Schellenger, Bill Long; Men's 45s (s): Buck Archer; Men's 45s (d): Buck Archer, Bob Spurrier; Men's 55s (s): Fred West; Men's 55s (d): Fred West, Allen Smith; Women's Open (s): Bev Cansler; Women's Open (d): Bev Cansler, Nina Cloaninger; Women's 35s (s): Mary Lou Jones; Women's 35s (d): Mildred Southern, Sylvia Gilley; Mixed: Mary Lou Jones, Sanji Arisawa; Father–Son: John and Lee Brummet

1972
Men's Open (s): Gene Hamilton; Men's Open (d): Jim Amaya, Tommy Dixon; Men's 35s: Norman Schellenger; Men's 35s (d): not listed; Men's 45s (s) Buck Archer; Men's 45s (d): Buck Archer, Bob Spurrier; Men's 50s (s): Bob Spurrier; Men's 50s (d):

Bob Spurrier, Frank Love; Men's 55s (s): Vince Connerat; Men's 55s (d): Unknown; Women's Open (s): Bev Cansler; Women's Open (d): Bev Cansler, Nina Cloaninger; Women's 35s (s): Unknown; Women's 35s (d): Unknown; Mixed Open: Bev Cansler, Norman Chambers; Father–Son: Dick and Richard McKee

1973
Men's Open (s): Jim Amaya; Men's Open (d): Jim Amaya, Tommy Dixon; Men's 35s: Norman Schellenger; Men's 35s (d): Norman Chambers, Herb Browne; Men's 45s (s): Buck Archer; Men's 45s (d): Buck Archer, Bob Spurrier; Men's 50s (s): Buck Archer; Men's 50s (d): Bob Spurrier, Frank Love; Men's 55s (s): Vince Connerat; Men's 55s (d): Harold Southern, Dick Legrand; Men's 60s (s): Vince Connerat; Men's 60s (d): unknown; Women's Open (s): Camey Timberlake; Women's Open (d): Camey Timberlake, Bev Culbertson; Women's 35s (s): Bev Culbertson; Women's 35s (d): Mary Lou Jones, Frances Hogan; Women's 45s (s): Mildred Southern; Women's 45s (d): June Derby, Helen Jones; Mixed Open: Camey Timberlake, Ray Lake; Father–Son: Dave and Tim Wilkison

1974
Men's Open (s): Bob Koury; Men's Open (d): Buster Brown, Gene Hamilton; Men's 35s: Norman Chambers; Men's 35s (d): Norman Chambers, Fred Farzanegan; Men's 45s (s): Buck Archer; Men's 45s (d): Buck Archer, Bob Spurrier; Men's 50s (s): Buck Archer; Men's 50s (d): Buck Archer, Bob Spurrier; Men's 55s (s): Fred West; Men's 55s (d): MB Allen, Allen Smith; Men's 60s (s): Vince Connerat; Men's 60s (d): unknown; Women's Open (s): Jane Preyer; Women's Open (d): Ginger Oakman, Liz Wagner; Women's 35s (s): Bev Culbertson; Women's 35s (d): Bev Culbertson, Sara Jones; Women's 45s (s): Sara Jones; Women's 45s

ADULT STATE CLOSED CHAMPIONS HISTORY (CONTINUED)

(d): Sara Jones, R. Fogartie; Mixed Open: Sally Schweppe, Herb McKim; Father–Son: Jerry Robinson, Sr. and Jerry Robinson, Jr.

1975
Men's Open (s): Tim Wilkison; Men's Open (d): Buster Brown, Gene Hamilton; Men's 35s: Allen Morris; Men's 35s (d): N. Schellenger, Jim Watson; Men's 45s (s): Buck Archer; Men's 45s (d): Buck Archer, Bob Spurrier; Men's 50s (s): Buck Archer; Men's 50s (d): Buck Archer, Bob Spurrier; Men's 55s (s): George Himadi; Men's 55s (d): MB Allen, Allen Smith; Men's 60s (s): Vince Connerat; Men's 60s (d): Vince Connerat, Ralph Rockett; Men's 70s (s): Rossie Shore; Men's 70s (d): Rossie Shore, Henry Sapp; Women's Open (s): Katherine Hogan; Women's Open (d): Jane Preyer, Beth Hamilton; Women's 35s (s): Bev Culbertson; Women's 35s (d): Bev Culbertson, Sara Jones; Women's 40s (s): June Sheppard; Women's 40s (d): Frances Hogan, Mary Lou Jones; Women's 45s (s): Mildred Southern; Women's 45s (d): Mildred Southern, Frances Hogan; Women's 50s (s): Mildred Southern; Women's 50s (d): Mildred Southern, Frances Hogan; Mixed Open: Ginger Oakman, Jim Amaya; Father–Son: Dewey and Dee Keesler

1976
Men's Open (s): Tim Wilkison; Men's Open (d): Tim Wilkison, Allen Farfour; Men's 35s: Allen Morris; Men's 35s (d): Bo Roddey, Herb Browne; Men's 40s (s): Maurice Everette; Men's 40s (d): Maurice Everette, Al Griffin; Men's 45s (s): Norman Schellenger; Men's 45s (d): Buck Archer, Norman Schellenger;

Men's 50s (s): Buck Archer; Men's 50s (d): Buck Archer, Bob Spurrier; Men's 55s (s): Bill Umstaedter; Men's 55s (d): Curt Walden, Frank Love; Men's 60s (s): Fred West; Men's 60s (d): Harold Southern, Dick Legrand; Men's 70s (s): H.S. McGinty; Men's 70s (d): H.S. McGinty, Rossie Shore; Women's Open (s): Susie Black; Women's Open (d): Jeanne Scott, Linda Matthews; Women's 35s (s): June Sheppard; Women's 35s (d): June Sheppard, Dickie Tyler; Women's 40s (s): June Sheppard; Women's 40s (d): Sylvia Gillery, Mary Lou Jones; Women's 45s (s): Sara Jones; Women's 45s (d): June Derby, Hazel Jones; Women's 50s (s): Romi Topp; Women's 50s (d): Hazel Jones, Phyllis Ingram; Women's 60s (s): Margery Mize; Women's 60s (d): Margaret Craver, Margaret Trotter; Mixed Open: Susie Black, Garry Cooper; Father–Son: Cy King, Cy King, Jr.

1977
Men's Open (s): Robbie Smith; Men's Open (d): Scott Dillon, Andy Andrews; Men's 35s: Bobby Andrews; Men's 35s (d): Bo Roddey, Herb Browne; Men's 40s (s): Maurice Everette; Men's 40s (d): Maurice Everette, Al Griffin; Men's 45s (s): Allen Morris; Men's 45s (d): Bo Roddey, Jack Warmath; Men's 50s (s): Buck Archer; Men's 50s (d): George Simkins, Norman Jarrard; Men's 55s (s): Frank Love; Men's 55s (d): Buck Archer, Frank Love; Men's 60s (s): Lloyd Hanson; Men's 60s (d): Bob Edmunds, Ed Armfield; Men's 65s (s): Vince Connerat; Men's 65s (d): Vince Connerat, Allen Smith; Men's 70s (s): H.S. McGinty; Men's 70s (d): H.S. McGinty, Rossie Shore; Women's Open (s): Jane Preyer; Women's Open (d): Susie Black, Kerry Young; Women's 35s (s): Dickie Tyler; Women's 35s (d): Ellen Adelman, Julia Anne Holt; Women's 40s (s): Julia Anne Holt; Women's 40s (d): June Sheppard, Sara Jones; Women's 45s (s): Julia Anne Holt; Women's

45s (d): Sara Jones, Mary Lou Jones; Women's 50s (s): Mildred Southern; Women's 50s (d): Hazel Jones, Phyllis Ingram; Women's 55s (s): Mildred Southern; Women's 55s (d): Mildred Southern, Kitty Harrison; Women's 60s (s): Unknown; Women's 60s (d): Margaret Craver, Margaret Trotter; Mixed Open: Elizabeth Tolson, Dee Blankenhorn; Mixed Open Over 40s: Mary Lou Jones, Maurice Everette; Father–Son: not held

1978
Men's Open (s): Mike Czarnecki; Men's Open (d): Mike Czarnecki, John Hill; Men's 35s: Keith Stoneman; Men's 35s (d): Keith Stoneman, Herb Browne; Men's 40s (s): Norman Chambers; Men's 40s (d): Buck Archer, Don Miller Men's 45s (s): Norman Schellenger; Men's 45s (d): Bo Roddey, Jack Warmath; Men's 50s (s): Buck Archer; Men's 50s (d):George Simkins, Norman Jarrard; Men's 55s (s): Curt Walden; Men's 55s (d): Buck Archer, Bob Spurrier; Men's 60s (s): Eugene Goodes; Men's 60s (d): Mac Allen, Allen Smith Men's 65s (s): Vince Connerat; Men's 65s (d): Vince Connerat, Allen Smith; Men's 70s (s): H.S. McGinty; Men's 70s (d): H.S. McGinty, Rossie Shore; Women's Open (s): Louise Allen; Women's Open (d): Louise Allen, Cindy Corey; Women's 35s (s): Liz Wagner; Women's 35s (d): Dickie Tyler, Bev Culbertson; Women's 40s (s): June Sheppard; Women's 40s (d): June Sheppard, Sara Jones; Women's 45s (s): June Sheppard; Women's 45s (d): Sara Jones, June Sheppard; Women's 50s (s): Mildred Southern; Women's 50s (d): Hazel Jones, June Derby; Women's 55s (s): Mildred Southern; Women's 55s (d): Mildred Southern, Hazel Jones; Women's 60s (s): Elizabeth Brown; Women's 60s (d): Frances Council, Velma Jean Clary; Mixed Open: Cindy Corey, Allen Farfour; Mixed Open Over 40s: Georgeanna Anderson and Don Anderson; Mixed Open Over 45s: Kent and Martha Hathaway; Father–Son: not held

1979

Men's Open (s): Buster Brown; Men's Open (d): Andy Avram, Mike Czarnecki; Men's 35s: William Poore; Men's 35s (d): Jack Warmath, Bo Roddey; Men's 40s (s): Norman Chambers; Men's 40s (d): Buck Archer, Norman Chambers; Men's 45s (s): Herb Browne; Men's 45s (d): Bo Roddey, Jack Warmath; Men's 50s (s): Buck Archer; Men's 50s (d): Bob Jones, Sam Wood Men's 55s (s): Buck Archer; Men's 55s (d): Buck Archer, Bob Spurrier; Men's 60s (s): Eugene Goodes; Men's 60s (d): Mac Allen, Allen Smith Men's 65s (s): J.L. Suttle; Men's 65s (d): Vince Connerat, Allen Smith; Men's 70s (s): William Powell; Men's 70s (d): William Powell, Sam McNeely; Women's Open (s): Louise Allen; Women's Open (d): Louise Allen, Cindy Corey; Women's 35s (s): Liz Wagner; Women's 35s (d): Dickie Tyler, Bev Culbertson; Women's 40s (s): Dickie Tyler; Women's 40s (d): June Sheppard, Dickie Tyler; Women's 45s (s): June Sheppard; Women's 45s (d): Sara Jones, June Sheppard; Women's 50s (s): Sara Jones; Women's 50s (d): June Derby, Hazel Jones; Women's 55s (s): Mildred Southern; Women's 55s (d): Mildred Southern, Hazel Jones; Women's 60s (s): Elizabeth Brown; Women's 60s (d): Frances Council, Velma Jean Clary; Mixed Open: Louise Allen, John Allen Farfour; Mixed Open Over 35s: Dan Elks, Penny Brawley; Mixed Open Over 45s: Maurice Everette, Vicki Everette; Father–Son: Sidney Martin and Sammy Martin; Mother–Daughter: Katherine Sammons and Chris Sammons

1980

Men's Open (s): Keith Richardson; Men's Open (d): Allen Farfour, Mike Czarnecki; Men's 35s: William Poore; Men's 35s (d): Norman Chambers, Maurice Everette; Men's 40s (s): Norman Chambers; Men's 40s (d): Norman Chambers, Maurice Everette; Men's 45s (s):

Jerry Robinson

Dick Makepeace; Men's 45s (d): Bo Roddey, Jack Warmath; Men's 50s (s): Buck Archer; Men's 50s (d): Bob Jones, Sam Wood Men's 55s (s): Art Culbertson; Men's 55s (d): Curt Walden, Frank Heberer; Men's 60s (s): Charles Eppinette; Men's 60s (d):Charles Eppinette, Paul Richardson; Men's 65s (s): Paul Guibord; Men's 65s (d): Vince Connerat, Allen Smith; Men's 70s (s): Vince Connerat; Men's 70s (d): Vince Connerat, Sam McNeely; Women's Open (s): Louise Allen; Women's Open (d): Cindy Corey, Susan Sadri; Women's 35s (s): Dickie Tyler; Women's 35s (d): Dickie Tyler, Bev Culbertson; Women's 40s (s): Julia Anne Holt; Women's 40s (d): Wendy Wilson, Helen Phillips; Women's 45s (s): June Sheppard; Women's 45s (d): Julia Anne Holt, Barbara Spencer; Women's 50s (s): Mildred Southern; Women's 50s (d): Hazel Jones, June Derby; Women's 55s (s): Romi Topp; Women's 55s (d): Mildred Southern, Hazel Jones; Women's 60s (s): Frances Council; Women's 60s (d): Mattie Canady, Margery Mize; Mixed Open: Dick Spong, Sharron Judy; Mixed Open Over 35s: Jim Haslam, Dickie Tyler; Mixed Open Over 40s: Maurice Everette, Vicki Everette; Mixed Open Over 50s: Bob Spurrier, June Derby; Father–Son: Dick Makepeace and Walton Makepeace; Mother–Daughter: Emily Preyer and Emily Preyer

1981

Men's Open (s): Bill Csipkay; Men's Open (d): Allen Farfour, Mike Czarnecki; Men's 35s: Norman Chambers; Men's 35s (d): Stan Cocke, Bill Eidson; Men's 40s (s): Keith Stoneman; Men's 40s (d): Stan Cocke, Bill Eidson Men's 45s (s): Buck Archer; Men's 45s (d): Maurice Everette, Al Griffin; Men's 50s (s): Jim Winstead; Men's 50s (d): John Tate, Tom Willson Men's 55s (s): Art Culbertson; Men's 55s (d): Curt Walden, Frank Heberer; Men's 60s (s): Paul Richardson; Men's 60s (d): Frank Love, Curt Walden; Men's 65s (s): Dick LeGrand; Men's 65s (d): J.L. Suttle, Dick LeGrand Men's 70s (s): J.L. Suttle; Men's 70s (d): Vince Connerat, Allen Smith; Men's 80s (s): Ben Bardin; Women's Open (s): Stephanie Rauch; Women's Open (d): Penelope Moor, Emily Preyer; Women's 35s (s): Liz Wagner; Women's 35s (d): Christy Edwards, Wendy Wilson; Women's 40s (s): June Sheppard; Women's 40s (d): June Sheppard, Dickie Tyler; Women's 45s (s): Julia Anne Holt; Women's 45s (d): Julia Anne Holt, Barbara Spencer; Women's 50s (s): Margaret Randle; Women's 50s (d): Bobbi Goodnough, Mildred Southern; Women's 55s (s): Mildred Southern; Women's 55s (d): Jeanne Scott, Mildred Southern; Women's 60s (s): Mildred Southern; Women's 60s (d): Elizabeth Brown, Mildred Southern; Mixed Open: Mike Czarnecki, Leigh Shepherd Mixed Open Over 35s: Jim Haslam, Dickie Tyler; Mixed Open Over 40s: Keith Stoneman, Dickie Tyler; Mixed Open Over 45s: Cody Williams, Sylvia Gilley; Mixed Open Over 50s: Bob Spurrier, June Derby; Father–Son: Moo Yancey and Gray Yancey

1982

Men's Open (s): Andy Avram; Men's Open (d): John A. Farfour, Jr., Chip Koury; Men's 25s (s): Doug Eller; Men's 25s (d): Doug Eller, Roger Martin; Men's 35s: Karl Coombes;

ADULT STATE CLOSED CHAMPIONS HISTORY (CONTINUED)

Men's 35s (d): Stan Cocke, Bill Eidson; Men's 40s (s): Norman Chambers; Men's 40s (d): Maurice Everette, Al Griffin; Men's 45s (s): Herb Browne; Men's 45s (d): Maurice Everette, Al Griffin; Men's 50s (s): Tom Willson; Men's 50s (d): Bob Jones, Sam Woods Men's 55s (s): David Smith; Men's 55s (d): Curt Walden, Frank Heberer; Men's 60s (s): Bob Spurrier; Men's 60s (d): Buck Archer, Frank Love; Men's 65s (s): Paul Guibord; Men's 65s (d): Lloyd Hansen, Mac Allen; Men's 70s (s): Vince Connerat; Men's 70s (d): Allen Smith, J.L. Suttle; Men's 80s (s): Rossie Shore; Women's 30s (s): Penelope Moor; Women's 30s (d): Sharron Judy, Susie Black; Women's 35s (s): Liz Wagner; Women's 35s (d): Bev Culbertson, Dickie Tyler; Women's 40s (s): Joan Kotas; Women's 40s (d): June Sheppard, Dickie Tyler; Women's 45s (s): Gloria Henninger; Women's 45s (d): Bev Culbertson, Julia Anne Holt; Women's 50s (s): Julia Anne Holt; Women's 50s (d): Julia Anne Holt, Barbara Spencer; Women's 55s (s): Mildred Southern; Women's 55s (d): Hazel Jones, Peggy Golden; Women's 60s (s): Mildred Southern; Women's 60s (d): Elizabeth Brown, Mildred Southern; Mixed Open: Scott Nichols, Penelope Moor; Mixed Open Over 35s: Jerry Patterson, Liz Wagner; Mixed Open Over 40s: Neill McGeachy, Ellen Adelman; Mixed Open Over 45s: Bob Bombauer, June Sheppard; Mixed Open Over 50s: Cody Williams, Julia Anne Holt; Father–Son: Moo Yancey and Gray Yancey

1983
Men's Open (s): Allen Farfour; Men's

Open (d): Dan Weant, Ken Whitaker; Men's 25s (s): Pravin Maharaj; Men's 25s (d): Doug Eller, Roger Martin; Men's 35s: Laird Griffin; Men's 35s (d): Doug Anderson, Bo Roddey; Men's 40s (s): Maurice Everette; Men's 40s (d): Maurice Everette, Al Griffin; Men's 45s (s): Maurice Everette; Men's 45s (d): Maurice Everette, Al Griffin; Men's 50s (s): Art Culbertson; Men's 50s (d): Bob Jones, Sam Woods Men's 55s (s): David Smith; Men's 55s (d): J.R. Jones, John McDonald; Men's 60s (s): David Smith; Men's 60s (d): Buck Archer, Frank Love; Men's 65s (s): Jim Hamilton; Men's 65s (d): Lloyd Hansen, Mac Allen; Men's 70s (s): J.L. Suttle; Men's 70s (d): David Morgan, J.L. Suttle; Women's 30s (s): Stephanie Rauch; Women's Open (d): Lindsey Linker, Jane Schroeder; Women's 25s (s): Sally Spetz; Women's 25s (d): Joan Cox, Wendy Wilson; Women's 35s (s): Liz Wagner; Women's 35s (d): Claudia Burkett, Harriet Smith; Women's 40s (s): Dickie Tyler; Women's 40s (d): Chris Edwards, Wendy Wilson; Women's 45s (s): Gloria Henninger; Women's 45s (d): Bev Culbertson, Julia Anne Holt; Women's 50s (s): Julia Anne Holt; Women's 50s (d): Julia Anne Holt, Barbara Spencer; Women's 55s (s): Betty Jones; Women's 55s (d): Hazel Jones, June Derby; Women's 60s (s): Mildred Southern; Women's 60s (d): M. Marsh, Mildred Southern; Mixed Open: Scott Dillon, Camey Dillon; Mixed Open Over 35s: Jim Haslam, Dickie Tyler; Mixed Open Over 40s: Jack McGinn, Penny Brawley; Mixed Open Over 45s: Bob Bombauer, June Sheppard; Mixed Open Over 50s: Cody Williams, Julia Anne Holt; Father–Son: Mike Corthum, Mike Corthum

1984
Men's Open (s): Pender Murphy; Men's Open (d): Matt McDonald, Pender Murphy; Men's 25s (s): Doug Eller; Men's 25s (d): Doug Eller,

Lendward Simpson

Roger Martin; Men's 30s (s): Rick Kinney; Men's 30s (d): Pal Mozingo, Don Swarthout; Men's 35s (s): Karl Coombes; Men's 35s (d): Doug Anderson, Herb Browne; Men's 40s (s): Norman Chambers; Men's 40s (d): Jeff Mullins, Terrell West Men's 45s (s): Norman Chambers; Men's 45s (d): Maurice Everette, Al Griffin; Men's 50s (s): Robin Gardner; Men's 50s (d): John Bremer, John McDonald; Men's 55s (s): Art Culbertson; Men's 55s (d): Bob Jones, John McDonald; Men's 60s (s): George Simkins; Men's 60s (d): Bob Jones, David Smith; Men's 65s (s): Jim Hamilton; Men's 65s (d): Mac Allen, Lloyd Hanson; Men's 70s (s): Paul Guibord; Men's 70s (d): Robert Edmunds, Paul Guibord; Men's 80s (s): Ben Barden; Women's Open (s): Penelope Moor; Women's Open (d): Lindsey Linker, Jane Schroeder; Women's 25s (s): Lindsey Linker; Women's 25s (d): Lindsey Linker, Gwynn Sasser; Women's 30s: June Sheppard; Women's 30s (d): Joan Cox, Wendy Wilson; Women's 35s (s): Liz Wagner; Women's 35s (d): Carmina Diaz, Helen Phillips 40s (s): Joan Kotas; Women's 40s (d): Missy Anderson, Dickie Tyler; Women's 45s (s): Julia Anne Holt; Women's 45s (d): Helen Phillips, Wendy Wilson; Women's 50s (s): Julia Anne Holt; Women's 50s (d): Julia Anne Holt, Barbara Spencer; Women's 55s (s): Peggy Golden; Women's 55s (d): Betty Henry, Sara Jones; Women's

60s (s): Mildred Southern; Women's 60s (d): Hazel Jones, Ellie McDowell; Women's 70s (s): Elizabeth Brown; Mixed Open: Randy Bailey, Jackie Jenkins; Mixed Open Over 35s: Jim Haslam, Dickie Tyler; Mixed Open Over 40s: Neill McGeachy, Wendy Wilson; Mixed Open Over 45s: Bob Bombauer, June Sheppard; Mixed Open Over 50s: Cody Williams, Julia Anne Holt; Father–Son: Neill McGeachy, Rod McGeachy; Mother–Daughter (d): Faye Thomas, Scotti Thomas

1985

Men's Open (s): Stephen Enochs; Men's Open (d): Andy Avram, Michael Gandolfo; Men's 25s (s): Dean Channell; Men's 25s (d): Randy Bailey, Dean Channell; Men's 30s (s): Doug Eller; Men's 30s (d): Bob Koury, Bruce Stanley; Men's 35s (s): Charlie Owens; Men's 35s (d): Charlie Owens, Robert Heald; Men's 40s (s): Norman Chambers; Men's 40s (d): Bill Cole, Terrell West Men's 45s (s): Herb Browne; Men's 45s (d): Maurice Everette, Al Griffin; Men's 50s (s): Al Griffin; Men's 50s (d): Jack McGinn, Terry Wise; Men's 55s (s): David Smith; Men's 55s (d): Bo Roddey, Sam Woods; Men's 60s (s): George Simkins; Men's 60s (d): Frank Heberer, George Simkins; Men's 65s (s): Charles Eppinette; Men's 65s (d): M.B. Allen, Lloyd Hanson; Men's 70s (s): Jim Hamilton; Men's 70s (d): Ed Armfield, Robert Edmonds; Men's 75s (s): Vince Connerat; Men's 80s (s): Ben Barden; Women's Open (s): Susan McDanald; Women's Open (d): Lindsey Linker, Jane Schroeder; Women's 30s (s): Stephanie Rauch; Women's 25s (s): Christy Cherry; Women's 25s (d): Lindsey Linker, Gwynn Sasser; Women's 30s: Dargan Williams; Women's 30s (d): Joan Cox, Wendy Wilson; Women's 35s (s): Faye Thomas; Women's 35s (d): Bev Culbertson, Dickie Tyler 40s (s): Joan Kotas; Women's 40s (d): Helen Phillips, Carmina Diaz; Women's 45s (s): Mary Ann Pinkerton; Women's

45s (d): Nettie Culp, Helen Phillips; Women's 50s (s): June Sheppard; Women's 50s (d): Sarah Jones, June Sheppard; Women's 55s (s): Peggy Golden; Women's 55s (d): Betty Henry, Sara Jones; Women's 60s (s): Mildred Southern; Women's 60s (d): Hazel Jones, Ellie McDowell; Mixed Open: Mark Dillon, Susan Sadri; Mixed 25s: Thomas Moore, Kathy Moore; Mixed 30s: Cecil Martin, Carol Stewart; Mixed Open Over 35s: Charlie Owens, Paula Van Every; Mixed Open Over 40s: Neill McGeachy, Wendy Wilson; Mixed Open Over 45s: Jack McGinn, June Sheppard; Mixed Open Over 50s: Billy Wilson, Audrey Johnson; Father–Son: Neill McGeachy, Rod McGeachy; Mother–Daughter (d): Jane Schroeder, Tory Schroeder

1986

Men's Open (s): Andy Avram; Men's Open (d): Allen Farfour, Laneal Vaughn; Men's 25s (s): John Ranthun; Men's 25s (d): Randy Bailey, Dean Channell; Men's 30s (s): Fred Robinson; Men's 30s (d): Jack Blankenhorn, Dee Blankenhorn; Men's 35s: Bobby Heald; Men's 35s (d): Dave Ashcraft, Jim Haslam; Men's 40s (s): Laird Griffin; Men's 40s (d): Maurice Everette, Bobby Heald; Men's 45s (s): Dan Elks; Men's 45s (d): Doug Anderson, Norman Chambers; Men's 50s (s): Maurice Everette; Men's 50s (d): Maurice Everette, Al Griffin; Men's 55s (s): Tom Willson; Men's 55s (d): Bob Jones, John McDonald; Men's 60s (s): Buck Archer; Men's 60s (d): Frank Heberer, George Simkins; Men's 65s (s): Curt Walden; Men's 65s (d): Mac Allen, Lloyd Hanson; Men's 70s (s): J.L. Suttle; Men's 70s (d): Vince Connerat, Ralph Rockett; Men's 75s (s): J.L. Suttle; Men's 80s (s): Ralph Moureau; Women's Open (s): Anneli Bennett; Women's Open (d): Laura Ballentine, Susan McDanald; Women's 25s (s): Lindsey Linker; Women's 25s (d): Lindsey Linker, Gwynn Sasser; Women's 30s:

Miriam Morey; Women's 30s (d): Joan Cox, Wendy Wilson; Women's 35s (s): Faye Thomas; Women's 35s (d): Joan Cox, Wendy Wilson; Women's 40s (s): Liz Wagner; Women's 40s (d): Helen Phillips, Carmina Diaz; Women's 45s (s): Roz Waitman; Women's 45s (d): Penny Brawley, Helen Phillips; Women's 50s (s): Julia Anne Holt; Women's 50s (d): Sarah Jones, June Sheppard; Women's 55s (s): Peggy Golden; Women's 55s (d): Betty Henry, Sara Jones; Women's 60s (s): Mildred Southern; Women's 60s (d): Hazel Jones, Mildred Southern; Women's 65s (s): Mildred Southern; Women's 65s (d): Mildred Southern, Evelyn White; Mixed Open: John Ranthun, Susan Saunders; Mixed 25s: Kenny House, Kim Clark; Mixed 30s: Rick Keller, Dargan Williams; Mixed Over 35s: Erik Witten, Ann Allen; Mixed 40s: Jim Haslam, Dickie Tyler; Mixed 45s: Bob Bambauer, Bev Culbertson; Mixed 50s: Cody Williams,, Julia Anne Holt; Father–Son: Gary Avram, Andy Avram; Mother–Daughter (d): Jane Schroeder, Tory Schroeder

1987

Men's Open (s): Wayne Hearn; Men's Open (d): James Krege, Thomas Tanner; Men's 25s (s): Mark Henry; Men's 25s (d): Brad Cherry, Bob Stiles; Men's 30s (s): Dan Weant; Men's 30s (d): Jack Blankenhorn, Dee Blankenhorn; Men's 35s: Jim Corn; Men's 35s (d): Karl Coombes, Bobby Heald; Men's 40s (s): J.W. Quick; Men's 40s (d): Maurice Everette, Bobby Heald; Men's 45s (s): Herb Browne; Men's 45s (d): Doug Anderson, Herb Browne; Men's 50s (s): Maurice Everette; Men's 50s (d): Maurice Everette, Al Griffin; Men's 55s (s): Tom Willson; Men's 55s (d): John Bowen, Tom Willson; Men's 60s (s): David Smith; Men's 60s (d): Bob Jones, John McDonald; Men's 65s (s): Curt Walden; Men's 65s (d): Bob Spurrier, Curt Walden; Men's 70s (s): Lloyd Hanson; Men's 70s (d): Mac Allen, Lloyd Hanson; Men's

ADULT STATE CLOSED CHAMPIONS HISTORY
(CONTINUED)

75s (s): Vince Connerat; Women's Open (s): Susan Saunders; Women's Open (d): Laura Ballentine, Susan McDanald; Women's 25s (s): Lindsey Linker; Women's 25s (d): Lindsey Linker, Gwynn Sasser; Women's 30s: Miriam Morey; Women's 30s (d): Sue Hamm, Dorothy Williams; Women's 35s (s): Anne Marshall; Women's 35s (d): Missy Anderson, Claudia Burkett; Women's 40s (s): Claudia Burkett; Women's 40s (d): Missy Anderson, Claudia Burkett; Women's 45s (s): Margrit Meier; Women's 45s (d): Katherine Shelburne, Wendy Wilson; Women's 50s (s): June Sheppard; Women's 50s (d): Julia Anne Holt, Helen Phillips; Women's 55s (s): Peggy Golden; Women's 55s (d): Betty Henry, Sara Jones; Women's 60s (s): Mildred Southern; Women's 60s (d): Hazel Jones, Mildred Southern; Women's 65s (s): Mildred Southern; Women's 65s (d): Elly McDowell, Mildred Southern; Mixed Open: Buck Stephenson, Becky Kopack; Mixed 25s: Jim Haslam, Christy Cherry; Mixed 30s: John Hobgood, Joan Jones; Mixed 35s: Karl Coombes, Paula Van Every; Mixed 40s: Neill McGeachy, Missy Anderson; Mixed 45s: Neill McGeachy, Penny Brawley; Mixed 50s: Cody Williams,, Julia Anne Holt; Mixed 60s: Harold Sauls, Mildred Southern; Father–Son: Neill McGeachy, Rod McGeachy; Mother–Daughter (d): Jane Schroeder, Tory Schroeder

1988
Men's Open (s): Stephen Enochs; Men's Open (d): Andy Avram, Mike Gandolfo; Men's 25s (s): Bill Schillings; Men's 25s (d): Bill Schillings, Fred Robinson; Men's 30s (s): Fred Robinson; Men's 30s (d): Bob Lake, Dan Weant; Men's 35s:

Fred Robinson; Men's 35s (d): Fred Robinson, Keith Richardson; Men's 40s (s): Bill Cole; Men's 40s (d): Dave Ashcraft, Jim Haslam; Men's 45s (s): William Poore; Men's 45s (d): Norman Chambers, Terrell West; Men's 50s (s): Norman Chambers; Men's 50s (d): Maurice Everette, Al Griffin; Men's 55s (s): Joe Dudley; Men's 55s (d): John Bowen, Tom Willson; Men's 60s (s): Buck Archer; Men's 60s (d): Bill Blackburn, Judd Bricker; Men's 65s (s): David Smith; Men's 65s (d): Frank Heberer, Bob Jones; Men's 70s (s): James Hamilton; Men's 70s (d): Mac Allen, Lloyd Hanson; Men's 75s (s): J.L. Suttle; Women's Open (s): Susan McDanald; Women's Open (d): Laura Ballentine, Susan McDanald; Women's 25s (s): Susan McDanald; Women's 25s (d): Leslie Lewis, Susan McDanald; Women's 30s: Lindsey Linker; Women's 30s (d): Lindsey Linker, Gwynn Sasser; Women's 35s (s): Liz Wagner; Women's 35s (d): Mary Lida Alexander, Liz Wagner; Women's 40s (s): Dickie Tyler; Women's 40s (d): Missy Anderson, Claudia Burkett; Women's 45s (s): Dickie Tyler; Women's 45s (d): Katherine Shelburne, Wendy Wilson; Women's 50s (s): Roz Waitman; Women's 50s (d): Nettie Culp, Helen Phillips; Women's 55s (s): June Sheppard; Women's 55s (d): Betty Henry, Sara Jones; Women's 60s (s): Peggy Golden; Women's 60s (d): Peggy Golden, Mildred Southern; Women's 65s (s): Rose Spalding; Women's 65s (d): Hazel Jones, Rose Spalding; Mixed Open: Phil Payne, Kim Vaughan; Mixed 25s: Fred Robinson, Susan McDanald; Mixed 30s: Jerry Patterson, Monti Smith; Mixed 35s: Karl Coombes, Paula Van Every; Mixed 40s: Jim Haslam, Dickie Tyler; Mixed 45s: Jerry Patterson, Liz Wagner; Mixed 50s: Maurice Everette, Vicki Everette; Mixed 60s: Harold Sauls, Mildred Southern; Father–Son: Herb Bolick, Bert Bolick; Mother–Daughter (d):

Faye Thomas, Scotti Thomas

1989
Men's Open (s): Stephen Enochs; Men's Open (d): Stephen Enochs, Mike Gandolfo; Men's 25s (s): Jeff Adams; Men's 25s (d): Tom McEvoy, Dan Weant; Men's 30s (s): Adam Brock; Men's 30s (d): Bob Lake, Dan Weant; Men's 35s: Fred Robinson; Men's 35s (d): Bill Ashley, Joe Antle; Men's 40s (s): J.W. Quick; Men's 40s (d): Bill Cole, Terrell West; Men's 45s (s): John Eatman; Men's 45s (d): John Eatman, Larry Hoyt; Men's 50s (s): Norman Chambers; Men's 50s (d): Maurice Everette, Al Griffin; Men's 55s (s): Larry McGee; Men's 55s (d): Robin Gardner, Jack McGinn; Men's 60s (s): Buck Archer; Men's 60s (d): Bob Jones, John McDonald; Men's 65s (s): Hal Cook; Men's 65s (d): Frank Heberer, George Simkins; Men's 70s (s): William Adolph; Men's 70s (d): Robert Bannin, Harold Southern; Men's 75s (s): Vince Connerat; Men's 75s (d): Claude Brown, Vince Connerat; Women's Open (s): Charlotte Haberstroh; Women's Open (d): Laura Ballentine, Susan McDanald; Women's 25s (s): Susan McDanald; Women's 25s (d): Lindsey Linker, Susan McDanald; Women's 30s: Lindsey Linker; Women's 30s (d): Lindsey Linker, Cynthia Wilhelm; Women's 35s (s): Miriam Morey; Women's 35s (d): Mary Lida Alexander, Liz Wagner-Smoake; Women's 40s (s): Sharron Frahm; Women's 40s (d): Mary Lida Alexander, Liz Wagner-Smoake; Women's 45s (s): Liz Wagner-Smoake; Women's 45s (d): Pat Cox, Peggy Thorne; Women's 50s (s): Dickie Tyler; Women's 50s (d): Pat Cox, Peggy Thorne; Women's 55s (s): June Shepherd Connerat; Women's 55s (d): June Shepherd Connerat, Sally Dillon; Women's 60s (s): Peggy Golden; Women's 60s (d): Betty Henry, Sara Jones; Women's 65s (s): Mildred Southern; Women's 65s (d): Hazel Jones, Mildred Southern; Mixed Open: Cooper Pulliam,

Susan Saunders; Mixed 25s: Lindsay Benton, Lindsey Linker; Mixed 30s: none; Mixed 35s: Karl Coombes, Paula Van Every; Mixed 40s: Fritz Gildemeister, Liz Wagner-Smoake; Mixed 45s: Bob Bambauer, Janet Bambauer; Mixed 50s: Maurice Everette, Vicki Everette; Mixed 55s: none; Mixed 60s: Frank Heberer, Helen Sizemore; Father–Son: Herb Bolick, Bert Bolick; Mother–Daughter (d): Jane Schroeder, Colee Schroeder

1990

Men's Open (s): Mike Pittard; Men's Open (d): Wells Brabham, Mike Pittard; Men's 25s (s): Jeff Adams; Men's 25s (d): Kenny House, Roger Martin; Men's 30s (s): Dan Weant; Men's 30s (d): Bob Lake, Dan Weant; Men's 35s: Fred Robinson; Men's 35s (d): Bill Ashley, Joe Antle; Men's 40s (s): J.W. Quick; Men's 40s (d): Jim Corn, Eric Witten; Men's 45s (s): John Eatman; Men's 45s (d): Doug Anderson, Herb Browne; Men's 50s (s): Norman Chambers; Men's 50s (d): Doug Anderson, Norman Chambers; Men's 55s (s): Herb Browne; Men's 55s (d): Bob Bambauer, Jack McGinn; Men's 60s (s): Tom Willson; Men's 60s (d): John Bowen, Tom Willson; Men's 65s (s): Harold Cook; Men's 65s (d): Frank Heberer, George Simkins; Men's 70s (s): Jim Chavasse; Men's 70s (d): Bob Bannin, Harold Southern; Men's 75s (s): J.L. Suttle; Men's 75s (d): Vince Connerat, J.L. Suttle; Men's 80s (s): Vince Connerat; Women's Open (s): Susan McDanald Open (d): Laura Ballentine, Susan McDanald; Women's 25s (s): Susan McDanald; Women's 25s (d): Lindsey Linker, Susan McDanald; Women's 30s: Lindsey Linker; Women's 30s (d): Susie Hill, Katherine Shelburne; Women's 35s (s): Wendy McColskey; Women's 35s (d): Mary Lida Alexander, Liz Wagner-Smoake; Women's 40s

(s): Sharron Frahm; Women's 40s (d): Mary Lida Alexander, Liz Wagner-Smoake; Women's 45s (s): Liz Wagner-Smoake; Women's 45s (d): Sharon Greene, Katherine Shelburne; Women's 50s (s): Dickie Tyler; Women's 50s (d): Julia Anne Holt, Barbara Spencer; Women's 55s (s): Julia Anne Holt; Women's 55s (d): Julia Anne Holt, Barbara Spencer; Women's 60s (s): Peggy Golden; Women's 60s (d): Betty Henry, Sara Jones; Women's 65s (s): Mildred Southern; Women's 65s (d): Hazel Jones, Mildred Southern; Mixed Open: Mike Dombrowski, Kelly Coleman; Mixed 25s: Lindsay Benton, Lindsey Linker; Mixed 30s: Terry Holder, Lindsey Linker; Mixed 35s: Ray Wheeler, Mary Lida Alexander; Mixed 40s: Scott Pollard, Dickie Tyler; Mixed 45s: Jim Hough, Carmina Diaz; Mixed 50s: Bill Marion, Carlene Marion; Mixed 55s: none; Mixed 60s: Bob Jones, Hazel Jones; Father–Son: Elwood Parker, Richard Parker; Mother–Daughter (d): Cynthia Wilhelm, Katherine Wilhelm Hilkey

1991

Men's Open (s): Mike Pittard; Men's Open (d): Bert Bolick, Jag Gowda; Men's 25s (s): John Sawyer; Men's 25s (d): Andy Avram, Chip Koury; Men's 30s (s): Dan Weant; Men's 30s (d): Bob Lake, Dan Weant; Men's 35s: Buster Brown; Men's 35s (d): Buster Brown, Gene Szymanski; Men's 40s (s): Jim Corn; Men's 40s (d): Norman Beam, Mike McHone; Men's 45s (s): Laird Griffin; Men's 45s (d): Norman Chambers, John Eatman; Men's 50s (s): Al Griffin; Men's 50s (d): Doug Anderson, Norman Chambers; Men's 55s (s): Al Griffin; Men's 55s (d): Herb Browne, Tom Willson; Men's 60s (s): Larry McGee; Men's 60s (d): Frank Heberer, George Simkins; Men's 65s (s): Bill Weathers; Men's 65s (d): Frank Heberer, George Simkins; Men's 70s (s): Charles Eppinette; Men's 70s (d): Charles Eppinette, Paul Richardson; Men's

75s (s): James Hamilton; Men's 75s (d): Dave Carey, Harold Southern; Men's 80s (s): J.L. Suttle; Women's Open (s): Susan McDanald Open (d): Laura Ballentine, Susan McDanald; Women's 25s (s): Mariana Routh; Women's 25s (d): Lindsey Linker, Mariana Routh; Women's 30s: Ellen Easter; Women's 30s (d): Ellen Easter, Telfair Stakias; Women's 35s (s): Sharron Frahm; Women's 35s (d): Sharron Frahm, Penelope Moore; Women's 40s (s): Liz Wagner-Smoake; Women's 40s (d): Chris Graham, Sharon Greene; Women's 45s (s): Liz Wagner-Smoake; Women's 45s (d): Sharon Greene, Katherine Shelburne; Women's 50s (s): Dickie Tyler; Women's 50s (d): Pat Cox, Katherine Shelburne; Women's 55s (s): None; Women's 55s (d): Julia Anne Holt, Barbara Spencer; Women's 60s (s): Peggy Golden; Women's 60s (d): Julia Anne Holt, Jane Reynolds; Women's 65s (s): Rose Spalding; Women's 65s (d): Hazel Jones, Mildred Southern; Women's 70s (s): Mildred Southern; Women's 70s (d): Julia Bannin, Lillian Thieme; Mixed Open: Mike Dombrowski, Kelly Coleman; Mixed 25s: Terry Holder, Lindsey Linker; Mixed 30s: Jeff Campbell, Darlene Tarlton; Mixed 35s: Norman Beam, Mary Lida Alexander; Mixed 40s: Norman Beam, Mary Lida Alexander; Mixed 45s: Robin Gardner, Linda Gardner; Mixed 50s: Bev Earle, Fritz Earle; Mixed 60s: Bob Jones, Hazel Jones; Father–Son: Neill McGeachy, Ron McGeachy; Mother–Daughter (d): Jane Schroeder, Colee Schroeder

1992

Men's Open (s): Michael Leonard; Men's Open (d): Stan Cocke, Mike Weidl; Men's 25s (s): Mike Dombrowski; Men's 25s (d): Steve MacDonald, Wayne Parrish; Men's 30s (s): Billy Roberts; Men's 30s (d): Billy Roberts, Jay Robinson; Men's 35s: Fred Robinson; Men's 35s (d): Tommy Dixon, Dan Weant; Men's 40s (s): Buster Brown; Men's 40s

ADULT STATE CLOSED CHAMPIONS HISTORY
(CONTINUED)

(d): David Barbin, Karl Coombes; Men's 45s (s): J.W. Quick; Men's 45s (d): Dave Barbin, Karl Coombes; Men's 50s (s): Maurice Everette; Men's 50s (d): Walter Brown, Walt Stamer; Men's 55s (s): Maurice Everette; Men's 55s (d): Fitz Earle, Jack McGinn; Men's 60s (s): Tom Willson; Men's 60s (d): John Bowen, Tom Willson; Men's 65s (s): Norman Jarrard; Men's 65s (d): Charles Oliver, Bill Weathers; Men's 70s (s): Paul Richardson; Men's 70s (d): Bill Adolph, Paul Richardson; Men's 75s (s): Wade MacDonald; Men's 75s (d): Dave Carey, Harold Southern; Men's 80s (s): J.L. Suttle; Women's Open (s): Susan McDanald Love; Women's Open (d): Laura Ballentine-Jeu de Vine, Susan McDanald Love; Women's 25s (s): Mariana Routh; Women's 25s (d): Mariana Routh, Mary Lloyd Seate; Women's 30s: Susan McDanald Love; Women's 30s (d): Susan McDanald Love, Lindsey Linker; Women's 35s (s): Penelope Moor; Women's 35s (d): Sharron Frahm, Dee Moore; Women's 40s (s): Sharron Frahm; Women's 40s (d): Susie Hill, Katherine Shelburne; Women's 45s (s): Sharon Greene; Women's 45s (d): Saundra Denny, Teresa Gilchrist; Women's 50s (s): Jane Sandridge; Women's 50s (d): Margrit Meier, Dickie Tyler; Women's 55s (s): Zoe Williams; Women's 55s (d): Beverly Earle, Julia Anne Holt; Women's 60s (s): Kay Wakley; Women's 60s (d): Barbara Spencer, Julia Anne Holt; Women's 65s (s): Kay Wakley; Women's 65s (d): Mildred Southern, Kay Wakley; Women's 70s (s): Mildred Southern;

Women's 70s (d): Mildred Southern, Rose Spaulding; Mixed Open: Bill Ashley, Mariana Routh; Mixed 25s: Terry Holder, Lindsey Linker; Mixed 30s: Mark Troutman, Susan McDanald Love; Mixed 35s: Norman Beam, Mary Lida Alexander; Mixed 40s: Clay Thomas, Faye Thomas; Mixed 45s: Jim Haslam, Dickie Tyler; Mixed 50s: Jack McGinn, Dickie Tyler Mixed 60s: Cody Williams, Julia Anne Holt; Father–Son: Elwood Parker, Richard Parker; Mother–Daughter (d): Dee Moore, Merryll McElwain

1993
Men's Open (s): Bryan Jones; Men's Open (d): Bert Bolick, Mike Pittard; Men's 25s (s): Matt Price; Men's 25s (d):Steve McDonald, Wayne Parrish; Men's 30s (s): Ray Thomas; Men's 30s (d): Jonathan Sawyer, Brad Smith; Men's 35s: Kenny House; Men's 35s (d): Karl Coombes, Craig Westman; Men's 40s (s): Buster Brown; Men's 40s (d): George Mauney, Scott Pollard; Men's 45s (s): Robert Heald; Men's 45s (d): Dave Barbin, Karl Coombes; Men's 50s (s): John Eatman; Men's 50s (d): Walter Brown, Walt Stamer; Men's 55s (s): Norman Chambers; Men's 55s (d): Gregory Grant, Jack McGinn; Men's

60s (s): Larry McGee; Men's 60s (d): Floyd Chandler, Larry McGee; Men's 65s (s): Bill Weathers; Men's 65s (d): Judah Bricker, Ed White; Men's 70s (s): : Buck Archer; Men's 70s (d): Buck Archer, Bob Jones; Men's 75s (s): Lloyd Hanson; Men's 75s (d): Lloyd Hanson, Wade MacDonald; Men's 80s (s): David Carey; Men's 80s (d): David Carey, J.L. Suttle; Women's Open (s): Cinda Gurney; Women's Open (d): Robyn Gurney, Cinda Gurney; Women's 25s (s): Wendy Gwathmey; Women's 25s (d): Susie Hill, Katherine Shelburne 30s: Mariana Routh; Women's 30s (d): Susan McDanald Love, Lindsey Linker; Women's 35s (s): Susie McDanald Love; Women's 35s (d): Mary Lida Alexander, Sharon Greene; Women's 40s (s): Sharron Frahm; Women's 40s (d): Saundra Denny, Teresa Gilchrist; Women's 45s (s): Sharon Greene; Women's 45s (d): Saundra Denny, Teresa Gilchrist; Women's 50s (s): Dickie Tyler; Women's 50s (d): Pat Cox, Katherine Shelburne; Women's 55s (s): Sue Baggett; Women's 55s (d): Julia Anne Holt, Barbara Spencer; Women's 60s (s): Peggy Golden; Women's 60s (d): Barbara Spencer, Julia Anne Holt; Women's 65s (s): Mildred Southern;

Women's 65s (d): Peggy Golden, Kay Wakley; Women's 70s (s): Mildred Southern; Women's 70s (d): Mildred Southern, Hazel Jones; Mixed Open: Buck Stephenson, Natalie Teague; Mixed 25s: Terry Holder, Cindy Shelly; Mixed 30s: Mark Troutman, Susan McDanald Love; Mixed 35s: Roger Sawyer, Libby Meiners; Mixed 40s: Clay Thomas, Faye Thomas; Mixed 45s: Neill McGeachy, Penny Brawley; Mixed 50s: Jack McGinn, Dickie Tyler Mixed 60s: Cody Williams, Julia Anne Holt; Mixed 70s: Bob Jones, Hazel Jones; Father–Son: Elwood Parker, Richard Parker; Mother–Daughter (d): Becky Weeks, Rebecca Weeks

1994

Men's Open (s): David Wolf; Men's Open (d): Peters Ayers, David Yett; Men's 25s (s): David Wolf; Men's 25s (d): Richard Parker, Buck Stephenson; Men's 30s (s): Donald Rutledge; Men's 30s (d): Jonathan Sawyer, Brad Smith; Men's 35s: Sammy Martin; Men's 35s (d): Sammy Martin, Ogi Mitra; Men's 40s (s): Buster Brown; Men's 40s (d): Karl Coombes, Craig Westman; Men's 45s (s): Robert Heald; Men's 45s (d): Karl Coombes, Bobby Heald; Men's 50s (s): Norman Chambers; Men's 50s (d): Maurice Everette, Al Griffin; Men's 55s (s): Norman Chambers; Men's 55s (d): Maurice Everette, Al Griffin; Men's 60s (s): Tom Willson; Men's 60s (d): Bill Weathers, Tom Willson; Men's 65s (s): Alan McGee; Men's 65s (d): Judah Bricker, Alan McGee; Men's 70s (s): : Buck Archer; Men's 70s (d): Frank Heberer, George Simkins; Men's 75s (s): Lyle Edwards; Men's 75s (d): Lyle Edwards, Paul Richardson; Men's 80s (s): David Carey; Men's 80s (d): David Carey, J.L. Suttle; Women's Open (s): Mariana Routh; Women's Open (d): Susie Hill, Katherine Shelburne; Women's 25s (s): Robin Ahearn; Women's 25s (d): Cathy Kiser, Karen Rembert 30s: Lindsey Linker; Women's 30s (d): Susie Hill,

Katherine Shelburne; Women's 35s (s): Susie Love; Women's 35s (d): Sheila Ernest, Wendy McColskey; Women's 40s (s): Sharron Frahm; Women's 40s (d): Saundra Denny, Teresa Gilchrist; Women's 45s (s): Sharron Frahm; Women's 45s (d): Susie Hill, Katherine Shelburne; Women's 50s (s): Liz Smoake; Women's 50s (d): Pat Cox, Katherine Shelburne; Women's 55s (s): Vicki Everette; Women's 55s (d): Nettie Culp, Helen Phillips; Women's 60s (s): Peggy Golden; Women's 60s (d): Barbara Spencer, Julia Anne Holt; Women's 65s (s): Kay Wakley; Women's 65s (d): Betty Henry, Sara Jones; Women's 70s (s): Mildred Southern; Women's 70s (d): Mildred Southern, Rose Spalding; Mixed Open: Derek Allen, Dana Allen; Mixed 25s: Bobby Heald, Nancy Arndt; Mixed 30s: Mark Troutman, Lindsey Linker; Mixed 35s: Tim Scott, Libby Meiners; Mixed 40s: Bill Ashley, Sharron Frahm; Mixed 45s: Scott Pollard, Margrit Meier; Mixed 50s: Jim Perkins, Marla Figard; Mixed 55s: Fritz Earle, Beverly Earle; Mixed 60s: Cody Williams, Julia Anne Holt; Father–Son: Elwood Parker, Richard Parker; Mother–Daughter (d): Becky Weeks, Rebecca Weeks

1995

Men's Open (s): Oscar Blacutt Men's Open (d): Andy Avram, Robert Phillips; Men's 25s (s): Andy Lake; Men's 25s (d): Andy Lake, Buck Stephenson; Men's 30s (s): Steve Price; Men's 30s (d): Jonathan Sawyer, Coy Shields; Men's 35s: Bill Schillings; Men's 35s (d): Andy Avram, Mark Dillon; Men's 40s (s): Fred Robinson; Men's 40s (d): Kim Dillard, Richard McKee; Men's 45s (s): Laird Griffin; Men's 45s (d): Laird Griffin, Bobby Heald; Men's 50s (s): Bill Cole; Men's 50s (d): Dan Elks, John Mitchell; Men's 55s (s): Norman Chambers; Men's 55s (d): Herb Browne, Jack McGinn; Men's 60s (s): Al Griffin; Men's 60s (d): Herb Browne, Jack McGinn;

Men's 65s (s): Bill Weathers; Men's 65s (d): Charlie Oliver, Bill Weathers; Men's 70s (s): : Buck Archer; Men's 70s (d): Bob Jones, Ed White; Men's 75s (s): Paul Richardson; Men's 75s (d): Lyle Edwards, Paul Richardson; Men's 80s (s): J.L. Suttle; Women's Open (s): Mariana Routh; Women's Open (d): Nancy Arendt, Mariana Routh; Women's 25s (s): Liz Smoake; Women's 25s (d): Nancy Arendt, Dale Heald; Women's 30s: Mariana Routh; Women's 30s (d): Susie Hill, Katherine Shelburne; Women's 35s (s): Susie Love; Women's 35s (d): Susie Love, Libby Meiners; Women's 40s (s): Sharron Frahm; Women's 40s (d): Saundra Denny, Teresa Gilchrist; Women's 45s (s): Faye Thomas; Women's 45s (d): Marla Figard, Sharon Greene; Women's 50s (s): Sharon Greene; Women's 50s (d): Pat Cox, Katherine Shelburne; Women's 55s (s): Barbara Fullwood; Women's 55s (d): Vicki Everette, Roz Waitman; Women's 60s (s): Caroline Clark; Women's 60s (d): Jane Reynolds, Julia Anne Holt; Women's 65s (s): Peggy Golden; Women's 70s (s): Mary Reams Maynard; Mixed Open: Oscar Blacutt, Mariana Routh; Mixed 25s: Bobby Heald, Nancy Arndt; Mixed 30s: Jesse Wilson, Mariana Routh; Mixed 35s: Tim Scott, Libby Meiners; Mixed 40s: Fritz Gildemeister, Susie Hill; Mixed 45s: Jim Haslam, Sharron Frahm; Mixed 50s: No champions—rain; Mixed 60s: No champions—rain; Father–Son: Mike Corthum, Michael Corthum; Mother–Daughter (d): Val Rothchild, Karen Rembert

1996

Men's Open (s): Robert Phillips Men's Open (d): Andy Avram, Robert Phillips; Men's 25s (s): Steve Price; Men's 25s (d): Richard Parker, Buck Stephenson; Men's 30s (s): Fred Robinson; Men's 30s (d): Doug Greenberg, Todd Hall; Men's 35s: Fred Robinson; Men's 35s (d): Billy Roberts, Jay Roberts; Men's 40s (s): Fred Robinson; Men's 40s (d): George Mauney, Scott Pollard; Men's 45s (s): Bobby Heald; Men's 45s (d): Bill Cole, Bobby Heald; Men's 50s (s): Bobby

ADULT STATE CLOSED CHAMPIONS HISTORY
(CONTINUED)

Heald; Men's 50s (d): John Mitchell, Jim Perkins; Men's 55s (s): Dan Elks; Men's 55s (d): Maurice Everette, Al Griffin; Men's 60s (s): Maurice Everette; Men's 60s (d): Herb Browne, Jack McGinn; Men's 65s (s): Bill Weathers; Men's 65s (d): Alan McGee, Larry McGee; Men's 70s (s): : Bill Weathers; Men's 70s (d): Frank Heberer, George Simkins; Men's 75s (s): Gordon Reynolds; Men's 75s (d): Jim Chavasse, Wade MacDonald; Men's 80s (s): Harold Southern; Men's 80s (d): Jim Hamilton, Harold Southern; Women's Open (s): Ralitza Bakita; Women's Open (d): Jane Schroeder, Tory Schroeder; Women's 25s (s): Ralitza Bakita; Women's 25s (d): Karen Rembert, Ralitza Bakita; Women's 30s: Mariana Routh; Women's 30s (d): Kathy Lewis, Mariana Routh; Women's 35s (s): Susie Love; Women's 35s (d): Susie Love, Libby Meiners; Women's 40s (s): Frances O'Sullivan; Women's 40s (d): Katherine Shelburne, Susie Hill; Women's 45s (s): Liz Smoake; Women's 45s (d): Katherine Shelburne, Susie Hill; Women's 50s (s): Liz Smoake; Women's 50s (d): Ellen Adelman, Liz Smoake; Women's 55s (s): Kathy Shelburne; Women's 55s (d): Pat Cox, Katherine Shelburne; Women's 60s (s): Billie Oxreider; Women's 60s (d): Jane Reynolds, Julia Anne Holt; Women's 65s (s): Caroline Clark; Women's 65s (d): Julia Anne Holt, Barbara Spencer; Women's 70s (s): Mildred Southern; Women's 70s (d): Mary Reams Maynard, Mildred Southern; Mixed Open: Buck Stephenson, Somer Khanlarian; Mixed 25s: Bobby Heald, Nancy Arndt; Mixed 30s: Mike Hollman, Mariana Routh; Mixed 35s: Tim Scott, Libby Meiners;

Mixed 40s: Kenny House, Kim Clark; Mixed 45s: Jim Perkins, Marla Figard; Mixed 50s: Jim Perkins, Marla Figard; Mixed 60s: Klaus Sabert, Mary Helen Bode; Mixed 70s: Wade MacDonald, Mildred Southern; Father–Son: Elwood Parker, Richard Parker; Mother–Daughter (d): Anne Gorrell, Katherine Gorrell

1997
Men's Open (s): Wayne Hearn Men's Open (d): Mike Weidl, Danny Colangelo; Men's 25s (s): Mike Weidl; Men's 25s (d): Richard Parker, Buck Stephenson; Men's 30s (s): Cliff Skakle; Men's 30s (d): Cliff Skakle, Mark Troutman; Men's 35s: Wayne Hearn; Men's 35s (d): Andy Avram, Wayne Hearn; Men's 40s (s): Cliff Skakle; Men's 40s (d): Bill Ashley, Doug Eller; Men's 45s (s): Bobby Heald; Men's 45s (d): Bill Cole, Bobby Heald; Men's 50s (s): JW Quick; Men's 50s (d): Bill Cole, Robert Heald; Men's 55s (s): Dan Elks; Men's 55s (d): Doug Anderson, Herb Browne; Men's 60s (s): Maurice Everette; Men's 60s (d): Maurice Everette, Al Griffin; Men's 65s (s): Bill Weathers; Men's 65s (d): Lindy Stevens, Ed White; Men's 70s (s): : Bill Weathers; Men's 70s (d): Buck Archer, Bob Light; Men's 75s (s): Paul Richardson; Men's 75s (d): Leo Fullwood, Paul Richardson; Men's 80s (s): David Carey; Men's 80s (d): David Carey, C.C. Herold; Women's Open (s): Carolina Blouin; Women's Open (d): Sara Dickson, Jamie Mayfield Women's Women's 25s (s): Frances O'Sullivan; Women's 25s (d): Nancy Arndt, Ralitza Bakita; Women's 30s: Mariana Routh Hollman; Women's 30s (d): Jane Poole, Mariana Routh Hollman; Women's 35s (s): Mariana Routh Hollman; Women's 35s (d): Susie Love, Mariana Routh Hollman; Women's 40s (s): Frances O'Sullivan; Women's 40s (d): Mary Lida Alexander, Frances O'Sullivan; Women's 45s (s): Sharron Frahm; Women's 45s (d): Kim Clark, Sharon

Greene; Women's 50s (s): Sharon Greene; Women's 50s (d): Susie Hill, Katherine Shelburne; Women's 55s (s): Pat Cox; Women's 55s (d): Pat Cox, Katherine Shelburne; Women's 60s (s): Billie Oxreider; Women's 60s (d): Sue Baggett, Sylvia Gaines; Women's 65s (s): Peggy Golden; Women's 65s (d): Julia Anne Holt, Barbara Spencer; Women's 70s (s): Kay Wakley; Women's 70s (d): Peggy Golden, Kay Wakley; Women's 75s (s): Mildred Southern; Women's 75s (d): Ruth Meighan, Mildred Southern; Mixed Open: Buck Stephenson, Somer Khanlarian; Mixed 25s: Bobby Heald, Nancy Arndt; Mixed 30s: Frances O'Sullivan, Mark Troutman; Mixed 35s: Wayne Hearn, Libby Meiners; Mixed 40s: Kenny House, Kim Clark; Mixed 45s: Rosemary Hill, Craig Westman; Mixed 50s: Jim Perkins, Marla Figard; Mixed 55s: Kendall Hetterly, Robert Hetterly; Mixed 60s: Billie Oxreider, Charles Oxreider; Mixed 65s: none; Mixed 70s: William Pool, Mildred Southern; Father–Son: none; Mother–Daughter (d): none

1998
Men's Open (s): Wayne Hearn Men's Open (d): Stuart Beauchamp, Adriano Blacutt; Men's 25s (s): Moses Igbinovia; Men's 25s (d): Michael Leonard, Matt Price; Men's 30s (s): Robert Stephens; Men's 30s (d): Kelly Hunter, Stuart Jackson; Men's 35s: Wayne Hearn; Men's 35s (d): Cliff Skakle, Wayne Hearn; Men's 40s (s): Sammy Martin; Men's 40s (d): Cliff Skakle, Mark Troutman; Men's 45s (s): Dennis Engelbrecht; Men's 45s (d): Dennis Engelbrecht, Clay Thomas; Men's 50s (s): Bobby Heald; Men's 50s (d): Bill Trott, Bobby Heald; Men's 55s (s): Bruce Brodie; Men's 55s (d): Jim Perkins, Walter Brown; Men's 60s (s): Norman Chambers; Men's 60s (d): Maurice Everette, Al Griffin; Men's 65s (s): Robert Hetterly; Men's 65s (d): John

Bowen, Tom Willson; Men's 70s (s): : Bill Weathers; Men's 70s (d): Norman Jarrard, Paul Stephanz; Men's 75s (s): Buck Archer; Men's 75s (d): Frank Heberer, David Smith; Men's 80s (s): Wade MacDonald; Men's 80s (d): Wade MacDonald, Harold Southern; Women's Open (s): Mariana Routh Hollman; Women's Open (d): Sara Dickson, Jaime Mayfield Women's Women's 25s (s): Sheila Milne; Women's 25s (d): Nancy Arndt, Ralitza Bakita; Women's 30s: Melony Bailey; Women's 30s (d): none; Women's 35s (s): Susan McDanal Love; Women's 35s (d): Susie Love, Susan McDanal Love; Women's 40s (s): Frances O'Sullivan; Women's 40s (d): Susie Hill, Frances O'Sullivan; Women's 45s (s): Sharron Frahm; Women's 45s (d): Mary Lida Alexander, Liz Smoake; Women's 50s (s): Liz Smoake; Women's 50s (d): Pat Cox, Tina Klaus; Women's 55s (s): Liz Smoake; Women's 55s (d): Pat Cox, Katherine Shelburne; Women's 60s (s): Vicki Everette; Women's 60s (d): Frances Kimball, Lois Walker; Women's 65s (s): Christiane Jackson; Women's 65s (d): Julia Anne Holt, Barbara Spencer; Women's 70s (s): Martha Norman; Women's 70s (d): Betty Henry, Sara Jones; Women's 75s (s): Mildred Southern; Women's 75s (d): Mildred Southern, Hazel Jones; Mixed Open: Sara Dickson, Wayne Hearn; Mixed 25s: Bobby Heald, Nancy Arndt; Mixed 30s: Hugh Grey, Melony Bailey; Mixed 35s: Wayne Hearn, Susan McDanal Love; Mixed 40s: Frances O'Sullivan, Mark Troutman; Mixed 45s: William Ashley, Sharron Frahm; Mixed 50s: Kathy Lewis, Mike Lewis; Mixed 55s: Jim Owens, Katherine Shelburne; Mixed 60s: Maurice Everette, Vicki Everette; Mixed 65s: none; Mixed 70s: Martha Norman, Harris Sanders; Father–Son: Elwood Parker, Richard Parker; Mother–Daughter (d): Cindi Khanlarian, Somer Khanlarian; Father–Daughter (d): Clif Patterson, Meggan Patterson;

Mother–Son (d): William Roberts, Patricia Hutton

1999
Men's Open (s): Miles Clouston; Men's Open (d): Miles Clouston, Jeff Zinn; Men's 25s (s): Richard Parker; Men's 25s (d): Richard Parker, Buck Stephenson; Men's 30s (s): Oscar Blacutt; Men's 30s (d): Richard Parker, Buck Stephenson; Men's 35s: Wayne Hearn; Men's 35s (d): Cliff Skakle, Wayne Hearn; Men's 40s (s): Craig Lemley; Men's 40s (d): Cliff Skakle, Mark Troutman; Men's 45s (s): Fred Robinson; Men's 45s (d): Bill Ashley, Doug Eller; Men's 50s (s): J.W. Quick; Men's 50s (d): Bobby Heald, Bill Cole; Men's 55s (s): Bob Adams; Men's 55s (d): Jim Perkins, John Mitchell; Men's 60s (s): Norman Chambers; Men's 60s (d): Willis Andrews, Greg Grant; Men's 65s (s): Bill Weathers; Men's 65s (d): Jack McGinn, Bill Weathers; Men's 70s (s): Bill Weathers; Men's 70s (d): Abe Ross, Jim Kelly; Men's 75s (s): Buck Archer; Men's 75s (d): Buck Archer, Gordon Reynolds; Men's 80s (s): Wade MacDonald; Men's 80s (d): Wade MacDonald, Harold Southern; Women's Open (s): Jackie Houston; Women's Open (d): Jennifer Goodling, Somer Khanlarian; Women's 25s (s): Ann Adams; Women's 25s (d): Myra Hill, Joan Jones; Women's 30s: Mariana Routh Hollman; Women's 30s (d): none; Women's 35s (s): Mariana Routh Hollman; Women's 35s (d): Susan McDanal Love, Mariana Routh Hollman; Women's 40s (s): Susie Love; Women's 40s (d): Susie Love, Lloyd Ford; Women's 45s (s): Miriam Morey; Women's 45s (d): Saundra Denny, Mary Rose; Women's 50s (s): Liz Smoake; Women's 50s (d): Sharon Greene, Susie Hill; Women's 55s (s): Tina Klaus; Women's 55s (d): Pat Cox, Katherine Shelburne; Women's 60s (s): Pat Cox; Women's 60s (d): Pat Cox, Julia Anne Holt; Women's 65s (s): Caroline Clark; Women's 65s (d): Jean Hilsby, Caroline Clark;

Women's 70s (s): Martha Norman; Women's 70s (d): Peggy Golden, Sara Jones; Women's 75s (s): Mildred Southern; Women's 75s (d): Mildred Southern, Hazel Jones; Mixed Open: Jennifer Goodling, Oscar Blacutt; Mixed 25s: David Carroll, Joan Jones; Mixed 30s: Jennifer Goodling, Mark Troutman; Mixed 35s: Wayne Hearn, Susan McDanal Love; Mixed 40s: Faye Thomas, Clay Thomas; Mixed 45s: Faye Thomas, Clay Thomas; Mixed 50s: Mike Harris, Susan Taylor; Mixed 55s: none; Mixed 60s: Maurice Everette, Vicki Everette; Mixed 65s: none; Mixed 70s: Hazel Jones, Charles Stevens; Father–Son: Elwood Parker, Richard Parker; Mother–Daughter (d): Cindi Khanlarian, Somer Khanlarian; Father–Daughter (d): Albert Khanlarian, Somer Khanlarian Mother–Son (d): Buck Stephenson, Rayma Stephenson; Women's Wheelchair: Harriet Enzor

2000
Men's Open (s): Michael Berger; Men's Open (d): Michael Berger, Ryan Shupe; Men's 30s (s): James Krege; Men's 30s (d): Kelly Hunter, Andy Ringlien; Men's 35s: Wayne Hearn; Men's 35s (d): George Husk, Wayne Hearn; Men's 40s (s): Cliff Skakle; Men's 40s (d): Cliff Skakle, John Arciero; Men's 45s (s): Dennis Engelbrecht; Men's 45s (d): Scott Stevenson, Dennis Engelbrecht; Men's 50s (s): Bobby Heald; Men's 50s (d): Bobby Heald, Bill Cole; Men's 55s (s): Bob Adams; Men's 55s (d): Jim Perkins, John Mitchell; Men's 60s (s): Norman Chambers; Men's 60s (d): Willis Anderson, Greg Grant; Men's 65s (s): Bill Weathers; Men's 65s (d): Morris Denton, Eric Moore; Men's 70s (s): : Bill Weathers; Men's 70s (d): John Bowen, Tom Willson; Men's 75s (s): Charles Lambeth; Men's 75s (d): Frank Heberer, George Simkins; Men's 80s (s): Wade MacDonald; Men's 80s (d): James Chavasse, Daniel Geller; Women's Open (s): Douglas Wink; Women's

ADULT STATE CLOSED CHAMPIONS HISTORY (CONTINUED)

Open (d): Jennifer Goodling, Somer Khanlarian; Women's 30s: Mariana Routh Hollman; Women's 30s (d): none; Women's 35s (s): Susan McDanald Love; Women's 35s (d): Mary Lloyd Barbera, Kelly Gaines; Women's 40s (s): Susie Love; Women's 40s (d): Susie Love, Lloyd Ford; Women's 45s (s): Faye Thomas; Women's 45s (d): Mary Lida Alexander, Liz Smoake; Women's 50s (s): Faye Thomas; Women's 50s (d): Dona Bowland, Katherine Shelburne; Women's 55s (s): Liz Smoake; Women's 55s (d): Saundra Denny, Marla Figard; Women's 60s (s): Pat Cox; Women's 60s (d): Pat Cox, Julia Anne Holt; Women's 65s (s): Caroline Clark; Women's 65s (d): Jean Hilsby, Caroline Clark; Women's 70s (s): Lois Walker; Women's 70s (d): Lois Walker, Sara Jones; Women's 75s (s): Mildred Southern; Women's 75s (d): Mildred Southern, Hazel Jones; Mixed Open: Jennifer Goodling, Oscar Blacutt; Mixed 30s: Mariana Routh Hollman, Buck Stephenson; Mixed 35s: Wayne Hearn, Susan McDanald Love; Mixed 40s: Edie Shepley, Sid Hanes; Mixed 45s: Faye Thomas, Clay Thomas; Mixed 50s: Audrey Beddingfield, Bob Beddingfield; Mixed 55s: Walter Brown, Katherine Shelburne; Mixed 60s: Maurice Everette, Vicki Everette; Mixed 65s: Charlotte Meyer, Gordon Alford; Mixed 70s: Allen Goslen, Mildred Southern; Father–Son: Robert Ormsby, Doug Ormsby; Mother– Daughter (d): Anne Gorrell, Catherine Gorrell; Father–Daughter (d): Clif and Meggan Patterson; Mother–Son (d): Patricia Hutton, William Roberts; Women's Wheelchair: Harriet Enzor

2001

Men's Open (s): Doug Root; Men's Open (d): Doug Root, Michael Berger; Men's 25s (s): Claes Persson; Men's 25s (d): Thomas Eek, N. Nilson; Men's 30s (s): Bill Schillings; Men's 30s (d): GK Fleming, George Newsome; Men's 35s: Wayne Hearn; Men's 35s (d): Wayne Hearn, Cliff Skakle; Men's 40s (s): Neil Alderman; Men's 40s (d): Larry Karageanes, Mark Troutman; Men's 45s (s): Cliff Skakle; Men's 45s (d): Bill Ashley, Doug Eller; Men's 50s (s): J.W. Quick; Men's 50s (d): George Mauney, Scott Pollard; Men's 55s (s): Bob Adams; Men's 55s (d): Bill Cole, Robert Heald; Men's 60s (s): Norman Chambers; Men's 60s (d): Maurice Everette, Al Griffin; Men's 65s (s): Al Griffin; Men's 65s (d): James Bland, Jack McGinn; Men's 70s (s): : Bill Weathers; Men's 70s (d): John Bowen, Tom Willson; Men's 75s (s): Bill Weathers; Men's 75s (d): Norman Jarrard, Bill Weathers; Men's 80s (s): Scott Mitchell; Men's 80s (d): Wade MacDonald, Harold Southern; Men's 90s (s): Vince Connerat; Women's Open (s): none; Women's Open (d): none; Women's 25s (s): Cara Robinette; Women's 25s (d): none; Women's 30s: Mariana Routh Hollman; Women's 30s (d): none; Women's 35s (s): Susan McDanald Love; Women's 35s (d): Jayne Andochick, Dale Hall; Women's 40s (s): Susie Love; Women's 40s (d): Nanette Huff, Wendy McColskey; Women's 45s (s): Janet Moseley; Women's 45s (d): Sharon Greene, Susie Hill; Women's 50s (s): Linda Chambers; Women's 50s (d): Sharron Greene, Susie Hill; Women's 55s (s): Liz Smoake; Women's 55s (d): Saundra Denny, Sharon Greene; Women's 60s (s): Pat Cox; Women's 60s (d): Pat Cox, Julia Anne Holt; Women's 65s (s): Sue Baggett; Women's 65s (d): Julia Anne Holt, Barbara Spencer; Women's 70s (s): none; Women's 70s (d): Julia Anne Holt, Jane Reynolds; Women's 75s

(s): Helen Lee; Women's 75s (d): none; Women's 80s (s): Helen Lee; Mixed Open: Cara Robinette, Cliff Skakle; Mixed 30s: Jennifer Goodling, Mark Troutman; Mixed 35s: Wayne Hearn, Susan McDanald Love; Mixed 40s: Russ Bernthal, Wendy McColskey; Mixed 45s: Faye Thomas, Clay Thomas; Mixed 50s: Sharon Greene, Mike McHone; Mixed 55s: Robert Beverly, Kay Beverly; Mixed 60s: Walter Brown, Katherine Shelburne; Mixed 65s: Charlotte Meyer, Gordon Alford; Father–Son: Robert Ormsby, Doug Ormsby; Mother–Daughter (d): Anne Gorrell, Catherine Gorrell; Father–Daughter (d): Clif and Meggan Patterson; Mother–Son (d): Sally Ormsby, Doug Ormsby; Women's Wheelchair (s): Harriet Enzor; Men's Wheelchair (s): Jeff Kegler; Men's Wheelchair (d): Jeff Kegler, Eddie Hawkins

2002

Men's Open (s): Doug Root; Men's Open (d): Doug Root, Marcio Torres; Men's 25s (s): Christopher Ehmeke; Men's 25s (d): Thomas Eek, Niclas Nilsson; Men's 30s (s): Bobby Hession; Men's 30s (d): Chris Cagle, Richard Parker; Men's 35s: Jon Stitt; Men's 35s (d): Andy Avram, Brad Cherry; Men's 40s (s): Wayne Hearn; Men's 40s (d): John Arciero, Michael Conroy; Men's 45s (s): Jim Schaefer; Men's 45s (d): Kenny House, Roger Martin; Men's 50s (s): J.W. Quick; Men's 50s (d): George Mauney, Scott Pollard; Men's 55s (s): Bill Cole; Men's 55s (d): Bill Cole, Robert Adams; Men's 60s (s): Ronnie Robinson; Men's 60s (d): John Benson, Walter Brown; Men's 65s (s): Maurice Everette; Men's 65s (d): Maurice Everette, Al Griffin; Men's 70s (s): : Lawrence McGee; Men's 70s (d): Joseph Dudley, Bill Weathers; Men's 75s (s): Bill Weathers; Men's 75s (d): Charles Lambeth, Bill Weathers; Men's 80s (s): Gordon Reynolds; Men's 80s (d): Gordon Reynolds, David Radcliffe; Women's Open (s): Brooke Skeen;

Women's Open (d): Brooke Skeen, Monica Galik; Women's 25s (s): Leigh Sink; Women's 25s (d): none; Women's 30s: Leigh Sink; Women's 30s (d): none; Women's 35s (s): Susan McDonald Love; Women's 35s (d): Tedi Mersky, Dale Hall; Women's 40s (s): Lloyd Ford; Women's 40s (d): Mariana Routh Hollman, Edie Shepley; Women's 45s (s): Lynn Thomas; Women's 45s (d): Sheila Ernest, Lynn Thomas; Women's 50s (s): Faye Thomas; Women's 50s (d): Saundra Denny, Chris Graham; Women's 55s (s): Sharon Greene; Women's 55s (d): Barbara Brown, Charlotte Meyer; Women's 60s (s): Jane Sandridge; Women's 60s (d): none; Women's 65s (s): June Connerat; Women's 65s (d): none; Women's 70s (s): Martha Norman; Women's 70s (d): Shirley Stump, Kathleen Tucker; Women's 75s (s): Martha Norman; Women's 75s (d): none; Women's 80s (s): Mildred Southern; Women's 80s (d): Mildred Southern, Elva Jones; Mixed Open: Doug Root, Brooke Skeen; Mixed 30s: none; Mixed 35s: John Arciero, Edie Shepley; Mixed 40s: Lloyd Ford, Scott Pollard; Mixed 45s: Dona Bowland, Robert Jones; Mixed 50s: Sharon Greene, Mike McHone; Mixed 55s: Susie Hill, Durham, Terry Wicker; Mixed 60s: Katherine Shelburne, Gordon Hammes; Mixed 65s: Barbara Brown, Joe White; Mixed 70s: Allen Goslen, Mildred Southern; Father–Son: Jon Davis, Jon Davis; Mother–Daughter (d): Gwen Highsmith-Quick, Winnie Quick; Father–Daughter (d): Barry Mabe, Elisha Mabe; Mother–Son (d): Sheila Ernest, Benjamin Ernest; Junior Wheelchair: Christian Felkl; Women's Wheelchair (s): Harriet Enzor; Women's Wheelchair (d): Harriet Enzor, Kelly Howell; Men's Wheelchair A (s): Jeff Kegler; Men's Wheelchair (d): Eddie Hawkins, Jeff Kegler; Men's Wheelchair B (s): Jeff Hall

2003

Men's Open (s): Mike Murray; Men's Open (d): Mark Brodie, John Isner; Men's 25s (s): Pertti Viskari; Men's 25s (d): Thomas Eek, Niclas Nilsson; Men's 30s (s): Oscar Blacutt; Men's 30s (d): Richard Parker, Buck Stephenson; Men's 35s: Wayne Hearn; Men's 35s (d): Andy Avram, Brad Cherry; Men's 40s (s): Robert Stephens; Men's 40s (d): Neil Alderman, Mark Tuttle; Men's 45s (s): Jim Schaefer; Men's 45s (d): Kenny House, Roger Martin; Men's 50s (s): Dennis Engelbrecht; Men's 50s (d): Bill Ashley, Doug Eller; Men's 55s (s): Bill Cole; Men's 55s (d): John Mitchell, James Perkins; Men's 60s (s): Ronnie Robinson; Men's 60s (d): Sam Bell, Vernon Hebert; Men's 65s (s): Al Griffin; Men's 65s (d): Maurice Everette, Al Griffin; Men's 70s (s): : Bill Weathers; Men's 70s (d): Joseph Dudley, Bill Weathers; Men's 75s (s): Bill Weathers; Men's 75s (d): Andrew Robinson, Bill Weathers; Men's 80s (s): Hal Cook; Men's 80s (d): Jim Chavasse, Frank Heberer; Women's Open (s): Brooke Skeen; Women's Open (d): Sue Haddon, Douglas Wink; Women's 25s (s): none; Women's 25s (d): Diane Mulkey, Kim Overman; Women's 30s: none; Women's 30s (d): none; Women's 35s (s): Susan McDonald Love; Women's 35s (d): Nina Cloaninger, Dale Hall; Women's 40s (s): Mariana Routh Hollman; Women's 40s (d): Mariana Routh Hollman, Edie Shepley; Women's 45s (s): Miriam Morey; Women's 45s (d): Sheila Ernest, Janet Moseley; Women's 50s (s): Faye Thomas; Women's 50s (d): Sharron Frahm, Wendy McColskey; Women's 55s (s): none; Women's 55s (d): Saundra Denny, Chris Graham; Women's 60s (s): Saundra Denny; Women's 60s (d): none; Women's 65s (s): Vicki Everette; Women's 65s (d): Vicki Everette, Julia Anne Holt; Women's 70s (s): Christiane Jackson; Women's 70s (d): Julia Anne Holt, Jane Reynolds; Women's 75s (s): Kay Wakley; Women's 75s (d): Peggy Golden, Kay Wakley; Mixed Open: Wayne Hearn, Brooke Skeen; Mixed 25s: Selin Nassi, Juan Sandoval; Mixed 30s: Jennifer Goodling, Donald Marriott; Mixed 35s: Wayne Hearn, Susan McDonald Love; Mixed 40s: Lloyd Ford, Scott Pollard; Mixed 45s: Margaret Bowles, Peter Popovich; Mixed 50s: Clay Thomas, Faye Thomas; Mixed 55s: Saundra Denny, Terry Wicker; Mixed 60s: Walt Brown, Katherine Shelburne; Mixed 65s: Barbara Brown, Joe White

2004

Men's Open (s): Ganiyu Adelekan; Men's Open (d): Ganiyu Adelekan, Raleigh, Yakuba Suleiman; Men's 25s (s): Christopher Ehmcke; Men's 25s (d): John Meyer, Juan Sandoval; Men's 30s (s): Oscar Blacutt; Men's 30s (d): Richard Parker, Matt Rowe; Men's 35s: Oscar Blacutt; Men's 35s (d): Thomas Eek, Wayne Hearn; Men's 40s (s): Neil Alderman; Men's 40s (d): Neil Alderman, Mark Tuttle; Men's 45s (s): Jim Schaefer; Men's 45s (d): Michael Martin, Dewey Stroud; Men's 50s (s): Douglas Eller; Men's 50s (d): Bill Cole, Doug Eller; Men's 55s (s): Scott Pollard; Men's 55s (d): Robert Adams, Bill Cole; Men's 60s (s): Robert Adams; Men's 60s (d): Robert Adams, Dan Elks; Men's 65s (s): Al Griffin; Men's 65s (d): Willis Anderson, James Gordon; Men's 70s (s): : Robin Gardner; Men's 70s (d): Herb Browne, Jack McGinn; Men's 75s (s): Bill Weathers; Men's 75s (d): Andrew Anderson, Bill Weathers; Men's 80s (s): William Walker; Men's 80s (d): Robert Boyce, Harold Southern; Men's 85s (s): Wade MacDonald; Men's 85s (d): Wade MacDonald, Jim Chavasse; Women's Open (s): Catherine Newman; Women's Open (d): Loni Worsley, Kara Worsley; Women's 30s s: Anna Zarate; Women's 30s (d): none; Women's 35s (s): Susan McDonald Love; Women's 35s (d): Melony

ADULT STATE CLOSED CHAMPIONS HISTORY (CONTINUED)

Bailey, Diane Mulkey; Women's 40s (s): Mariana Routh Hollman; Women's 40s (d): none; Women's 45s (s): Faye Thomas; Women's 45s (d): none; Women's 50s (s): Miriam Morey; Women's 50s (d): Sharron Frahm, Wendy McColskey; Women's 55s (s): Christina Klaus; Women's 55s (d): none; Women's 60s (s): Jane Sandridge; Women's 60s (d): Patricia Cox, Christina Klaus; Women's 65s (s): Patricia Cox; Women's 65s (d): Patricia Cox, Julia Anne Holt; Women's 70s (s): Caroline Clark; Women's 70s (d): Julia Anne Holt, Jane Reynolds; Women's 75s (s): Martha Norman; Women's 75s (d): none; Women's 80s (s): Mildred Southern; Women's 80s (d): Mildred Southern, Mary Weaver; Mixed Open: Tanner Haddon, Sue Haddon; Mixed 25s: none; Mixed 30s: Todd Campbell, Maaret Voutilainen; Mixed 35s: Wayne Hearn, Susan McDonald Love; Mixed 40s: Mariana Routh Hollman, Jeffrey Zinn; Mixed 45s: Margaret Bowles, Peter Popovich; Mixed 50s: Clay Thomas, Faye Thomas; Mixed 55s: Karol Beverly, Robert Beverly; Mixed 60s: Carlene Marion, Bill Marion; Mixed 65s: June Connerat, Goetz Reinbold; Mixed 70s: Robert Meyer, Charlotte Meyer; Father–Son: Michael Criscoe, Keith Criscoe; Mother–Daughter (d): Gwen Highsmith-Quick, Winnie Quick; Father–Daughter (d): Terry Wood, Cayce Wood; Mother–Son (d): Lee Bailey, Rhonda Bailey; Senior Father–Son: Mike Corthum, Michael Corthum; Men's Wheelchair Open (s): Jeff Kegler; Men's Wheelchair A (s): Gregory Taylor; Men's Wheelchair B (s): Tim Underhill; Men's Wheelchair Open (d): Eddie

Hawkins, Jeff Kegler; Women's Wheelchair Open (s): Harriet Enzor

2005

Men's Open (s): Daniel McCain; Men's Open (d): William Noblitt, Mason Schermerhorn; Men's 25s (s): Robert McAdoo; Men's 25s (d): Robert Phillips, Clint Weathers; Men's 30s (s): Matthew Rowe; Men's 30s (d): Richard Parker, Matt Rowe; Men's 35s: Wayne Hearn; Men's 35s (d): Oscar Blacutt, Mike Weidl; Men's 40s (s): Neil Alderman; Men's 40s (d): Neil Alderman, Mark Tuttle; Men's 45s (s): Pender Murphy; Men's 45s (d): Andy Avram, Mark Dillon; Men's 50s (s): Dennis Engelbrecht; Men's 50s (d): Bill Ashley, Doug Eller; Men's 55s (s): Scott Pollard; Men's 55s (d): Robert Adams, Bill Cole; Men's 60s (s): Robert Adams; Men's 60s (d): John Mitchell, James Perkins; Men's 65s (s): Willis Anderson; Men's 65s (d): Willis Anderson, James Gordon; Men's 70s (s): Al Griffin; Men's 70s (d): Robin Gardner, James Bailey; Men's 75s (s): Bill Weathers; Men's 75s (d): Floyd Chandler, Bill Weathers; Men's 80s (s): Norman Dawson; Men's 80s (d): Norman Dawson, Harold Southern; Men's 85s (s): Wade MacDonald; Women's Open (s): Kelly McCain; Women's Open (d): Gwen Highsmith-Quick, Winnie Quick; Women's 30s: Chrisann Parr Ricciardi; Women's 30s (d): none; Women's 35s (s): Diane Mulkey; Women's 35s (d): Susan McDonald Love, Diane Mulkey; Women's 40s (s): none; Women's 40s (d): none; Women's 45s (s): Dale Hall; Women's 45s (d): Lynne Davis, Aimee Norris; Women's 50s (s): Miriam Morey; Women's 50s (d): Miriam Morey, Gay Engelbrecht; Women's 55s (s): Faye Thomas; Women's 55s (d): none; Women's 60s (s): Christina Klaus; Women's 60s (d): Saundra Denny, Marla FIgard; Women's 65s (s): Vicki Everette; Women's 65s (d): Patricia Cox, Julia Anne Holt;

Women's 70s (s): Christiane Jackson; Women's 70s (d): Julia Anne Holt, Jane Reynolds; Women's 75s (s): Jean Hilsby; Women's 75s (d): none; Women's 80s (s): Mildred Southern; Women's 80s (d): Mildred Southern, Mary Weaver; Mixed Open: Kelly McCain, Daniel McCain; Mixed 25s: Diane Mulkey, Clint Weathers; Mixed 30s: none; Mixed 35s: Wayne Hearn, Susan McDonald Love; Mixed 40s: Mariana Routh Hollman, Junior Luffman; Mixed 45s: Kenny House, Miriam Morey; Mixed 50s: Wendy McColskey, Mike McHone; Mixed 55s: Sharon Greene, Mike McHone; Mixed 60s: Marla Figard, James Perkins; Mixed 65s: Vicki Everette, Maurice Everette; Mixed 70s: Gordon Alford, Martha Norman; Father–Son: Gary Whitman, Troy Whitman; Mother–Daughter (d): Gwen Highsmith-Quick, Winnie Quick; Father–Daughter (d): Clif Patterson, Meggan Patterson; Mother–Son: Deborah Louden, Brian Louden; Senior Father–Son: Elwood, Richard Parker; Men's Wheelchair A (s): David Kiley; Men's Wheelchair A (d): William Eno, Jeff Kegler; Men's Wheelchair C (s): Jeff Dills; Men's Wheelchair C (d): Jasmin Bambur, Jeff Dills; Quad Wheelchair: (s): Gregory Taylor

2006

Men's Open (s): Brett Ross; Men's Open (d): Brett Ross, Derrick Spice; Men's 25s (s): Tanner Haddon; Men's 25s (d): Tanner Haddon, Chad York; Men's 30s (s): Christopher Ehmcke; Men's 30s (d): Tyler Haney, Shawn Cooke; Men's 35s: Oscar Blacutt; Men's 35s (d): Robert Phillips, Brad Cherry; Men's 40s (s): Neil Alderman; Men's 40s (d): Neil Alderman, Mark Tuttle; Men's 45s (s): Robert Stephens; Men's 45s (d): Andy Avram, Mark Dillon; Men's 50s (s): Michael Martin; Men's 50s (d): Kenny House, Michael Martin; Men's 55s (s): Scott Pollard; Men's 55s (d): Scott Pollard, George Mauney; Men's 60s (s): Robert Adams; Men's

60s (d): Robert Adams, Bill Cole; Men's 65s (s): Al Griffin; Men's 65s (d): Frank Douglas, Walter Brown; Men's 70s (s): : Gordon Hammes; Men's 70s (d): Gordon Alford, Goetz Reinbold; Men's 75s (s): Bill Weathers; Men's 75s (d): William Campbell, Bill Weathers; Men's 80s (s): Bill Weathers; Men's 80s (d): Jim Chavasse, Frank Heberer; Men's 85s (s): Jim Chavasse; Women's Open (s): Kelly McCain; Women's Open (d): Jennifer Stone, Melissa Wolf; Women's 30s: Kristen Deskevich; Women's 30s (d): Nancy Chirino, Christine Thompson; Women's 35s (s): Katherine Cheek; Women's 35s (d): Susan McDanald Love, Diane Mulkey; Women's 40s (s): Mariana Routh Hollman; Women's 40s (d): none; Women's 45s (s): Susan McDanald Love; Women's 45s (d): Dale Hall, Aimee Norris; Women's 50s (s): Miriam Morey; Women's 50s (d): Sharron Frahm, Wendy McColskey; Women's 55s (s): none; Women's 55s (d): none; Women's 60s (s): Christina Klaus; Women's 60s (d): Christina Klaus, Pat Cox; Women's 65s (s): none; Women's 65s (d): none; Women's 70s (s): Caroline Clark; Women's 70s (d): Julia Anne Holt, Jane Reynolds; Women's 75s (s): Caroline Clark; Women's 75s (d): Julia Anne Holt, Jane Reynolds; Mixed Open: Oscar Blacutt, Cory Ann Avants; Mixed 30s: Shawn Cooke, Chrystal Rhodes; Mixed 35s: Mark Dillon, Susan McDanald Love; Mixed 40s: Neil Alderman, Nanette Huff; Mixed 45s: Debbie Carmazzi, Tom Parker; Mixed 50s: Wendy McColskey, Mike McHone; Mixed 55s: Randy Chamberlain, Christian Drury; Mixed 60s: Karol Beverly, Robert Beverly; Mixed 65s: Gordon Alford, Charlotte Meyer; Mixed 70s: Sue Baggett, Robert Baggett; Father–Son: John McGovern, Jonathan McGovern; Mother–Daughter (d): Susan McCain, Kelly McCain Father–Daughter (d): Mark Troutman, Mari Taylor Troutman

Mother–Son: Sheila Ernest, Benjamin Ernest

2007

Men's Open (s): Paul Goode; Men's Open (d): Toby Curtis, Dipesh Rao; Men's 25s (s): Tanner Haddon; Men's 25s (d): Tanner Haddon, William York; Men's 30s (s): Richard Parker; Men's 30s (d): Jeffrey Cato, Kasper Nielsen; Men's 35s: Oscar Blacutt; Men's 35s (d): Oscar Blacutt, Chris Cagle; Men's 40s (s): Richard Green; Men's 40s (d): Wade Jackson, Andy Wilkison; Men's 45s (s): John Arciero; Men's 45s (d): David Williams, Jonathan Robinson; Men's 50s (s): George Phillips; Men's 50s (d): Kenny House, Michael Martin; Men's 55s (s): Buster Brown; Men's 55s (d): Robert Adams, Bill Cole; Men's 60s (s): Robert Adams; Men's 60s (d): John Mitchell, James Perkins; Men's 65s (s): Al Griffin; Men's 65s (d): Walter Brown, Dan Elks; Men's 70s (s): : Gordon Hammes; Men's 70s (d): Al Griffin, Jack McGinn; Men's 75s (s): Bill Weathers; Men's 75s (d): John Bowen, Tom Willson; Men's 80s (s): Bill Weathers; Men's 80s (d): Robert Clutts, Raeford Turner; Women's Open (s): Cory Ann Avants; Women's Open (d): Cory Ann Avants, Kristin Koenig; Women's 25s (s): Melony Bailey; Women's 30s (s): Diana West; Women's 30s

(d): none; Women's 35s (s): Diane Mulkey; Women's 35s (d): Melony Bailey, Diane Mulkey; Women's 40s (s): Elizabeth Edwards; Women's 40s (d): none; Women's 45s (s): Margy Pettit; Women's 45s (d): Robin Edwards, Carolyn McGarry; Women's 50s (s): Margy Pettit; Women's 50s (d): Deborah Foster, Dee Wilson; Women's 55s (s): none; Women's 55s (d): none; Women's 60s (s): Christina Klaus; Women's 60s (d): Christina Klaus, Pat Cox; Women's 65s (s): Margarita Wamholtz; Women's 65s (d): none; Women's 70s (s): Emma Frye; Women's 70s (d): Barbara Brown, Charlotte Meyer; Women's 75s (s): Caroline Clark; Women's 75s (d): Caroline Clark, Jean Hilsby; Women's 80s S; Martha Norman; Women's 80s (d): Hazel Anderson, Martha Norman; Mixed Open: Oscar Blacutt, Cory Ann Avants; Mixed 25s: Scott Ross, Joy Ross; Mixed 30s: none; Mixed 35s: Diane Mulkey, W. Clint Weathers; Mixed 40s: none; Mixed 45s: John Arciero, Aimee Norris; Mixed 50s: Wendy McColskey, Mike McHone; Mixed 55s: Clay Thomas, Faye Thomas; Mixed 60s: Ronald Keiger, Alice Keiger; Mixed 65s: Cindy Hall, Richard Hall; Mixed 70s: Thomas Sayetta, Anne Sayetta; Father–Son: Robert Lake, Robert Lake; Mother–

ADULT STATE CLOSED CHAMPIONS HISTORY (CONTINUED)

Daughter (d): Carla Huffman, Tori Huffman; Father–Daughter (d): Terry Wood, Cayce Wood

2008

Men's Open (s): William Noblitt; Men's Open (d): David Stone, Will Plyler; Men's 25s (s): Chad Carlson; Men's 25s (d): Chad Carlson, Ashley Shaw; Men's 30s (s): Chris Cagle; Men's 30s (d): Chris Cagle, Mike Weidl; Men's 35s: John Chatlak; Men's 35s (d): Marc Kantor, Clint Weathers; Men's 40s (s): Neil Alderman; Men's 40s (d): Neil Alderman, Mark Tuttle; Men's 45s (s): John Arciero; Men's 45s (d): John Chatlak, Wayne Hearn; Men's 50s (s): Bradley Wyckoff; Men's 50s (d): Kenny House, Michael Martin; Men's 55s (s): Doug Eller; Men's 55s (d): Bill Ashley, Doug Eller; Men's 60s (s): Robert Adams; Men's 60s (d): Robert Adams, Bill Cole; Men's 65s (s): Dan Elks; Men's 65s (d): Sam Bell, Walter Brown; Men's 70s (s): : Norman Chambers; Men's 70s (d): Willis Anderson, Jack McGinn; Men's 75s (s): James Bland; Men's 75s (d): Herbert Browne, Joseph Dudley; Men's 80s (s): Bill Weathers; Men's 80s (d): Bill Weathers, Gene Nolan; Women's Open (s): Kelly McCain; Women's Open (d): Cory Ann Avants, Mary Pate; Women's 25s (s): Diane Mulkey; Women's 25s (d): none; Women's 30s (s): Barbara Simpson; Women's 30s (d): none; Women's 35s (s): none; Women's 35s (d): none; Women's 40s (s): Barbara Simpson; Women's 40s (d): Nanette Huff, Lloyd Ford; Women's 45s (s): Margy Pettit; Women's 45s (d): Tina Gray, Robin Edwards; Women's 50s (s): Margy Pettit; Women's 50s

(d): Paula Conley, Billie Oxrieder; Women's 55s (s): Beverly Ranger; Women's 55s (d): Gay Engelbrecht, Faye Thomas; Women's 60s (s): Christina Klaus; Women's 60s (d): Christina Klaus, Pat Cox; Women's 65s (s): none; Women's 65s (d): Emma Frye, June Wasoll; Women's 70s (s): Vicki Everette; Women's 70s (d): none; Women's 75s (s): none; Women's 75s (d): none; Women's 80s S; Martha Norman; Women's 80s (d): Elizabeth Henry, Dorothy Maloney; Mixed Open: Paul Goode, Cory Ann Avants; Mixed 25s: Massimo Bosso, Julie Tanner; Mixed 30s: none; Mixed 35s: Scott Figel, Stacey Schefflin; Mixed 40s: Dora Burdzinska-Drezek, David Myers; Mixed 45s: John Arciero, Aimee Norris; Mixed 50s: Wendy McColskey, Mike McHone; Mixed 55s: Dennis Engelbrecht, Gay Engelbrecht; Mixed 60s: Ronald Keiger, Alice Keiger; Mixed 65s: none; Mixed 70s: Gordon Alford, Barbara Brown; Father–Son: Michael Chriscoe, Michael Chriscoe; Mother–Daughter (d): Gwen Highsmith-Quick, Winnie Quick; Father–Daughter (d): Christy Core, Hap Core

2009

Men's Open (s): Robbye Poole; Men's Open (d): Brad Pomeroy, Robbye Poole; Men's 25s (s): Michael Criscoe; Men's 25s (d): none; Men's 30s (s): Tyler Haney; Men's 30s (d): none; Men's 35s: Christopher Ehmcke; Men's 35s (d): Scott Figel, Charles Reiney; Men's 40s (s): Oscar Blacutt; Men's 40s (d): David Johnson, Mathew Menzi; Men's 45s (s): John Arciero; Men's 45s (d): Ricky McElreath, Jonathan Sawyer; Men's 50s (s): John Arciero; Men's 50s (d): H. Fred Pfuhl, James Roueche; Men's 55s (s): Dennis Englebrecht; Men's 55s (d): Elbert Brown, Al Mack; Men's 60s (s): Scott Pollard; Men's 60s (d): Scott Pollard, George Mauney; Men's 65s (s): Zoltan Fabian; Men's

65s (d): John Mitchell, Jim Perkins; Men's 70s (s): Gordon Hammes; Men's 70s (d): Willis Anderson, Al Griffin; Men's 75s (s): Gordon Hammes; Men's 75s (d): Gordon Hammes, James Bland; Men's 80s (s): Bill Weathers; Men's 80s (d): Raeford Turner, Newman Way; Men's 85s (s): Jim Chavasse; Men's 90s (s): Jim Chavasse; Women's Open (s): Christina Lee; Women's Open (d): none; Women's 25s (s): none; Women's 25s (d): none; Women's 30s (s): Cynthia Staton; Women's 30s (d): none; Women's 35s (s): Carolina Blouin; Women's 35s (d): none; Women's 40s (s): Amy Dillingham; Women's 40s (d): none; Women's 45s (s): Susan McDanald Love; Women's 45s (d): none; Women's 50s (s): none; Women's 50s (d): Anne Frautschi, Kris McDonald; Women's 55s (s): Faye Thomas; Women's 55s (d): Christian Drury, Beth Lambeth; Women's 60s (s): Judith McAllister; Women's 60s (d): none; Women's 65s (s): none; Women's 65s (d): none; Women's 70s (s): none; Women's 70s (d): Vicki Everette, Sylvia Gaines; Women's 75s (s): Caroline Clark; Women's 75s (d): none; Women's 80s (s): Martha Norman; Women's 80s (d): none; Mixed Open: Brian Ford, Caroline Newman; Mixed 25s: none; Mixed 30s: Shawn Cooke, Chrystal Rhodes; Mixed 35s: Diane Mulkey, Clint Weathers; Mixed 40s: Amy Dillingham, David Wolf; Mixed 45s: Mark Dillon, Susan McDanald Love; Mixed 50s: Wendy McColskey, Mike McHone; Mixed 55s: Clay Thomas, Faye Thomas; Mixed 60s: Audrey Beddingfield, Robert Beddingfield; Mixed 65s: none; Mixed 70s: Ronald Keiger, Alice Keiger; Father–Son: Robert Lake, Steve Lake; Mother–Daughter (d): Brittney Williams, Angelia Williams; Father–Daughter (d): Terry Wood, Cayce Wood; Senior Mother–Son (d): Cindi Khanlarian, Shane Khanlarian; Senior Father–Son: Willis Anderson, David Anderson

2010

Men's Open (s): Robbye Poole; Men's Open (d): Jonathan Stokke, Stephen Ward; Men's 25s (s): Gregory Artzt; Men's 25s (d): David Johnson, Ashley Shaw; Men's 30s (s): none; Men's 30s (d): Matthew Rowe, Michael Weidl; Men's 35s: Claes Persson; Men's 35s (d): Anders Persson, Claes Persson; Men's 40s (s): Christopher Ehmcke; Men's 40s (d): David Johnson, Adam Thomson; Men's 45s (s): George Husk; Men's 45s (d): John Deering, James Demos; Men's 50s (s): John Arciero; Men's 50s (d): Fred Pfuhl, James Roueche; Men's 55s (s): Gary McGrath; Men's 55s (d): Junior Luffman, Mike Martin; Men's 60s (s): Scott Pollard; Men's 60s (d): Mike McHone, John Walton; Men's 65s (s): Bill Cole; Men's 65s (d): Walt Brown, Bill Cole; Men's 70s (s): Al Griffin; Men's 70s (d): Willis Anderson, David Ringler; Men's 75s (s): Al Griffin; Men's 75s (d): Al Griffin, Jack McGinn; Men's 80s (s): Sharf Zinovy; Men's 80s (d): Raeford Turner, Newman Way; Men's 85s (s): Norman Dawson; Women's Open (s): Catherine Newman; Women's Open (d): Catherine Newman, Caroline Newman; Women's 25s (s): none; Women's 25s (d): none; Women's 30s (s): Amy Dillingham; Women's 30s (d): none; Women's 35s (s): Carolina Blouin; Women's 35s (d): none; Women's 40s (s): Amy Dillingham; Women's 40s (d): none; Women's 45s (s): Susan McDanald Love; Women's 45s (d): Dale Hall, Aimee Norris; Women's 50s (s): Frances O'Sullivan; Women's 50s (d): Frances O'Sullivan, Judi Stiff; Women's 55s (s): Dee Wilson; Women's 55s (d): Debbie Carmazzi, Joann Crolley; Women's 60s (s): Judith McAllister; Women's 60s (d): Alice Keiger, Rhonda Sykes;

Women's 65s (s): Christina Klaus; Women's 65s (d): none; Women's 70s (s): none; Women's 70s (d): none; Women's 75s (s): none; Women's 75s (d): none; Women's 80s (s): Martha Norman; Women's 80s (d): none; Mixed Open: Catherine Newman, Robbye Poole; Mixed 25s: none; Mixed 30s: none; Mixed 35s: Diane Mulkey, Clint Weathers; Mixed 40s: Mariana Routh Hollman, George Phillips; Mixed 45s: none; Mixed 50s: Mike McHone, Janet Moseley; Mixed 55s: Sharon Mitchell, Tom Parker; Mixed 60s: Ronald Keiger, Rhonda Sykes; Mixed 65s: none; Mixed 70s: Ronald Keiger, Alice Keiger; Father–Son: James Roueche, James Roueche; Mother–Daughter (d): Dona Bowland, Michelle Johnson Father–Daughter (d): Laneal Vaughn, Lauren Vaughn; Mother–Son (d): Deborah Louden, Brian Louden; Senior Father–Son: Willis Anderson, David Anderson

2011

Men's Open (s): Robbye Poole; Men's Open (d): John Haywood, Robert Haywood; Men's 25s (s): Keith Criscoe; Men's 25s (d): none; Men's 30s (s): none; Men's 30s (d): Mike Weidl, Tanner Haddon; Men's 35s: Michael Roper; Men's 35s (d): Scott Fligel , Lawrence Fuller; Men's 40s (s): Brad Hobday; Men's 40s (d): David Johnson, Adam Thomson; Men's 45s (s): Brad Cherry; Men's 45s (d): Brad Hobday, Leslie McIver; Men's 50s (s): John Arciero; Men's 50s (d): William Annear, George Phillips; Men's 55s (s): Scott Pollard; Men's 55s (d): Mike Martin, Dewey Stroud; Men's 60s (s): Scott Pollard; Men's 60s (d): Mike McHone, John Walton; Men's 65s (s): Richard

Shipman; Men's 65s (d): William Trott, William Cole; Men's 70s (s): : Jimmy Washington; Men's 70s (d): Walter Brown, Jerrold Hinton; Men's 75s (s): Al Griffin; Men's 75s (d): Gordon Alford, Hugh Wise; Men's 80s (s): Richard Stennett; Men's 80s (d): Joe Dudley, Richard Stennett; Men's 85s (s): Norman Dawson; Women's Open (s): Jennifer Ansari; Women's Open (d): none; Women's 25s (s): none; Women's 25s (d): none; Women's 30s (s): Kimberly Culbreth; Women's 30s (d): none; Women's 35s (s): Carolina Blouin; Women's 35s (d): none; Women's 40s (s): Michele Sawyer; Women's 40s (d): none; Women's 45s (s): Adelyn Lutz Parker; Women's 45s (d): Elizabeth Meiners, Monica Nee; Women's 50s (s): Janet Moseley; Women's 50s (d): none; Women's 55s (s): Beverley Ranger; Women's 55s (d): none; Women's 60s (s): Judith McAllister; Women's 60s (d): Sharron Frahm, Christina Klaus; Women's 65s (s): Christina Klaus; Women's 65s (d): none; Women's 70s (s): none; Women's 70s (d): none; Women's 75s (s): none; Women's 75s (d): none; Women's 80s (s): Martha Norman; Women's 80s (d): none; Mixed Open: Taylor Davidson, Kevin Le; Mixed 25s: none; Mixed 30s: none; Mixed 35s: Carolina Blouin, William Poore; Mixed 40s: none; Mixed 45s: none; Mixed 50s: Janet Moseley, George Phillips; Mixed 55s: Debbie Carmazzi, Frank Carmazzi; Mixed 60s: Sharron Frahm, Mike McHone; Mixed 65s: Caroline Beverly, Bob Beverly; Mixed 70s: none; Father–Son: James Roueche, James Roueche; Mother–Daughter (d): Michele Sawyer, Erica Sawyer; Father–Daughter (d): Wade Jackson, MaryBeth Jackson; Mother–Son (d): none; Senior Father–Son: John McGovern, Jonathan McGovern

NORTH CAROLINA ADULT STATE CLOSED NTRP CHAMPIONS HISTORY

1994

Men's 2.5 (s): Tracey Smith; Men's 3.0 (s): Lee Whitacre; Men's 3.0 (d): Ben Parsons, Matt Rhodes; Men's 3.5 (s): Robert Krall; Men's 3.5 (d): Patrick Egan, Doug Hershey; Men's 4.0 (s): Joel Carmichael; Men's 4.0 (d): Garlan Homes, Wilson, Ras Homes; Men's 4.5 (s): Tom Wilson; Men's 4.5 (d): Marcel Janssen, Hani Nassar; Men's 5.0 (s): Matt Mason; Women's 3.0 (s): Hilda Savin; Women's 3.5 (s): Brenda Hatchell; Women's 3.5 (d): Sherrie Austin, Wanda Davis; Women's 4.0 (s): Vicki Goodwin; Women's 4.5 (s): Debbie Carmazzi; Women's 4.5 (d): Janet Patterson, Kathy Vartanian; Mixed 4.0: Freddie Johnson, Tarina Diaz-Llaneza

1995

Men's 3.0 (s): Tracy Smith; Men's 3.5 (s): Clyde Penry; Men's 3.5 (d): Keith Edwards, Robert Womack; Men's 4.0 (s): Joe Garrison; Men's 4.0 (d): Doug Dutton, Ken Kreidler; Men's 4.5 (s): Bob Ormsby; Men's 4.5 (d): Jim Elliott, Bob Ormsby; Men's 5.0 (s): Steve Wagel; Women's 3.5 (s): Nancy Tuchscherer; Women's 3.5 (d): Lori Andrews, Becky Custer; Women's 4.0 (s): Lewvenia Parks; Women's 4.5 (s): Debbie Carmazzi; Mixed 3.5: Tom Whitfield, Valerie Whitfield; Mixed 4.0: Cliff Durkee, Gail Deese

1996

Men's 3.0 (s): Tim Schaubroeck; Men's 3.5 (s): Clyde Penry; Men's 3.5 (d): Gregg Herbert, Jim Yau; Men's 4.0 (s): Chris Mallott; Men's 4.0 (d): Doug Dutton, Ken Kreidler; Men's 4.5 (s): Matthew Pascale; Men's 4.5 (d): Bob Keyho, Gary Ma; Women's 3.0 (s): Debbie Gawrych; Women's 3.0 (d): Sue Daly, Debbie Gawrych; Women's 3.5 (d): Regina Pinsker, Sarah Williams; Women's 4.0 (s): Heather Edwards; Women's 4.5 (s):

Debbie Carmazzi; Mixed 4.0: Mike Price/ Michelle Barford; Mixed 5.0: Mark Hoerbelt, Joanna Scott

1997

Men's 3.0 (s): Howard Talley; Men's 3.5 (s): Gerry Dudley; Men's 4.0 (s): Robert Womack; Men's 4.0 (d): Paul Finch, Johnny Gregory; Men's 4.5 (s): David Gandee; Women's 3.0 (s): Emily Peeples; Women's 3.0 (d): Anne Cober, Sue Sinclair; Women's 3.5 (s): June Anderson; Women's 4.0 (s): Sally Ormsby; Women's 4.0 (d): Mary Anne Nixon, Penny Bowlin; Mixed 3.5: Andy Watkin, Ann Oakley; Mixed 4.0: Joe Garrison, Jeanne Roller

1998

Men's 3.0 (s): Rick Weinstock; Men's 3.5 (s): Gerry Dudley; Men's 3.5 (d): Rob Bencini, Dennis Sterns; Men's 4.0 (s): Tony Baker; Men's 4.0 (d): Jeff Lloyd, Adam Davis; Men's 4.5 (s): Barry Sumner; Men's 4.5 (d): Art Lomax, Rashed Simpson; Men's 5.0 (s): Rick Peters; Women's 3.0 (s): Ann Cober; Women's 3.0 (d): Tara Santosuosso, Sue Sinclair; Women's 3.5 (s): Tara Santosuosso; Women's 4.0 (s): Lori Gibson; Women's 4.0 (d): Sherrie Austin, Bud Ware; Women's 5.0 (s): Laura Loehr; Mixed 3.5: Bud Faulkenberry, Kim Faulkenberry; Mixed 4.0: Joe Garrison, Jeane Roller; Mixed 4.5: Bob Ormsby, Sally Ormsby

1999

Men's 3.0 (s): Rick Weinstock; Men's 3.5 (s): Dudley Gerald; Men's 3.5 (d): Cliff Ormsby, Doug Fields; Men's 4.0 (s): Joe Garrison; Men's 4.0 (d): Robert Womack, Jim Yau; Men's 4.5 (s): Barry Sumner; Men's 4.5 (d): Russ Parmale, Rod Schwartz; Men's 5.0 (s): Luke Sargent; Men's 5.0 (d): Will Hancock, Rip Robbins; Women's 3.0 (s): Donna Lee; Women's 3.0 (d): Elizabeth Yedell, Dagmar Reddig; Women's 3.5 (s): Cynthia Ayers; Women's 3.5 (d): Tara Santosuosso, Susan Sinclair; Women's 4.0 (s): Anne Clark; Women's 4.0 (d): Bobbi

Lucas, Nancy Reece; Women's 4.5 (s): Sally Ormsby; Women's 4.5 (d) Maria Britt, Sandi Mitchell; Mixed 3.5: Jim Pfefferkorn, Tara Santosuosso; Mixed 4.0: Joe Garrison/ Jeanne Roller; Combo Mixed 6.5: David Fisher, Linda Fisher; Combo Mixed 7.5: Nick Villa, Cindy Ayers, Charlotte; Combo Mixed 9.5: David Riggsbee, Lori Tomlin

2000

Clay Court

Men's 3.0 (s): Robert Witherspoon; Men's 3.5 (s): Michael McKeown; Men's 3.5 (d): Robert Bean, Doug Driver; Men's 4.0 (s): Lorenza Kearns; Men's 4.0 (d): Jim Yau, Lorenza Kearns; Men's 4.5 (s): Kevin Leary; Men's 4.5 (d): Russell Parmele, Rod Schwartz; Men's 5.0 (s): Brent Foushee; Women's 3.0 (s): Kim Comer; Women's 3.5 (s): Renee Jones; Women's 3.5 (d): Connie Morgan, Marie Sladky; Women's 4.0 (s): Darla Fogle; Women's 4.0 (d): Beth Cornell, Mary Ann Lang; Women's 4.5 (s): Gwen Highsmith-Quick; Women's 4.5 (d): Kathy Bell, Dona Bowland; Combo Mixed 6.5: Sean Conneen, Tracy Conneen; Combo Mixed 7.5: Cynthia Ayers, Nick Villa

Hard Court

Men's 3.0 (s): Shelby Williams; Men's 3.5 (s): Bob Kent; Men's 3.5 (d): Kurt Stork, Rocky Davis; Men's 4.0 (s): Larry Spruill; Men's 4.0 (d): Larry Spruill, Tony Thompson; Men's 4.5 (s): Freddie Lacewell; Men's 4.5 (d): John Merritt, Bobby Taylor; Women's 3.0 (s): Suzan Lawler; Women's 3.5 (s): Dela Clark; Combo Mixed 6.5: Erica Houston, Robert Jones; Combo Mixed 8.5: Marion Edwards, Fran Hooks

2001

Clay Court

Men's 3.0 (s): Steven Floyd; Men's 3.5 (s): Brian Garlick; Men's 3.5 (d):

Robert Bean, Robert Bencini; Men's 4.0 (s): Mark Caradori; Men's 4.0 (d): Abraham Lopez, Jim Yau; Men's 4.5 (s): Zachary Crutchfield; Men's 4.5 (d): Michael Cahall, Richard McClenny; Men's 5.0 (s): Pertti Viskari; Women's 3.0 (s): Vicky Schrader; Women's 3.0 (d): Vicky Schrader, Wendy Utley; Women's 3.5 (s): Allison Bumgardner; Women's 4.0 (s): Nancy Chirino; Women's 4.0 (d): Bud Ware, Sherrie Austin; Women's 4.5 (s): Beverly Ranger; Combo Mixed 6.5: Diane Tomerlin, Harold Dean Wright; Combo Mixed 7.5: Nick Villa, Cynthia Ayers

Hard Court

Men's 3.0 (s): Ernie McDrew; Men's 3.5 (s): Mark Aycock; Men's 3.5 (d): Donald Clark, Jack Jennings; Men's 4.0 (s): Lorenza Kearns; Men's 4.0 (d): Mike Gray, Brad Fowler; Men's 4.5 (s): Mitch Peyton; Men's 4.5 (d): Gene Autry, Lorenza Kearns; Women's 3.0 (s): Jennifer Moats; Women's 3.0 (d): Beth Chester, Kathy Pruitt; Women's 3.5 (s): Dela Clark; Women's 3.5 (d): Jean Haas, Veineta Howard; Women's 4.0 (s): Leigh Best; Combo Mixed 6.5: James Hanson, Mary Jo Hundley; Combo Mixed 75: Beth Chester, Tim Huryn

2002

Clay Court

Men's 3.0 (s): Brad Mann; Men's 3.5 (s): Joseph Faske; (d): Robert Bean, Robert Bencini; Men's 4.0 (s): JD Heuer; (d): John Bruckel, David McLeod; Men's 4.5 (s): Job Zarate; (d): Shawn Cooke, Pertti Viskari; Men's 5.0 (s): Pertti Viskari; Women's 3.0 (s): Karen Richter; (d): Ann Hartley, Karen Rhew; Women's 3.5 (s): Esmeralda Canales; (d): Tina Bailey, Roberta Rohan; Women's 4.0 (s): Ann Clark; Mixed Combo 7.5: Janet Nicol, Mike McKeown; Mixed Combo 8.5: David Gandee, Debra Thoburn; Mixed Combo 9.5: Darla Fogle, Robert McAdoo

Hard Court

Men's 3.0 (s): Richard Nelson; Men's 3.5 (s): Brian Garlick; Men's 3.5 (d): Jim Freeman, Mike Russell; Men's 4.0 (s): Jeffrey Smith; Men's 4.0 (d): Bryant Langston, Chuck Winslow; Men's 4.5 (s): Richard McClenny; Men's 4.5 (d): Michael Cahall, Richard McClenny; Women's 2.5 (s): Sara Moore; Women's 3.0 (s): Holly Mace; Women's 3.5 (s): Dela Clark; Women's 3.5 (d): Carrie Handley, Carol Taylor; Women's 4.0 (s): Elaine Ashley; Mixed Combo 6.5: Lin Hall, Michelle Jernigan; Mixed Combo 8.5: Kris Broadwell, Richard McClenny

2003

Clay Court

Men's 3.0 (s): Chip Ashley; Men's 3.0 (d): Chip Aprile /Brad Vice; Men's 3.5 (s): Ronnie Digh; Men's 3.5 (d): Steve Cannon, Skip Hepburn; Men's 4.0 (s): Jeremy East; Men's 4.0 (d): Ron Bryant, Thomas Griffin; Men's 4.5 (s): Mitchell Peyton; Men's 4.5 (d): Scott Fowler /Erik Witten; Men's 5.0 (s): Nicolas Ecos-Ossio; Women's 3.0 (s): Debbie McBride; Women's 3.0 (d): Karen McKelvev/Rhonda Wood; Women's 3.5 (s): Jimmie Welch; Women's 3.5 (d): Jennifer Cornelius, Karen Love; Women's 4.0 (s): Juanita Pope; Women's 4.0 (d): Betsy Darden, Stacey Venditti; Women's 4.5 (s): Cathy Kiser; Women's 4.5 (d): Cheryl Moger/Diane Ward; Combo Mixed 6.5: Caroline Pickup/ Charles Spraggs; Combo Mixed 7.5: George Jackson, Jean Little; Combo Mixed 8.5: Mario Gonzalez, Tisha Vandemore

Hard Court

Men's 3.0 (s): Michael Wilson; Men's 3.0 (d): Ross Gordon, Thomas Krisulewicz; Men's 3.5 (s): Danny Brown; Men's 4.0 (s): Jimmy Davis; Men's 4.5 (s): Jeff Smith; Men's 5.0 (s): Kabiru Ibrahim; Men's 5.0 (d): Michael Cahall, Russ Grewe; Women's 3.0 (s): Suzanne Gray; Women's 3.5 (s): Della Clark; Women's 3.5 (d): Jean Hass, Mary

Sauls; Women's 4.0 (s): Patricia Blackwell; Combo Mixed 8.5: Patricia Blackwell, Malcolm Harris

2004

Clay Court

Men's 3.0 (s): David Dickson; Men's 3.5 (s): Michael Alivio; Men's 3.5 (d): David Barnes, Bill Shaw; Men's 4.0 (s): Jeremy East; Men's 4.0 (d): Ron Bryant, Thomas Griffin; Men's 4.5 (s): Kevin Potts; Men's 4.5 (d): Christopher Butler, Paul Miller; Men's 5.0 (s): Christopher Ehmcke; Women 3.0 (s): Brenda Cooke; Women 3.0 (d): Brenda Cook, Elaine Liddy; Women 3.5 (s): Tina Bailey-Richardson; Women 3.5 (d): Tina Bailey-Richardson, Roberta Rohan; Women 4.0 (s): Bonnie Newell; Women 4.0 (d): Nancy Chirino, Kathy Stafford; Women 4.5 (s): Lynn Chambers; Mixed Combo 6.5: Dora Burdzinska-Drezek, Mike Drezek; Mixed Combo 7.5: Amy Adams, Scott Jones; Mixed Combo 8.5: Oscar Nieto, Jean Miller

Hard Court

Men's 3.0 (s): Michael Wilson; Men's 3.5 (s): Robert Jones; Men's 3.5 (d): Marion Edwards, Robert Jones; Men's 4.0 (s): Jimmy Davis; Men's 4.5 (s): Freddie Lacewell; Men's 4.5 (d): Jarvis James, Adrian Baluyot; Men's 5.0 (s): Adrian Baluyot; Women 2.5 (s): Lynnette Worthington; Women 3.0 (s): Suzanne Gray; Women 3.5 (s): Jennifer Moats; Women 3.5 (d): Kimberly King, Jennifer; Women 4.0 (s): Sunny Orr; Women 4.0 (d): Sunny Orr, Mew Boey; Mixed Combo 7.5: Danny Brown, Lisa Sowers; Mixed Combo 8.5: Patricia Blackwell, Malcolm Harris

2005

Clay Court

Men's 3.0 (s): David Vega; Men's 4.0 (s): Kanwar Singh; Men's 4.0 (d): Baker Arrowood, Hao Dang; Men's 4.5 (s): Scott Fowler; Men's 4.5 (d): Christopher Butler, Doug

NORTH CAROLINA ADULT STATE CLOSED NTRP CHAMPIONS HISTORY
(CONTINUED)

Knox; Women's 3.0 (s): Minqxin Xu; Women's 3.0 (d): Bonnie DePaolis, Felicia Dean; Women's 3.5 (s): Roberta Rohan; Women's 3.5 (d): Donna Riggi, Nilda Willis; Women's 4.0 (s): Lisa Scott; Women's 4.0 (d): Tina Bailey-Richardson, Roberta Rohan; Women's 4.5 (s): Lynn Chambers; Mixed 6.0: Karen Brown, Kenji Krzywoszki; Mixed 7.0: Christine Thompson, William Hirata; Mixed 8.0: Martin Schoeberl, Kirsten Shields; Mixed 9.0: Melony Bailey, Josh Oxendine

Hard Court

Men's 2.5 (s): Sam Steed; Men's 3.0 (s): William Jackson; Men's 3.0 (d): Michael Wilson, Jesse Parks; Men's 3.5 (s): Scott Reeder; Men's 3.5 (d): Gary Kowalski, David Segur; Men's 4.0 (s): Lucious Smith; Men's 4.0 (d): Stephen Arnold, Joseph Smith; Men's 4.5 (s): William Jones; Men's 5.0 (s): Grant Hollard; Women's 2.5 (s): Crystal Zabala; Women's 3.0 (s): Lynnette Worthington; Women's 3.0 (d): Julie Jackson, Nancy Wilson; Women's 3.5 (s): Julie Harper; Women's 4.0 (s): Burnett Herrick; Women's 4.0 (d): Shelley Gibbons, Kandis Maynard; Mixed 8.0: Sunny Orr, Anthony Stewart

2006

Clay Court

Men's 3.0 (s): Duane Floyd; Men's 3.5 (s): Eric Rhew; Men's 3.5 (d): Brad Erlandson, Jeff Oler; Men's 4.0 (s): Shawn Cooke; Men's 4.0 (d): Mark Carnes, Jeff Latham; Men's 4.5 (s): Shaun Sumner; Men's 4.5 (d): Martin Schoeberi, Christopher Butler; Men's 5.0 (s): Robert Stephens; Women's 2.5 (s): Rada Washington; Women's 2.5 Double: Tiffany Morgan, Tina

Smith; Women's 3.0; (d): Shannon Bookter, Sheri Sparks; Women's 3.5 (s): Andreina Morris; Women's 3.5 (d): Felicia Dean, Bonnie Depaolis; Women's 4.0 (s): Sunny Orr; Women's 4.0 (d): Kathy Stafford, Sharon Kerns; Women's 4.5 (s): Amy Dillingham; Women's 4.5 (d): Betsy Darden, Kari Andrews; Mixed 7.0: Caroline Pickup, Tony McGraw; Mixed 8.0: Jeremy Caslin, Flora Robinson; Mixed 9.0: Kristen Deskevich, Hugh Grey

Hard Court

Men's 3.5: (d): David Pope, Bill Stevenson; Men's 4.0: (d): Tony Johnson, Dominic Wainwright; Men's 4.5 (d): Shaun Sumner, Stefan Sumner; Men's 5.0 (s): Kevin Fleck; Women's 3.0 (d): Jean Harrington, Lynnette Worthington; Women's 3.5 (d): Shelley Gibbons, Lorie Stevenson; Women's 4.0 (s): Nicole Earnhardt

2007

Clay Court

Men's 3.0 (s): Michael Baldeli; Men's 3.0 (d): Chris Rupert, John Bosak; Men's 3.5 (s): Sameer Shaik; Men's 3.5 (d): Mickey Gallegos, David Savage; Men's 4.0 (s): Brad Erlandson; Men's 4.0 (d): Mark Carnes, Mauro Coruzzi; Men's 4.5 (s): Scott Fowler; Men's 4.5 (d): Drew Crawford, David Stroman; Men's 5.0 (s): Greg May; Men's 5.0 (d): Bradley Hobday, Keith Kye; Women's 3.0 (s): Shumbriar Ostapko; Women's 3.0 (d): Geneva Bosak, Marlene Katter; Women's 3.5 (d): Cissie Dickson, Alice Hansen; Women's 4.0 (s): Sunny Orr; Women's 4.0 (d): Janet Baker, Kirsten Shields; Women's 4.5 (s): Lynn Chambers; Women's 4.5 (d): Lynn Chambers, Warner Riley; Mixed 6.0: Geneva Bosak, John Bosak; Mixed 7.0: Scott Abrams, Mary Hamilton Chiles; Mixed 8.0: Oscar Nieto, Dora Burdzinska-Drezek; Mixed 9.0: Robert Fryer, Christine ThompsonWaxhaw

Hard Court

Men's 3.0 (s): Michael Sloop; Men's 3.5 (s): George Richardson; Men's 3.5 (d): Timothy Simmons, Bill Stevenson; Men's 4.0 (s): Tom Wilson; Men's 4.0 (d): Tony Johnson, Paul Cory; Men's 4.5 (s): Linwood Hall; Men's 4.5 (d): Mrinal Das, Todd Garcia; Men's 5.0 (s): Shaun Sumner; Women's 3.5 (s): Dela Clark; Women's 4.0 (s): Sunny Orr; Mixed 7.0: Arnie Grieves, Carol Taylor; Mixed 8.0: Sunny Orr, Tony Johnson; Mixed 9.0: Chad Oxendine, Tracy Conneen

2008

Clay Court

Men's 3.0 (s): Christian Karaslewicz; Men's 3.5 (s): Jeff Moser; Men's 3.5 (d): Louis Duncan, James Epler; Men's 4.0 (s): Evan Shaw; Men's 4.0 (d): Baker Arrowood, Bradley Hubacher; Men's 4.5 (s): Kevin Potts; Men's 4.5 (d): Drew Crawford, David Stroman; Men's 5.0 (s): Nicolas Ecos-Osso; Women's 3.0 (d): Patricia Arrowood, Karla Williams; Women's 3.5 (s): Vishwanthini Cook; Women's 3.5 (d): Saundra Holloman, Mala Lee; Women's 4.0 (s): Anita Klendjian; Women's 4.0 (d): Dora Burdzinska-Drezek, Sharon Roberts; Women's 4.5 (s): Lynn Chambers; Mixed 7.0: Mala Lee, Randy McVane; Mixed 8.0: Amy Adams, James Hendrix; Mixed 9.0: Massimo Bosso, Julie Tanner

Hard Court

Men's 3.0 (s): Jake Howering; Men's 3.0 (d): Loren Ota, Michael Sloop; Men's 3.5 (s): George Richardson; Men's 4.0 (s): Raul Suarez; Men's 4.0 (d): Vivian Karimakwenda, Bill Stevenson; Men's 4.5 (s): Kevin Coghill; Men's 5.0 (s): Lee Bailey; Women's 3.0 (s): Vanessa Bailey; Women's 4.0 (s): Anita Klendjian; Mixed 7.0: Mindy Dehaven, Ken Dehaven; Mixed 8.0: Ray Boehmer, Michelle Bass; Mixed 9.0: Tracy Conneen, Chad Oxendine

2009

Clay Court

Men's 3.0 (s): David Griffin; Men's 3.5 (s): George Garest; Men's 3.5 (d): Ted Mitchell, Ross Nethery; Men's 4.0 (s): Shawn Cooke; Men's 4.0 (d): Shawn Cooke, Robert Roxcroft; Men's 4.5 (s): Timothy Sneed; Men's 4.5 (d): Christopher Butler, Drew Crawford; Men's 5.0 (s): Kevin Potts; Women's 3.0 (s): Dana Griffin; Women's 3.0 (d): Wendy Fairer, Gretchen Mann; Women's 3.5 (s): Cristen Morgan; Women's 3.5 (d): Pamela Bender, Denise Hamme; Women's 4.0 (s): Kristy Donaldson; Women's 4.0 (d): Amy Adams, Andreina Morris; Women's 4.5 (s): Lynn Chambers; Mixed 6.0: David Griffin, Dana Griffin; Mixed 7.0: Mary Jones, Russell Walker; Mixed 8.0: Amy Adams, James Hendrix

Hard Court Championships

Men's 3.0 (s): Dail Spencer; Men's 3.5 (s): Joshua Cooper; Men's 3.5 (d): Steven Davis, TJ Thomas; Men's 4.0 (s): Jimmy Davis; Men's 4.0 (d): William Hancock, Travis Robbins; Men's 4.5 (s): Michael Boothman; Men's 4.5 (d): Christopher Baum, Scott Rickel; Men's 5.0 (s): Lee Bailey; Women's 3.0 (s): Latisha Alford; Mixed 7.0: John Alford, Latisha Alford

2010

Clay Court

Men's 3.0 (s): AntonioPorretta; Men's 3.5 (s): Tommy Barbour; Men's 3.5 (d): Michael Guest, Jim Illing; Men's 4.0 (s): Eugene Brycki; Men's 4.0 (d): Chuck Capehart, Scott Darden; Men's 4.5 (s): Michael Earl; Men's 4.5 (d): Mark Allen, Raul Rodriguez; Men's 5.0 (s): Bradley Hobday; Men's 5.0 (d): Bradley Hobday, James Lowe; Women's 3.0 (s): Stephanie Durovic; Women's 3.0 (d): Paige McGuirk, Alyson Wharton; Women's 3.5 (s): Nicole Yudin; Women's 3.5 (d): Zanthia Hastings, Ernestine Staton; Women's 4.0 (s): Diofra Azucenas; Women's 4.0 (d): Diofra Azucenas, Alessandra Scottbey; Women's 4.5 (s): Nancy Chirino; Women's 4.5 (d): Nancy Chirino, Dee Dee Samples; Mixed 6.0: Ted Mitchell, Melissa Mitchell; Mixed 7.0: Michelle Potuzak, Kevin Snyder; Mixed 8.0: Todd Sommers, Cindy Sommers; Mixed 9.0: Kirsty Donaldson, Raul Rodriguez

Hard Court

Men's 3.0 (s): Jeff Atkinson; Men's 3.0 (d): Jeff Atkinson, Gregg White; Men's 3.5 (s): W Troutman; Men's 4.0 (s): Raul Suarez; Men's 4.0 (d): Jobe Makar, Robert Skinner; Men's 4.5 (s): Nicholas Holloman; Women's 3.0 (s): Gloria Quick; Mixed 9.0: Carol Aro, Diogo Miranda

2011

Clay Court

Men's 3.0 (s): Justin Abbott; Men's 3.5 (s): Marko Durovic; Men's 3.5 (d): Kevin Snyder, Cole Wilson; Men's 4.0 (s): Nickel Thomas; Men's 4.0 (d): Chuck Capehart, Scott Darden; Men's 4.5 (s): Jeffrey Campbell; Men's 4.5 (d): Baker Arrowood, Michael Brady; Men's 5.0 (s): Kelly Hunter; Men's 5.0 (d): Bradley Hobday, Jesse Hutchinson; Women's 3.0 (s):Leila O'Brien; Women's 3.0 (d): Susan Duncan, Robin Illing; Women's 3.5 (d): Elizabeth Krogstie, Gina Nichols; Women's 4.0 (s): Jessica Polonsky; Women's 4.0 (d): Mary Hamilton Chiles, Sharon Roberts; Women's 4.5 (s): Diofra Azucenas; Women's 4.5 (d): Nancy Chirino, Dee Dee Samples; Mixed 6.0: Ray Helms, Mary Wilson; Mixed 7.0: Jennie Carruth, Kevin Snyder; Mixed 8.0: Jackie Hege, Andrew Smith; Mixed 9.0: Kate Meiners, Josh Oxendine

Hard Court

Men's 3.5 (s): Jonathan Parker; Men's 4.0 (s): Vivian Karimakwenda; Men's 4.5 (s): Dan Sarisky; Men's 5.0 (s): Vijay Shankar; Women's 3.0 (s): Natalie Quilter; Women's 3.5 (s): Ashley Richards; Women's 3.5 (d): Kasia Headley, Natalie Quilter; Women's 4.5 (s): Allison Ostrander

USTA NATIONAL AWARDS WON BY NORTH CAROLINIANS

The Eve Kraft USTA Community Service Award

Honors volunteer tennis leaders for significant contributions made to tennis development in their respective communities.
1974 Mildred Southern
2002 Kathy Kim

The Barbara Williams Leadership Award

Recognizes a female volunteer who through her leadership and by her example has encouraged and inspired others to become volunteers and assume leadership roles at the community, sectional, and/or national levels of the United States Tennis Association.
2009 Judy Utley

Gold Slam Award

Established in 2002, the Gold Slam Award recognizes adult and senior competitive players who have won all of the national championships played in the same division throughout the year.
2010 Super Senior Father–Son: Carl Erikson, Asheville, N.C., and John Erikson, Oberlin, Ohio

Seniors' Service Award

A trophy for service to senior tennis is awarded each year to the person the USTA Adult/Senior Competition Committee deems most deserving of the respect and honor of all seniors. It is awarded on the basis of the recipient's willingness, cooperation and participation, either in play or organizational work for the betterment and furtherance of senior competition.
1979 Buck Archer
1991 Mildred Southern
1994 Art Rondeau

Service Bowl Award

"To the Woman Tennis Player Who Yearly Makes the Most Notable Contribution to the Sportsmanship, Fellowship, and Service of Tennis."
1997 Mildred Southern

Super Senior Service Award

The Super Senior Service Award is given annually to the person who, in the opinion of the Super Senior Tennis Board of Directors, has made a notable contribution to the promotion of tennis for the 55-and-over USTA-recognized age divisions.
1991 Buck Archer
1994 Dick Covington

Dr. Allen B. Stowe Sportsmanship Award

Trophy to be presented annually to the Junior Boys' 18s player who, in the opinion of the National Junior and Boys' Championships Committee, best combines the qualities of outstanding sportsmanship and outstanding tennis ability.
1986 Stephen Enochs
1995 Tripp Phillips
2002 Jonathan Stokke

Bobby Kaplan Sportsmanship Award

Presented annually at the USTA Boys' 16s National Championships, the Bobby Kaplan Sportsmanship Award is awarded to that boy who best combines sportsmanship and outstanding tennis ability.
2000 Jonathan Stokke

USTA Girls' 18s National Championship Sportsmanship Award

The USTA Girls' 18s National Championship Sportsmanship Award is presented each year at the USTA Girls' 18s National Championships to the girl who, in the opinion of the committee of judges, exemplifies outstanding sportsmanship, conduct and character.
1989 Kim Kessaris

USTA NJTL of the Year Award

The USTA Tennis NJTL Chapter of the Year Award is designed to honor an outstanding USTA Tennis NJTL chapter or chapters that have demonstrated continued excellence in recreational tennis.
1996 Raleigh Parks and Recreation

Outstanding Tennis Facility Award

The Tennis Facility Awards Program honors outstanding tennis facilities and encourages excellence in future construction and/or renovation. Facilities must be under the jurisdiction of: (1) a parks and recreation department, (2) an educational institution or (3) an industrial complex.
1990 Jimmy Powell Tennis Center Elon College
1997 Burlington Tennis Center
2000 Sheffield Tennis Center Duke University
2002 Wake Forest Tennis Center
2002 Charlotte Racquet Club North
2004 J.W. Isenhour Tennis Center NC State University
2006 Cary Tennis Park
2007 North Hills Club

USTA Girls' Sportsmanship Trophy Award

The USTA Girls' Sportsmanship Trophy Award was presented annually at the close of the International Girls' 18s Grass Court Championships to the player in the championship who, in the opinion of the committee of judges, most nearly approaches the ideal in sportsmanship, appearance, court manners and tactics.
2002 Katrina Tsang

Harry Fogleman Memorial Trophy

The Harry Fogleman Memorial Trophy was awarded each year at the USTA Boys' 12s National Championships to the boy who, in the opinion of the Tournament Committee, exemplified outstanding sportsmanship, conduct, character and tennis ability.
1980 Stephen Enochs
1987 J.J. Jackson

William M. Johnston Award

The William M. Johnston Trophy is awarded to that male player who, by character, sportsmanship, manners, spirit of cooperation and contribution to the growth of the game, ranks first in the opinion of the selection committee.
2000 Tim Wilkison

USTA SOUTHERN PRESIDENTS FROM NORTH CAROLINA

1976–77 Marshall Happer
1982–83 Mildred Southern
1984–85 Charlie Morris
1995–96 Herman Enochs
2007–08 Judy Utley

SOUTHERN TENNIS HALL OF FAME

1985 Allen Morris
1992 Mildred Southern
1993 Buck Archer
1995 Dick Covington
1995 Marshall Happer
2000 Charlie Morris
2000 Tim Wilkison
2006 John Peddycord
2008 Bill Weathers

JACOBS BOWL

The highest honor presented by the USTA Southern Section, this award is presented to a volunteer who has exhibited outstanding service in the USTA Southern Section.
1954 Allan Morris
1976 Marshall Happer
1982 Charlie Morris
1983 Mildred Southern
1984 John Peddycord
1986 Herman Enochs
1999 Harold Southern
2005 Paula Hale
2008 Judy Utley

CHARLIE B. MORRIS JR. SERVICE AWARD

Presented in memory of Charlie Morris to the volunteer who best exhibits exemplary volunteer spirit at the local, State, Sectional and/or National levels.
1995 John Peddycord
1998 Mildred Southern
2008 Vicki Everette
2011 Judy Utley

NCTA DISTINGUISHED SERVICE AWARD

Highest award given by the N.C. Tennis Association, given from time to time when appropriate. (Recommended by Hall of Fame Council to the NCTA Management Committee)
1979 Carl Easterling
1980 H.S. (Mac) McGinty, Jasper Memory
1991 Lenoir Keesler, Dewey Keesler, Lacy Keesler, Ted Keesler
1992 Judge Frank Dupree
1995 Tom Norfleet
2000 Leon Meadows
2002 Harry Fogleman
2007 Bob and Hazel Jones
2012 Tom Peatross

MARY MILAM AWARD

Given to a deserving volunteer who played junior tennis in NC and now gives back as an adult.
2011 Palmer Sugg
2010 Shane Wells
2009 Chris Cagle
2008 Richard Holderness
2007 Andy Andrews
2005 Kelly Gaines
2004 Billy Trott
2003 Karen Rembert
2000 Alex Rucker
1999 Mary Lloyd Barbera
1998 John Eatman
1997 Henry Hostetler
1996 Cy King

Index

Endnotes

SECTION ONE

1. This pasture would in 19 years become Coker Arboretum.

2. At this point in time tennis was still sometimes called "sphairistike".

3. Research paper entitled "The Early Days of Tennis in Moore County" by Harry Richard Watson, of Whispering Pines and a student at Union Pines High School

4. N.C. High School Athletic Association website

5. *North Carolina Tennis History*, Carlyle Lewis

6. The Grady Elmore Award is given annually to a journalist who supports tennis.

7. Carrington, Arthur, Black Tennis, *An Archival History from 1890-1962.*

SECTION TWO

8. NCTA files

9. In addition to the vice presidents, Jack Warmath was appointed as chairman of the North Carolina Closed Tournament and Sam Daniel was appointed chairman of the 1960 Ranking Committee.

10. http://www.lib.unc.edu/mss/uars/ead/40094.html

SECTION THREE

11. USTA.com

SECTION FOUR

12. League Division in North Carolina:

    USTA Adult & Senior League (20) – Adult Women 2.5, 3.0, 3.5, 4.0, 4.5, 5.0; Adult Men 3.0, 3.5, 4.0, 4.5, 5.0, 5.5; Senior Men & Women 3.0, 3.5, 4.0, 4.5

    USTA League Super Seniors (14) – 60s M & W 3.0, 3.5, 4.0, 4.5; 70s M & W 3.0, 3.5, 4.0

    USTA League Mixed Doubles (13) - Adult 5.0, 6.0, 7.0, 8.0, 9.0, 10.0; Senior 6.0, 7.0, 8.0, 9.0; Super Senior 6.0, 7.0, 8.0

    Southern Combo Doubles (25)- Adult Women's 5.0, 5.5, 6.5, 7.5, 8.5, 9.5; Adult Men 5.5, 6.5, 7.5, 8.5, 9.5; Senior M & W 6.5, 7.5, 8.5, 9.5; Super Senior M & W 6.5, 7.5, 8.5

    NCTA Singles League (14) – Adult Women 2.5, 3.0, 3.5, 4.0, 4.5; Adult Men 3.0, 3.5, 4.0, 4.5; Senior Women 3.5, 4.0; Senior Men 3.5, 4.0, 4.5

    NCTA Tri-Level League (3) – Women 2.5/3.0/3.5, 3.0/3.5/4.0, 3.5/4.0/4.5

13. Albemarle; Capital Area; Central Carolina; Coastal Plains; Eno River; Foothills; Lake Norman, Metro; Neuse River; Piedmont; Sandhills; South East Tennis (SET); Western NC; Yadkin Valley

14. Registrations per league in 2011; USTA Adult & Senior League – 22,781; USTA League Super Seniors – 1,636; USTA League Mixed Doubles – 8,270; Southern Combo Doubles – 18,022; NCTA Singles League - 515; NCTA Tri-Level League – 715

Photos

Old Salem Court	Courtesy of Old Salem Museum and Gardens
Venable Court	Courtesy of the North Carolina Collection, University of North Carolina at Chapel Hill Library
Franklin St. Scene	Courtesy of the North Carolina Collection, University of North Carolina at Chapel Hill Library
Grove Park	Courtesy of Grove Park Inn
Sylva Tennis Club	Courtesy of Special Collections, Hunter Library Western Carolina University Library
Bo Roddey	Courtesy of Bo Roddey
Royster Stadium	Courtesy of Cy King
Hanes Park	Courtesy of Digital Forsyth, Forsyth County Public Library
Women's College	Courtesy Documenting the American South, The University of North Carolina at Chapel Hill Libraries.
Biltmore Forest CC	Courtesy of Biltmore Forest Country Club
NC State Tennis Team	Courtesy of NC State Athletic Department
ECTA players	Courtesy of Marshall Happer
Irwin Holmes	Courtesy of NC State Athletic Department
Clark Family	Courtesy of Blanche Clark
RRC Membership Certificate	Courtesy of Cy King
Joe White sign	Courtesy of Bob Dostal
RRC Southerns Patch	Courtesy of Cy King
Olde Providence RC	Courtesy of Olde Providence Racquet Club
RRC Groundbreaking	Courtesy of Cy King
Paul Bredenburg	Courtesy of Cy King
Keith Stoneman	Courtesy of Keith Stoneman
Patrons Ticket	Courtesy of Cy King
Gene Hamilton	Courtesy of Gene Hamilton
Stan Smith	Courtesy of Mark Dillon

NC State Tennis Team	Courtesy of NC State Athletic Department
National Tennis Center	Courtesy of Russ Adams Photography
Spencer Love	Courtesy of Mark Falcon
Ball Machine	Courtesy of Metaltek
Guilford women	Courtesy of Guilford College Department of Athletics
NC Central Team	Courtesy of North Carolina Central University Archives and Records
Cone Kenfield	Courtesy of Andrew Parker
Elon Tennis Center	Courtesy of Elon University Dept of Athletics
Henry Hostetler	Courtesy of Kelly Gaines
Hanes Park Bridge	Courtesy of Bob Dostal
Raleigh Edge	Courtesy of Duane Long
Olde Providence	Courtesy of Olde Providence Racquet Club
Charlie Morris	Courtesy of John Peddycord
The Richardson Preyers	Courtesy of the Richardson Preyer Family
Bobby Taylor	Courtesy of Bobby Taylor
Buster Brown	Courtesy of Buster Brown
Duke 2009 Women's Team	Courtesy of Duke University Dept. of Athletics
Jeff Frank	Courtesy of Davidson College
Fred Robinson	Courtesy of Fred Robinson
Winston-Salem Open	Courtesy of Winston-Salem Open
John Isner	Courtesy of Lagardère Unlimited Tennis
Jane Preyer	Courtesy of Duke University Dept. of Athletics
Rebel Good	Courtesy of Rebel Good
Judy Utley	Courtesy of Judy Utley
Old Racquet Collection	Courtesy of Bill Guilfoil

Donors

The North Carolina Tennis Foundation would like to extend a special thanks to the following donors who by their generosity made this project possible:

$1000 or more
Herb Browne
Kelly Key Gaines
Mary Lou Jones
Cyrus B. King Jr
Neill R. McGeachy, Jr
John Peddycord
Harold T. and Mildred F. Southern
William M. Trott
Dargan and Blount Williams
John and Judy Utley
Bonnie & Michael Vandegrift
Keith Stoneman
Raleigh Tennis Foundation

$500-$999
Andy Andrews
Sharron Frahm
Druid Eggert Michaels
Alex Rucker & Family
Ronnie Watson
Western Wake Tennis Association

$250-$499
Andy Avram Family
John Benson
Carl and Marianne Britt
Brian Burchfield
Coley, Christopher & Tammy Stutts

Jack Warmath
The Jim Corn Family
Vicki & Maurice Everette
Al & Marilyn Griffin
Paula Hale
Marshall Happer
Katherine G. Harrison
Burnett Herrick
Julie & Richard Holderness
Jim & Julia Anne Holt
Mr. and Mrs. Henry Hostetler
Karen K. Johnson
Robin and Alan Jones
Jeff and Patty Joyce
J. Frank Love, Jr.
Jack McGinn
The Tom Peatross Family
Bill Peeler Family, Josh, Matt and Nathan
Jane Preyer
The Raleigh Racquet Club
Sunset Ridge Racquet & Swim Club–Ted & Jennifer Reese
Christopher C. Rhyne
Keith & Marilyn Richardson
The Skakle Family
Debbie Southern
Susan (Susie) Black Wall
Shane Wells & Family
Molly and Barden Winstead

The Long and the Short of It
Two North Carolina treasures, Kelly Gaines,
longtime NCTA executive director, and John
Isner, North Carolina's first world's top tenner.